REVELATION

H. A. IRONSIDE

An Ironside Expository Commentary

REVELATION

H. A. IRONSIDE

Kregel
Academic & Professional

Revelation: An Ironside Expository Commentary

Originally published in 1920. Reprinted in 2004 by Kregel Publications, a division of Kregel, Inc., P.O. Box 2607, Grand Rapids, MI 49501.

Unless otherwise noted, Scripture quotations are from the King James Version of the Holy Bible.

Scripture quotations marked RV are from the Revised Version of the Holy Bible (Church of England, 1885).

Scripture quotations marked WEYMOUTH are from *Weymouth's New Testament in Modern Speech* (1903), reprinted in 1978 by Kregel Publications.

ISBN 978-0-8254-2909-5

Printed in the United States of America

07 08 09 10 11 / 7 6 5 4 3

CONTENTS

PREFACE TO THE 1930 EDITION

The eleven years that have elapsed since these lectures were first issued in printed form, have but added proof that the system of interpretation followed is scriptural. The word of prophecy is confirmed by the passing of the years. Everything in the church, in Jewry, and in the world continues exactly as predicted in the Holy Scriptures.

The author is sincerely gratified that, in his preparing a new edition in response to the ever-increasing demand for this unpretentious volume, he has no interpretation to discard or matter of any importance to alter. A few typographical errors have been corrected, an occasional sentence has been recast, and here and there an entire paragraph has been altered, but only to make the teaching less ambiguous or to change awkward expressions to clarify the whole. Otherwise, this edition is practically the same as that of 1919.

May God continue to use it to the awakening of believers to the imminence of the Lord's return and to the arousing of the unsaved that they may come to Christ before the door of grace is closed.

—H. A. IRONSIDE

PREFACE

In reproducing these lectures in book form, I simply accede to the requests of many people who heard them, in either Oakland or other cities where I have spoken on the same book in recent years. Heretofore, I have always refused to bring out a volume on the Apocalypse because it seemed to me, so many were already in print that were better than any I could hope to write. Although this fact remains as true today as ever, the Great War and other colossal movements of the past five years have combined to so emphasize and clarify much that abler brethren had written in earlier years, that it now seems to me that a need exists for some later exposition of the last prophetic book of the Bible that would consider or include these many significant events.

Sober students of prophecy must be gratified to find that their position is only strengthened and their previous conclusions confirmed by recent happenings. On the other hand, those of the self-styled optimistic school, who have ever closed their eyes to the solemn facts of prophecy, might well be humiliated to find their vain-glorious prognostications proven so utterly false and their confidence in human brotherhood, as a preventive of war and cruelty, shown to be a foolish hallucination that ignored the Word of God and the corruption of the human heart.

In preparing these addresses for the press, I have not changed their form materially, although here and there I have altered ambiguous sentences and occasionally enlarged some theme for the sake of clarity. The first lecture was only partially reported and therefore had to be almost completely recast. The others are largely as delivered.

Trusting that the book may be used to arouse an interest in the study of prophecy and to prepare a people for the Lord's return, I send it forth in His Name.

—H. A. IRONSIDE

THE INTRODUCTION

Revelation 1:1–8

It is certainly cause for deep regret that the book of Revelation seems to many Christians to be what God never intended—a sealed book. The book of Daniel was to be sealed until the time of the end (Dan. 12:9), but of Revelation it is written, "Seal *not* the sayings of the prophecy of this book: for the time is at hand" (22:10, emphasis added). This portion of Holy Scripture clearly was given for our instruction and edification, but thousands of the Lord's people permit themselves to be robbed of blessing by ignoring it.

Significantly enough, it is the one book of the Bible that both begins and ends with a blessing on those who read and keep what is written therein (1:3; 22:7). Surely God did not mean to mock us by promising a blessing on all who keep what they cannot hope to understand! Only unbelief would reason thus. Faith delights to appropriate every part of the sacred record and finds that "they are all [clear] to him that understandeth" (Prov. 8:9).

The true title is given us in the opening verse. It is "The Revelation of Jesus Christ," not "The Revelation of St. John the Divine." No authority exists in any manuscript for the latter designation, and it shows all too plainly how far some early editor had slipped from first principles. John was a saint, as all believers are saints, but he was *not* divine! Such a title would have amazed him beyond measure.

Nor is the book the revelation of John or of any other servant of God; it is the revelation of Jesus Christ Himself.

The word rendered *revelation,* and sometimes *apocalypse,* means literally an unveiling, or manifestation. So this book is the unveiling of our Lord Jesus Christ; He is its one great theme. It presents Him as the Son of Man in the midst of the churches during the current dispensation and as the Judge and the King in the dispensations to come. If you would learn to appreciate Christ more, read this book frequently and prayerfully. It reveals Him as the Lamb rejected but soon to reign in glory—the Lamb on the throne!

And observe that the title is not in the plural. People often speak of the book of "Revelations." No such book is in the Bible. It is *the* Revelation—one blessed, continuous manifestation of God's unique Son, the anointed Prophet, Priest, and King. Revelation is the crowning book of the Bible. It is like the headstone of Zechariah 4:7 that completes and crowns the whole wondrous pyramid of truth.

Of this vast pyramid, the Pentateuch of Moses forms the broad, solid foundation. Upon that is built the Covenant History, then Psalms and the Poetic Books, and then the Prophetic Series of the Old Testament. Higher up are the Gospels and Acts andhen the Epistles with their deep spiritual instruction. Completing the glorious structure, this last solemn but exceedingly precious book, the Revelation, links all of the others with the soon-to-be-manifested glory of God.

Or, if you think of Holy Scripture as a great golden circle of truth, we start with Genesis, the book of beginnings, and go on through the Testaments until we come to Revelation—the book of the last things, and, lo, we find that it dovetails perfectly into the book of Genesis, thus perfecting the inspired ring! The Word of God is one absolutely perfect, unbroken, and unbreakable circle.

A comparison of Genesis and Revelation will readily make this truth plain and show how we have the types in Genesis and the completion of the truth in Revelation—in the one book the beginning and in the other book the consummation.

Genesis gives us the creation of the heavens and the earth; Revelation presents a new heaven and a new earth.

Genesis shows us the earthly paradise, with the Tree of Life and the river of blessing lost through sin; Revelation gives us the Paradise of God, with the Tree of Life and the pure river of Water of Life proceeding out of the throne of God and the Lamb—Paradise regained through Christ's atonement.

In Genesis, we see the first man and his wife set over all of God's creation; in Revelation, we behold the Second Man and His bride ruling over a redeemed world.

In Genesis, we are told of the first typical sacrificial lamb; in Revelation, the Lamb once slain is in the midst of the throne.

In Genesis, we learn of the beginning of sin, when the serpent first entered the garden of delight to beguile Adam and Eve with his sophistries; in Revelation, that old Serpent, called the Devil and Satan, is cast into the lake of fire.

In Genesis, we have the first murderer, the first polygamist, the first rebel, the first drunkard, and so forth; in Revelation, all such people, who refuse to accept God's grace in Christ Jesus, are banished from His presence forever.

In Genesis, we view the rise of Babel, or Babylon; in Revelation, we are called to contemplate its doom.

In Genesis, we see the city of man; in Revelation, we see the city of God.

Genesis shows us how sorrow, death, pain, and tears—the inevitable accompaniments of sin and rebellion—came into the world; Revelation does not close until we have seen God wiping away all tears and welcoming His redeemed into a home where sin, death, pain, and sorrow never come.

And so we might go on for an hour, contrasting and comparing these two books, but enough has been cited, I trust, to stir each interested believer to study for himself. What we get from our Bibles for ourselves is, in the presence of God, is worth far more than all that another person can pass on to us. We may learn from each other, but it is best to take nothing for granted, but rather, like Ruth the Moabitess, to "beat out that [which we have] gleaned" (Ruth 2:17) through meditation and prayer.

But before we examine with some degree of care the opening verses of this remarkable book, it might be good to point out that those who seek to comment upon or expound the book of Revelation present three distinct views of it: the Preterist, the Historical, and the Futurist views. Each of the three systems of interpretation might be subdivided into various, conflicting schools, but the names give the main point of view in each case.

As a rule, the preterists see very little in the book beyond a weird religio-political document supposedly written by some unknown person who took the name of John to give acceptance to his writings, or some other John than the apostle of that name whose real object was to comfort his Christian brethren in a time of great persecution under one of the Roman emperors by portraying the final outcome of the stern conflict as a great victory for the saints that would result in the overthrow of paganism and the recognition of a glorious city of God in its place.

Scholars of the historical school believe that they see in the momentous events of the last nineteen hundred years, the fulfillment of the seals, trumpets, and vials and the other special visions of the book. According to this view, no under-standing of Revelation is possib le apart from a thorough knowledge of the his-tory of the nations comprising Christendom, the sphere that nominally acknowledges Christ's authority. Many and varied are the schools of interpreta-tion founded on this supposition or hypothesis.

Generally speaking, the futurists consider that the largest part of the book applies to a period still future, and that only the first three chapters refer to the current church dispensation. Some extreme futurists also relegate even these three chapters to the end-times and therefore do not see the church in Revelation at all.

As we attempt to expound the book, the reader will see that our own position coincides with that of the futurists first mentioned, but we reserve for a later lecture the ground upon which we base this view.

Turning again to the text, we note in verse 1 that the Revelation of Jesus Christ was given by the Father to the Son, as David revealed to Solomon all of his plans in connection with the building of the future temple. God is repre-sented as being in counsel with our Lord Jesus Christ concerning "things which must shortly come to pass" and that it is the joy of His heart to communicate to His servants. An angel becomes the medium to make everything known to the beloved apostle John, who, in this sense, is to tarry in the church until the com-ing of the Lord—that is, his line of ministry carries us on to that blessed event. Note, then, the order through which the revelation came to us. God gave it to Jesus Christ, who sent it by His angel to His servant John to show to His ser-vants the coming things.

He is said to have *signified* it; that is, He made it known by signs or symbols. It is important to remember this fact. This book is a book of symbols, but the careful student of the Word need not exercise his own ingenuity to think out the meanings of the symbols. A principle of first importance is that *every symbol used in Revelation is explained or alluded to somewhere else in the Bible.* Therefore, he who would get God's mind as to this portion of His Word must study with earnest and prayerful attention every other part of Holy Scripture. Undoubt-edly, this is why so great a blessing is in store for those who read and hear the words of this prophecy and keep the things written therein (v. 3).

Verses 4–8 comprise the salutation. The book is particularly addressed, as a great general epistle, to "the seven churches in Asia." By the term *Asia* we are not to understand the continent that now bears that name, nor yet what we speak of as Asia Minor, but a Roman proconsular province that of old was distinctively denominated "Asia." In John's day, many Christian churches already had been established in that province; of these, seven are selected to be especially addressed. If anyone asks why these seven churches were selected rather than others (as, for instance, Colosse and Hierapolis, both cities in which were important churches), my answer is that the geographical position of these churches was in keeping with the vision presented in verses 12–18. They formed a rough circle in the midst of which the seer beheld Christ standing in His priestly garb, taking note of all that was going on.

But there was more than this: the internal conditions prevailing in these churches were suited to portray the state of the whole sphere of Christian profession in seven distinct periods, from the apostolic days to the close of the church's testimony on earth. Even the very names of the seven cities, when interpreted, help to make this fact plain; they become, so to speak, keys to the different periods to which they apply. But the proof of this truth must be reserved for the next three addresses.

Observe how the three Persons of the Holy Trinity are linked in the salutation: "He who is, and who was, and who is to come" is Jehovah. This is the literal meaning of the mystic name communicated to Moses. "Jehovah" is a compound formed from three words; the first meaning *He is;* the second, *He was;* the third, *He will be* or *He will come.* Jehovah is the triune God; hence, the Father, the Son, and the Spirit are alike called by this name. But the current passage clearly has God the Father in view. The Spirit comes before us in the next clause: "and from the seven Spirits [that] are before his throne." If it is hard to understand how the one, eternal Holy Spirit can be so pictured, turn to Isaiah 11:1–2, where we read of the seven spirits who rest upon the Branch of Jehovah, our Lord Jesus Christ. Note the order given.

1. The Spirit of the Lord
2. The Spirit of Wisdom
3. The Spirit of Understanding
4. The Spirit of Counsel
5. The Spirit of Might
6. The Spirit of Knowledge
7. The Spirit of Fear of the Lord

In this passage, we see the one Spirit in the sevenfold plenitude of His power. Seven, mentioned so frequently in this book, is the number of perfection and is so used here. Then, with the Father and the Spirit, we have Jesus Christ as "the faithful witness" when He was here on earth, "the first begotten of the dead" in resurrection glory, and "the prince of the kings of the earth" when He comes again to reign.

No wonder an outburst of praise and worship follows (v. 5) at this full revelation of His glories: "Unto him that loveth us, and hath loosed us from our sins by his own blood, and hath made us a kingdom, priests to God and his Father, to him be glory and dominion for ever and ever. Amen." John's heart was full and could contain no longer. Adoration and praise were the spontaneous result of contemplation of Christ's person and offices as Prophet, Priest, and King.

Then John heralds the glad news of His coming again. He is going to return—not as a babe, born of woman, but as the glorified One, descending from heaven, and, by a stupendous miracle, every eye shall see Him while "all tribes of the land shall mourn because of him." This, I am persuaded, is the true meaning and refers to Zechariah 12, where the prophet sees all of the tribes of restored Israel mourning over their past rejection of Christ and lamenting their folly while awaiting His return. John speaks for all of the church when he cries with rapture, "Even so. Amen!" Does *your* heart take up the same glad welcoming shout, or can it be that you are unready to meet Him and would dread His return?

In the eighth verse, it is the Son who speaks, and now He declares Himself to be Jehovah, too, One eternally with the Father. He is the Alpha and Omega—the first and the last letters of the Greek alphabet—the beginning and the ending: He created all things; He will wind up all things and bring in the new heavens and the new earth. He is, and was, and will be the coming One, *El Shaddai,* who of old appeared to Abraham—the Almighty. May our hearts be occupied with Him, and may His return always be for us "that blessed hope" (Titus 2:13).

THE FIRST VISION

Revelation 1:9–20

In our study of the first chapter last week, we got down to the first vision of the book. The apostle John tells us that he was a prisoner banished to "the isle called Patmos"—a little rocky island in the Mediterranean Sea—for the sake of the name of the Lord Jesus Christ. There, shut away from all Christian fellowship, John had a greater God-given mission for him than he had ever known.

You remember that when the Lord Jesus had restored Peter's soul after his fall, He told him how when he was old another would gird him and lead him whither he would not, thus signifying by what death he should glorify God. Then Jesus said, "Follow me" (John 21:19). Peter turned and saw the disciple whom Jesus loved following, and said, "Lord, what shall this man do?" (v. 21). The Lord answered, "If I will that he tarry till I come, what is that to thee? Follow *thou* me" (v. 22). Note that in that sentence the Lord Jesus very clearly sets forth two things that some Christian teachers often confuse—death and the second coming of Christ. He says, "If I will that he tarry till I come, what is that to thee?" and He clearly puts "tarry till I come" in contrast with Peter's dying before He comes. There is no place in Scripture where death and our Lord's second coming are confused. Death, instead of being the second coming of the Lord, is that which is to be swallowed up in victory at that Second Coming. But most of us are extremists, so when the Lord said to Peter, "If I will that he tarry till I come," we are told that this saying "went abroad among the brethren that that disciple should *not* die: yet Jesus said not unto him, He shall not die; but, If I will that he tarry till I come" (v. 23). And, of course, time proved their hasty conclusion to be incorrect.

And John also died long years ago, but some years before the end of his earthly life, while he was on that desolate island of Patmos, where he was banished for his faithfulness, a wonderful vision of truth connected with our Lord Jesus' second coming unfolded before him, by means of which *his ministry abides with us until Christ shall come again.* John is absent from the body but present with the Lord—as he has been for more than eighteen hundred years. But through the ministry given to us in this wonderful book of Revelation, John abides still until Jesus comes, throwing light upon all of the complex problems that God's people would have to meet in the current dispensation, and he wants us to understand, as no other ministry does, the great program that God Himself is soon going to carry out.

So we see that the Devil really overreached himself when Domitian banished John to the isle of Patmos; if John had remained ministering the Word to the saints and preaching to the unsaved, he might not have been able to write the book of Revelation, and we might not have the visions that this book gives us. But there on that lonely isle, with him shut off from all of his service, the veil was rolled back, enabling him to give us this wonderful record of the unveiling of Jesus Christ.

John tells us that he was "in the Spirit on the Lord's day." The Lord's Day is a divinely given designation for the first day of the week. I know that some people tell us that the Lord's Day here is the Jewish Sabbath, which in the Old Testament is called the Sabbath of the Lord; and they tell us that inasmuch as nowhere in the New Testament is the Jewish Sabbath done away with, it should still be observed. But, in answer to that, we may notice that nowhere in all of the New Testament, after the resurrection of the Lord Jesus Christ from the dead, do we ever have any special honor paid to the seventh day—Israel's Sabbath. On that day, the Lord lay in the tomb. On the morning of the first day of the week, "when the Sabbaths were past"—as Matthew 28:1 puts it, that is, when the Jewish Sabbaths were ended—the Lord rose in triumph from the dead, and that new day became distinctly the Lord's Day.

You find in the Word of God that "on the first day of the week the disciples came together to break bread" and on the first day of the week the Lord met with His own in the Upper Room. In connection with their gathering thus, see

1 Corinthians 16:2: "Upon the first day of the week let every one of you lay by him in store, as God hath prospered him." Thus, Christian giving and the weekly remembrance of the Lord are linked. It is safe to say that if Christians everywhere carried this out, there would be no "financial problem" in the church of God today.

The first day of the week is preeminently the day for Christians. Whenever the earliest Christian writers refered to the term "Lord's Day," they spoke of it as the first day of the week, the day after the Jewish Sabbath, the day we Christians call "the Lord's Day." I venture to say that people who lived from fifty to two hundred years after the apostle John were far more likely to know what was meant by the term "Lord's Day" than are people who live eighteen hundred years after. I know there are some students of prophecy who confuse the Lord's Day with the "great day of the Lord," but a decided difference exists between the two terms. The Lord's Day is in the possessive case in the original. The word translated "Lord's" is an adjective. If it were permissible to say the Lordian day, you would have the exact meaning of this word. Such an adjective has been formed from the word *Christ*. We say a "Christian spirit" and so forth. So the Lordian or Lordly Day is the day on which the Lord Jesus Christ broke asunder the bonds of death and rose, never more to die, and we Christians love to keep this day in memory of Him.

On that day, John says, "I was in the Spirit." John was far away from any Christian assembly, but he found his pleasure in the things of God. Some Christians you know go to meeting every Lord's Day when they are at home, but when they are on their vacations or out of town, the Lord's Day is just like any other day because nobody knows them in those places. But John, shut away from any Christian association, was "in the Spirit on the Lord's day." It is good to see a Christian take his Bible with him on a vacation and have daily communication with the Lord, or look up someone who does not know Jesus Christ and seek to make Him known to that needy one. See to it that you are in the Spirit on the Lord's Day.

Being "in the Spirit" on the Lord's Day, John had a glorious vision of the Lord Himself. First, he heard a voice, and then he saw a form. He heard a voice saying, "I am Alpha and Omega, the first and the last. What thou seest, write in a book," and so forth. "And being turned, I saw seven golden lampstands." If I understand it aright, these were not like the candlesticks in the temple and in the tabernacle. Those were seven-branched; they had six side branches, and the central shaft made the seven. But John saw seven separate lamp stands. Christ is represented by the seven-branched candlestick in the holy place, and the Spirit of God is represented by the seven lamps upon it. But during His absence—during the time of His priesthood up there in heaven—His people are to be lights for Him in this world. So John sees in this first vision not one candlestick with seven branches, but seven distinct lampstands in the form of a circle, and in the midst of them he sees One like unto the Son of Man girt about the breasts with a golden girdle. It is the Lord judging in the midst of His assemblies.

Then we learn what these lampstands symbolize. They are the seven churches in the Roman proconsular province of Asia, and these seven churches were selected from all of the assemblies of God that they might illustrate for us the whole course of the church's history until the coming again of our Lord Jesus Christ. In His absence, the church of God is responsible to keep a light burning in the midst of the darkness. You remember that He said while He was here on earth, "I am the light of the world" (John 8:12; 9:5), and so forth, and before He went away, He said to His disciples, "Ye are the light of the world" (Matt. 5:14). He has gone up to the glory, and we—all of the members of His church—are to shine for Him here. What kind of light are you giving out for Jesus? Do your next-door neighbors appreciate your Christianity? Do the people with whom do business think much of it? What about the tradesmen and your business associates—all of the folks with whom you have to do so much of the time? I would rather get the testimony of the people with whom you have to do than of those you meet in the public assemblies. When a man is really converted, it changes him through and through.

The church of God and individual assemblies of Christians are in this world to shine for Christ. We are here not merely to enjoy the things of Christ ourselves, but to hold up Christ to the world. Speaking of the Lord's Supper, the apostle says in 1 Corinthians 11:26, "For as often as ye eat this bread, and drink this cup, ye do shew the Lord's death till he come." The word translated "shew" in that passage is the same word that is used elsewhere for preaching: "you preach the Lord's death." It is a testimony to sinners as well as something for the church to enjoy. The church of God is here to shine for Christ, and we shine for Him as He is exalted in our gatherings and manifested in our lives.

"I saw seven golden [lampstands]; and in the midst . . . one like unto the Son of man." In many respects, He seemed different from how John remembered Him, except when they were on the Mount of Transfiguration. But he knew who He was—"one like unto the Son of man." John had known Him well on earth, and he knew Him the moment He appeared in that glorious vision.

Note how He is described "clothed with a garment down to the foot"—the priestly garment. He is there in the long, white garments of the high priest and girt about the breasts with a golden girdle. The girdle speaks of service. We read of the servant girding himself and waiting upon the table. Here it is a high-priestly service. Our blessed Lord is now serving us at God's right hand. Looking back to the Cross, where Jesus hung in sacrifice for us, we rejoice to remember His dying words, "It is finished" (John 19:30). Nothing can be added to and nothing taken away from that completed work. But He is now carrying on another work for His people. Although He is up there in the glory, He is still serving us. His people need His help all along the way. The moment you belong to the Lord Jesus, you are brought into living union with our great High Priest at God's right hand. "He is able to save to the uttermost" all those who come to God through faith by Him, seeing "He ever liveth to make intercession for them" (Heb. 7:25). He does not ask you to go in your own strength. Trust Him as Savior, and let *Him* fill your heart and control your life. He will live His life in you, to His praise and glory. We are to come boldly to a throne of grace, that we may obtain mercy and find seasonable help. The girdle is a *golden* one, and Christ's service is in full accord with God's holy and righteous ways.

Notice verse 14: "His head and his hairs were white like wool, as white as snow; and his eyes were as a flame of fire." I said last Sunday night that every figure and every symbol found in this book is explained somewhere else in the Bible. Turn now to Daniel 7:9–13, where we read of the Ancient of Days and the Son of Man. Note that John said that the One in the midst of the seven lampstands was "like unto the Son of man." He was undoubtedly linking that with the seventh chapter of Daniel. He goes on to describe Him as one whose hair is "as white as snow." He had the appearance of great age although the Lord Jesus was cut off at the age of thirty-three.

Observe again Daniel 7:9: "And the Ancient of days did sit . . . and the hair of his head was like the pure wool," and so forth. Who is the Ancient of Days? In Daniel 7, He is the Jehovah of Israel, and to Him the Son of Man comes. But we learn that the Son of Man is Himself the Ancient of Days. In other words, the Jehovah of the Old Testament is the Jesus of the New Testament. Christ is Himself "God manifest in the flesh."

Turn to Micah 5:2, "But thou, Bethlehem Ephratah, though thou be little among the thousands of Judah, yet out of thee shall he come forth unto he that is to be ruler in Israel; whose goings forth have been from of old, from everlasting." Who is the Savior born in Bethlehem? He is the One "whose goings forth have been from of old, from everlasting." The Lord Jesus Christ is the Ancient of Days, and this is one of the truths for which Christians are called to contend in these times of apostasy. Ministers are telling people that we are all sons of God.

They deny Christ's virgin birth and deity and say that He is simply the greatest of all teachers sent from God. But that is not enough for the Christian. Christ is God—or we and those in heaven are idolaters—because it is He who is worshiped there and here. The Unitarian believes in God the Father but not in the Son. He says, "Don't draw the lines too straight—Jesus is only a creature." If that Unitarian is right, I am an idolater because I am worshiping Jesus Christ. I worship, not Buddha, not Brahma, but Jesus and acknowledge Him as God. Yet some people would tell me that it does not make any difference! It makes a tremendous difference for both time and eternity. It is going to mean the difference between heaven and hell because the Lord Jesus says, "Except ye believe that I am, ye shall die in your sins, and whither I go ye cannot come" (John 8:21). Jesus Christ is God manifest in the flesh, the Only-begotten Son of God, the anointed One who came in grace to save lost, guilty sinners. Are you trusting Him as your Savior?

So we see that this One in the midst is the Son of Man, yet God Himself. The Lord Jesus has that double character, and His place is always in the midst. Jesus in the midst! No company of believers deserves to be called a Christian company that does not give Him that place. But "Where two or three are gathered together unto my name," He says, "there am I in the midst" (Matt. 18:20). You remember that when He hung on that cross between two thieves, He saved one of them who turned to Him in faith. When He rose from the dead and His disciples were gathered in the Upper Room, "Then came Jesus and stood in the midst" (John 20:26). In the fifth chapter of Revelation, John looked and saw the Lamb "in the midst of the throne, in the midst of the elders, and in the midst of the living creatures." This is the place that ever belongs to the Lord Jesus—the central place, the preeminent place. God must have Jesus in the midst.

But let us turn back to our chapter. "His eyes were as a flame of fire." John did not know Him in that way on earth, except perhaps as He rebuked the Pharisees. But remember that all who do not accept Him now are going to see His eyes like a flame of fire. Nothing will be hidden from those eyes. They will discern everything that you would fain hide. All will be out in the light and brought into judgment. Oh, have everything out with Him *now*. Do you realize that the first time you meet God, you must meet Him with all of your sins upon your soul? Have you had a meeting with Him yet? If the first time you meet Him is at the day of judgment, it will be too late. You can have your first meeting with Him in this world. You can meet Him by faith. Do not try to improve or make yourself better. Come just as you are, without one plea, but that He is the sinner's Savior and invites you to come. You will find that those eyes, that are as a flame of fire and look into the depths of your soul, will become filled with the most tender love and will draw you to Himself.

But John's description goes on to say, "His feet were like molten brass." Brass in the Old Testament is the symbol of judgment. The brazen altar that stood before the tabernacle was that on which the fire of God's judgment was burning continually. It was of brass[1] because brass could stand the fire. You will find throughout Scripture that brass is a symbol of judgment. And here He has feet like brass because His ways are in righteousness unyielding. The day is coming when He shall put His feet on everything contrary to truth and righteousness. Everything unholy will be stamped out in divine judgment.

His voice is as the sound of many waters. When you stand on the cliff by the seaside and hear the sound of many waters, you are awed by their power. The ship that looks so large and strong at the docks is a helpless thing when the ocean rouses itself in furious anger. His voice is as the sound of the billows of the sea— a voice of power. That power, put forth in grace, means your salvation; the same power, put forth in judgment, means your eternal damnation! You may pass from death unto life by hearing His voice now. He can speak to your poor soul and in a moment create your heart anew. Here is what He says: "The hour is coming, *and now is,* when the dead shall hear the voice of the Son of God; and they that hear shall live" (John 5:25, emphasis added). Hearing His voice, believing His Word, you live! Have you heard that voice of power? Soon, His people will hear that same mighty voice calling them from earth away, "for the Lord himself shall descend from heaven with a shout, . . . and the dead in Christ shall rise first" (1 Thess. 4:16), and the living saints shall be changed. Sometimes Christians become discouraged, but when that voice, like the sound of many waters, says from heaven, "Arise, my love, my fair one, and come away" (Song 2:10, 13), we will be caught up in a moment to meet Him in the air.

"He had in his right hand seven stars." The stars speak of ministry committed to His saints, as responsible to shine by His light and for Him in this world. "They that turn many to righteousness shall shine as the stars forever and ever" (Dan. 12:3). He holds the stars in His right hand. "Out of his mouth went forth a sharp two-edged sword." It is the Word of God (Heb. 4:12). Men are trifling with that two-edged sword, but they will find out soon that it is powerful and irresistible.

"His countenance was as the sun shining in his strength." Malachi 4:2: "But unto you that fear my name, shall the Sun of righteousness arise with healing in his wings." When Saul of Tarsus was stricken down, remember what he saw—a light above the brightness of the sun. It was the glory of God in the face of Christ

Jesus. That is what John saw, and he fell at His feet. But He laid His right hand upon John, and said, "Fear not, I am the first and the last. I am [the Living One. I] was dead, but I am alive for evermore. I have the keys of death and of hades."

What is death? It is the body without the spirit: "The body without the spirit is dead" (James 2:26). There is no such thing in the Bible as soul sleeping. The spirit of the man is not in the grave. The body goes down to the grave, but the spirit is in the unseen world. Hades is the condition of the spirit without the body. Christ has the keys of both death and hades.

In verse 19, we get the threefold division of the book of Revelation: "Write the things which thou hast seen, and the things which are, and the things which shall be hereafter"—or "after these things."

"*The things which thou hast seen*" are the things of chapter 1—the *first* division of the book of Revelation.

"*The things which are*" follow in the next two chapters and make the *second* division. "The things which are" have to do with the current dispensation. The seven churches give us a picture of the whole professing church's history from the apostolic period to the coming of the Lord Jesus. These two chapters portray the condition of the church on earth in seven distinct periods. The church's history ends at the Rapture, when Jesus comes as the Bright and Morning Star. That event closes the current dispensation.

"*The things which shall be after these things,*" chapters 4 to the end, make the *third* and last division of the book—the things which shall take place after the church's history ends: the Great Tribulation, the kingdom, and the eternal state.

But our time is up, and I must close for tonight.

THE SEVEN CHURCHES

Revelation 2

We now turn to the letters addressed to the first four churches as found in chapter 2. In the last address, I tried to make clear that the key to the structure of the book is 1:19. We have already been occupied with the things that the apostle John had seen—that is, the first vision of the book, where he beheld the glorified Lord in the midst of the lampstands. The third revision is clearly indicated in the opening words of chapter 4, where we read in the Revised Version, *"After these things I* looked, and behold, a door was opened in heaven." Necessarily, then, the second division must take in simply what we have in chapters 2 and 3—"the things which are" (present, continuous tense)—the things that are now in progress. This is the only part of the Apocalypse that has to do specifically with the present, the church period, although it is all written for our instruction, warning, and encouragement.

In fact, I believe that the real value of the Revelation consists in this: that it gives us the full-grown trees that we now see as developing saplings. We need this book to judge aright the various movements that are now going on. For myself, I am sure that if I did not know something of the teaching of this book, I would long since have been identified with many movements that I have come absolutely to distrust because I believe that I can see, by a careful study of the Apocalypse, what the end of them will be.

Let me illustrate. Someone asks about the so-called "Church Federation scheme." Wouldn't it be a wonderful thing if all of the churches united? If we simply had one great organization, wouldn't it be grand? Everyone could agree to accept a common creed so worded that everyone could subscribe to it, and so the shame of Christendom's divisions would be at an end. Now, why not go in for something like that? Would not that be the fulfillment of the prayer of our Lord, "that they all may be one"?

Well, I might be caught by such a proposal, but I turn to the book of Revelation and learn that just such a religious federation is going to arise after the church of God has been caught away to be with the Lord Jesus Christ, and it is designated in the seventh chapter as "Babylon the Great." This will be the big world church. The current movement is just a preparation for that world church, and when I have the light from heaven shining upon it in the book of Revelation, I say that if that is the way it is going to end, the thing to do is to have no part in it now. Separation from evil—not fusion of diverse systems—is the divine order. So we see that the prophetic book throws the light of the future upon events and movements that are now in progress that we may take warning and be preserved from that which is contrary to the mind of God.

Before we begin our study of "the things which are," let me give you this parable. Some time ago, while some people were rummaging through an old castle, they came across a very strange-looking old lock that secured a stout door. They shook the door and tried unsuccessfully to open it. They tried first one way and then another to move the lock, but they could not turn it. By and by, somebody picked up a bunch of old keys from some rubbish on the floor and said, "Maybe I can unlock it." He tried one key, but it made no impression. He tried another key, and the lock gave a little, another and it gave a little more, and so on. But no key would open the lock. At last, he came to a peculiar old key. He slipped it into the lock, gave a turn, and the lock was open. They said, "Undoubtedly, this key was meant for this lock."

You will understand my parable if I draw your attention to the fact that, in the twentieth verse of the first chapter, we are told that a mystery was connected with the seven lampstands. The seven lampstands are said to symbolize the seven churches of Asia, but a mystery was connected with them. Although some people have tried one key and other people have tried another (all kinds of efforts have been made to interpret this mystery), no solution was found until some devout students of Scripture weighing this portion said, "Might it not be that, inasmuch as this section of the book presents 'the things which are,' God has been pleased to give us here a prophetic history of the church for the entire dispensation?" But would the key fit the lock? They compared the first part of the church's history with the letter to Ephesus. Here it fitted perfectly. They went on and compared the letter to Smyrna with the second part of the church's history, and the agreement was most marked. They went right on down to the end, and when they came to Laodicea, they found that what is written to the church of Laodicea answers exactly to the condition of the professing church in the days in which we live, and they said, "There, the mystery is all clear. The lock has been opened; therefore, we have the right key."

For myself, I have no question that this was in very truth the mind of the Lord in sending these letters to the seven churches. Seven churches were chosen because seven in Scripture is the number of perfection; and you have only to read these seven letters and then take any good, reliable church history and see for yourself how perfectly the key fits the lock.

The very names of the churches are significant. It would be impossible to reverse any of these names. If the order were changed, they would not apply. Take the first one, for example. *Ephesus* means "desirable," such a term as a Greek applied to the maiden of his choice. Ephesus gives us a picture of the church as it was in the beginning, when the Lord held the stars (His servants) in His hand and controlled their ministry. He sent them here and there, just as He would, to proclaim the glad gospel of His grace and to minister to His saints. But human systems have largely changed all of that. He walked in the midst of His churches. His eyes were upon everything, and He was there to admonish, correct, and control. Observe that in the beginning His Name was the only center, and unto Him was the gathering of His saints. Read the second and third verses:

> I know thy works, and thy labour, and thy patience, and how thou canst not bear them which are evil: and thou hast tried them which say they are apostles, and are not, and hast found them liars: and hast borne, and hast patience, and for my name's sake hast laboured, and hast not fainted.

The early church was walking in separation from the world. The Greek word *ecclesia,* translated "church" in our Bibles, means a called-out company. This is God's ideal, and every effort to amalgamate the church and the world is opposed to His mind and must end in confusion because the church will never convert the world in the current dispensation. Someone once asked Dr. A. T. Pierson, "Don't you really think that the world is getting converted already?" "Well," he said, "I admit that the world has become a little churchy, but the church has become immensely worldly." If it were possible that the church could convert the world, that would be the end of the church. What do I mean? Simply this: the church is a *called-out* company, and if the world were converted, there would not be anything else left out of which to call the church.

In the days of Ephesus, believers could not bear those who were evil. In our day, discipline in the church is almost at an end. In many quarters, anyone is welcome to full participation in all church privileges, particularly if they have a good bank account, but in the beginning it was very different. That little Ephesian assembly said, "We don't want numbers if they are not *holy* numbers. We don't want growth at the expense of holiness." More than that, they were loyal to the truth. They tried those who claimed to be apostles, and if they found that they were deceivers, they refused them as liars, instead of saying, "Oh well, you know, Dr. So-and-so comes with such good recommendations, he is such a lovely man and so cultured, and though he doesn't happen to believe in the Virgin Birth, the deity of Christ, or His atonement, and so forth, still he has so many good qualities that we mustn't be hard on him." The early church would have said, "Are you a servant of the Lord Jesus Christ?" and put a few serious questions to him. If he was not what he professed to be, they soon unmasked him and refused his unholy ministrations. But today, teachers can deny almost any truth of Scripture, and the professing church never knows the difference. Oh, for more of the zeal and piety of early days!

In verse 3, we learn that these saints were suffering for the name of the Lord Jesus. They were not suffering for the name of any denomination nor yet for some special theories or usages. They were suffering for Christ's sake. For His name's sake, they bore trial and endured persecution.

And yet, even then, we have the evidence of early decline. Verse 4 says, "But I have . . . against thee, because thou hast left thy first love." They had left their first love. Their heart was drifting away from Christ. The decline that began in those first days of the church has continued. There has been no corporate recovery. That spirit of declension has continued increasing until the current Laodicean day.

In the next letter, we see that the Lord, whose love never changes, permitted something to take place to arouse His people from their lethargy.

> And unto the angel of the church in Smyrna write; These things saith
> the first and the last, which was dead, and is alive; I know thy works,

and tribulation, and poverty, (but thou art rich) and I know the blasphemy of them which say they are Jews, and are not, but are the synagogue of Satan. (vv. 8–9)

Smyrna means "myrrh." It is frequently mentioned in Scripture in connection with the embalming of the dead. Myrrh had to be crushed for it to emit its fragrance. This description sets forth the period when the church was crushed beneath the iron heel of pagan Rome, yet it never gave out such sweet fragrance to God as in those two centuries of almost constant martyrdom.

"These things saith the first and the last, which was dead, and is alive." What a blessed thing to know that the children of God are linked with a resurrected Christ! The power of His resurrection works in them. He says, "I know thy works, and tribulation and poverty, but thou art rich." This was a day when the church was hated, outlawed, and persecuted. Instead of worshiping in magnificent buildings, they gathered in caves, catacombs, and other hidden places, with sentries posted to warn them of the approach of their foes. Despised by the world and condemned as enemies of the empire because of their faith in and loyalty to Christ, their lives were precious to God. They were in His eyes rich. They were poor in this world's goods, but they were rich in faith.

But even then, all was not perfection, so He says, "I know the blasphemy of them which say they are Jews, and are not, but are the synagogue of Satan," referring to the Judaizing movement that came into the church in the early centuries. It was the leaven of Galatianism that had never been wholly judged and that made astonishing progress in the second and third centuries. He says, "Fear not . . . thou shalt have tribulation ten days." It is significant that in the two centuries of Roman persecution, which began with Nero and terminated in A.D. 312, ten distinct edicts demanded that governors seek out Christians everywhere and put them to death. The last edict was under Diocletian. He was the tenth persecutor. The early Christians believed that he would be the last, and he was. "The blood of the martyrs is the seed of the church," said Augustine. The testimony of the dying Christians again and again led their very persecutors to receive the Lord Jesus Christ as their Savior because of the convincing power of the truth manifested in the martyrs. Satan's effort to destroy Christianity by persecution was in vain. But those were days when it meant something to be a Christian. When God's people were being crushed like myrrh, what a sweet odor of devotion, what fragrance of Christian love was wafted up to the very throne of God!

Pergamos has two meanings: "marriage" and "elevation." It speaks of the time when the church was elevated to a place of power and was married to the world. It depicts the time when church and state were united under Constantine and his successors.

Read verses 12–13:

> And to the angel of the church in Pergamos write; These things saith he which hath the sharp sword with two edges; I know thy works, and where thou dwellest, even where Satan's seat is: and thou holdest fast my name, and hast not denied my faith, even in those days wherein Antipas was my faithful martyr, who was slain among you, where Satan dwelleth.

The Lord Jesus judges everything by the Word. The word that He spoke will judge men in the last day. If you reject it *now,* it will judge you *then.* "I know . . . where thou dwellest," He says, even on "Satan's throne." What was Satan's throne? If you had asked any of the Smyrna believers, they would have pointed you to the emperor's throne in Rome. In Pergamos, you find the very church of God sitting upon the imperial throne. How did that happen?

Those of you who are familiar with Roman history and church tradition will recall that after the death of Diocletian and Glarius, Constantine and Maxentius contended for the throne. Constantine is said to have seen a vision of a cross of fire and to have heard a voice saying, "In this sign, conquer." He wondered what the vision could mean. He was told that the cross was the sign of the Christian religion, and that it must mean that the God of the Christians was calling him to be the champion of the Christian religion, that if he obeyed the voice, he would be victor over the hosts of Maxentius and become emperor of the world. He called for Christian bishops and asked them to explain their religion to him. He accepted the new doctrine and declared himself to be its God-appointed patron and protector. Some writers make a great deal of this so-called conversion of Constantine, but it is questionable if he ever became a child of God by faith in Christ Jesus. He won a great victory over his opponent and thus became emperor of the world, and one of his first acts was to liberate the Christians and to stop all persecution. He bestowed unwonted honors on the bishops; they sat on thrones with the nobles of the empire.

During this time, the truth of the second coming of Christ was forgotten. Before the days of Constantine, the church was looking for Him. That was their expectation and hope. But after the great change in their circumstances, they largely lost sight of this truth. Christian bishops said, "We have been looking for

Christ's reign, but we have been wrong; *Constantine's* empire is Christ's kingdom." They thought that the church was already reigning, so it went on until the days of the Reformation, when the light began to dawn again.

But now note a most interesting thing: at the very time that the Lord said, "I know . . . where thou dwellest, even where Satan's seat [or throne] is," He goes on to say, "Thou holdest fast my name, and hast not denied my faith," and so forth. Here is something very remarkable. At the same time that Christ sees them sitting on Satan's throne, He can yet commend them for holding fast His Name.

During that time, the Arian controversy was fought. Arius denied the eternity of the Word. John says, "In the beginning was the Word" (John 1:1)—He always existed. When everything that had a beginning began, the Word *was*. Arius declared that the Word was the greatest of all beings that ever emanated from God. His opponents insisted that the Word was one with the Father, in one eternal Trinity—Father, Son, and Holy Spirit: one God in three persons. It was the most tremendous issue the church had ever been called to face, and, for more than a century, it was the issue that provoked heated controversy everywhere. For years, the church was almost rent asunder over two words— *"homoiosian"* and *"homoousian."* The former word meant "of *like* substance"; the latter word meant "of the *same* substance." The first was the battle cry of the Arians; the second was that of the orthodox, headed by Athanasius, Bishop of Alexandria. So irreconcilable were the contending parties that Constantine himself at last decided to take a hand in the matter, and he called a great church council, which convened in the city of Nicea, where they debated the question of what the apostolic teaching really had been. Was Jesus truly God, or was He only the greatest being that God had ever brought into existent? More than three hundred bishops met, and Constantine, sitting on a golden throne, presided as the acknowledged head of the Christian church at the very time that he still bore the title Pontifex Maximus, or High Priest of the Heathen—the same title that the pope now bears.

They examined the matter in question from all sides. Again and again Constantine had to quell disturbances because feelings ran so high. On one occasion, a brilliant Arian seemed to have almost silenced opposition, and the great assemblage seemed to be about to cast its vote in favor of the damnable Unitarian heresy, when a hermit from the deserts of Africa sprang to his feet, clad chiefly in tiger's skin. He tore the cloak from his back, disclosing great scars (the result of having been thrown into the arena among the wild beasts, which dreadfully disfigured his back with their claws), crying dramatically, "These are the brand marks of the Lord Jesus Christ, and I cannot hear this blasphemy." Then he proceeded to give so stirring an address, setting forth so clearly the truth as to Christ's eternal deity, that the majority of the council realized in a moment that it was indeed the voice of the Spirit of God. Whether this story is actually true I cannot say, but it well sets forth the spirit pervading many who were in attendance, most of whom had passed through the terrible persecution of Diocletian. The result was that the council of Nicea went on record as confessing the true deity of our Lord Jesus Christ, "Very God of Very God," "Light of Lights," "perfection of perfection"—God and man in one blessed person, nevermore to be separated. Thus was settled once and forever, publicly, the acknowledged faith of the church of God, which held fast to His Word and would not deny His Name.

What would have been the case if the council had decided the other way? It would have meant that Unitarianism would have henceforth borne the stamp of orthodoxy, and the truth of the deity of Christ would have been branded as heresy.

We have no record as to who the Antipas referred to in the latter part of the preceding quoted verses was, but it is singular that the word means "against all." Many years after the Council of Nicea, when the Arian party was again largely in the ascendancy, Athanasius, that doughty old champion of the truth, was summoned before the Arian emperor Theodosius, who demanded that he cease his opposition to the teaching of Arius—who, by the way, had long since died—and admit the Arians to the Lord's Table. This Athanasius refused to do. Theodosius reproved him bitterly for what he considered his rebellious spirit and asked sternly, "Do you not realize that all the world is against you?" The champion of the truth drew himself up and answered the emperor, "Then I am against all the world." He was a true Antipas, a faithful witness to the end of his days, despite banishment and opposition of various kinds.

Oh, my brethren, God wants just such men today, men of God, who, for the truth's sake, are willing to stand, if need be, against all the world!

We now consider another phase of things in the Pergamos period—the introduction of the doctrine of Balaam and the teaching of the Nicolaitanes in the church. Balaam taught Balak to cast a stumbling block before the sons of Israel by leading them to make unholy alliances with the Midianitish women, as recorded in Numbers 25:1–9. In figure, this incident is the union of the church and the world. During the Smyrna period, Satan sought to destroy the church by persecution. In the next three centuries, he tried different tactics: he endeavored to ruin the testimony by worldly patronage from without and the introduction of false principles from within. You know that it is far more dangerous for the church to be patronized by the world than when the world is openly arrayed against it. Take any of the different denominations in Christendom. When were they shining most brightly for the Lord? It was in the days of their first love, when they were suffering from the world and were the objects of its bitter persecution. But when those days had passed, when the period of persecution ended and the world began to look upon them with complacency, to greet them with the outstretched hand and the smiling face, instead of with the sword and the frown, in every instance decline set in. So it was in the Pergamos period. Constantine's patronage did what Diocletian's persecution could not do: it corrupted the church, and she forgot her calling as a chaste virgin espoused to an absent Lord. Then she gave her hand in marriage to the world that had crucified Him, thus entering into an unholy alliance of which she has never really repented.

In close connection with this, we have the introduction of wrong principles within—the teaching of the Nicolaitanes. Others have often pointed out that this is an untranslated Greek word meaning "rulers over the people." Nicolaitanism is really clerisy—the subjugation of those who were contemptuously styled "the laity" by a hierarchical order that lorded it over them as their own possessions, forgetting that it is written, "One is your Master, even Christ; and all ye are brethren" (Matt. 23:8). In the letter to Ephesus, the Lord commended them for hating the deeds of the Nicolaitanes, those who, like Diotrephes, loved to have the preeminence among them. But, in the Pergamos letter, we have Nicolaitanism designated as a distinct system of teaching. That was when clerisy was accepted as of divine origin and therefore something to which one must bow.

All of this prepared the way for the Thyatira period, according to the letter that follows.

I have already tried to point out that every one of these names seems to be significant. Thyatira is perhaps the most difficult of all to define. Scholars tell us that it comes from two words, one meaning a sacrifice, or an incense offering, and the other meaning that which goes on continually. A suggested interpretation, therefore, is "continual sacrifice." This interpretation is very significant because Thyatira undoubtedly sets forth the period that was the result of the union of church and state, which we have already noticed. In the seventh century, the Bishop of Rome was first regularly recognized as Christ's vicegerent and the visible head of the church. This was, properly speaking, the beginning of the papacy. No Roman Catholic Church existed, in the full sense, until the pope was the acknowledged head of Christendom. It is important for Protestants to remember this fact. You will often hear papists say, "You know the first church was the Roman Catholic Church, and all of the different branches of the Protestant church have simply broken off from Rome. There was no Protestant church until the days of Luther." That is an absolute sophistry. No such thing as the papacy existed until the seventh century of the Christian era. For six centuries before that, the church was becoming more and more corrupt, drifting farther away from the Word of God, until, in the seventh century, men professing themselves to be servants of God were ready to acknowledge the pope as the head of all Christendom.

A Roman Catholic once asked a bright Protestant school girl, "Where was your church before the days of Henry the VIII?" "Why, sir, where yours never was, *in the Bible,*" she sensibly and correctly replied. It is a far cry from the simplicity of early Christianity, when in the seventh century they were ready to acknowledge the pretensions of the bishop of Rome.

I said that Thyatira seemed to imply a continual sacrifice. You will see the significance of this meaning in the great fundamental error of the church of Rome—the sacrifice of the Mass. The Roman Catholic priests declare that, in the Mass, they offer a continual sacrifice for the sins of the living and the dead. Other errors of the church of Rome spring from that error. Protestants might be able to condone many things, but this is the central, the root, blasphemy—the denial of the *finished* work of the Lord Jesus on Calvary's Cross—the one, only, and all-sufficient offering for the sins of a guilty world. Every time the priest stands at Rome's altar to offer the sacrifice of the Mass, he denies the unchanging efficacy of the work wrought by the Lord Jesus on Calvary's Cross. I have often pressed this question home to Catholic priests: "What is your function as a sacrificing priest?" They say, "It is my privilege to offer up the Lord Jesus from time to time a continual sacrifice for the sins of the living and the dead."

I generally put it like this: "Well, Christ has to be slain that He may be offered up; doesn't He?"

"Yes."

"You claim, then, that every time you offer the sacrifice of the Mass, every time you pronounce the blessing, you are sacrificing Christ for the sins of the living and the dead?"

"Yes."

"Well, then, you kill Christ afresh every time you offer that sacrifice!" Then they begin to hedge. But there is no escape from this horrible conclusion. The Roman priest says that when he offers the sacrifice of the Mass, he is presenting

Christ again for the sins of the living and the dead. And the only way that Christ can be a sacrifice is to be put to death; therefore, the priest kills Him afresh every time he offers Mass. They cannot get away from it. The apostle Peter said at Pentecost, "Him, being delivered by the determinate counsel and foreknowledge of God, ye have taken, and by wicked hands have crucified and slain: whom God hath raised up." If Christ has to be offered continually, then every priest is guilty of murdering the Lord Jesus Christ in the sight of God.

God is going to judge Rome in a little while, so Christ's letter to Thyatira properly speaks of this central blasphemy of the church of Rome. Continual sacrifice? Never! No other sacrifice is needed. The dignity of the Lord is so great, the value of His blood is so absolutely infinite, that it is vain for you or any other man to speak about a new sacrifice.

You may say, "I agree with you, sir." Well, now let me ask, Have *you* a personal interest in that one offering made once upon the Cross? I hope you can say, "Thank God, He gave Himself a propitiation for *my* sins, and He is *my* Savior. I need no other sacrifice. My soul is resting on the finished work of Christ. I require nothing more on which to enter the presence of God."

But let us turn to the Lord's address to Thyatira:

> And unto the angel of the church in Thyatira write; These things saith the Son of God, who hath his eyes like unto a flame of fire, and his feet are like fine brass. (v. 18)

It is very significant the way the Lord presents Himself in each of these letters, so as to meet the special condition in which the church is found. When He addresses Himself to the church of Thyatira, He speaks solemnly as "the Son of God." Why does the Lord Jesus Christ emphasize the fact of His deity here? Because Rome everywhere has accustomed people to think of Him as the Son of Mary. I once talked with a woman who told me that she would sooner go to Mary than to Christ or the Father. She said, "There is nobody that has so much influence with a son as his mother, and if Jesus Christ is inclined to be a bit hardhearted, I just go to His good, kind mother, and I ask her to please say a good word to Him for me."

What a caricature of our Lord Jesus Christ! Think of having to go to anybody else to win His favor. Who else could be compared with Him? Thus, Christ is degraded into the position of the Son of Mary rather than being acknowledged as the Son of God, who came in infinite grace to save poor sinners.

But notice that He has "eyes like unto a flame of fire, and his feet are like fine brass." This speaks of His holiness and righteousness. He must judge all that is evil. And yet He never overlooks what can be commended. He goes on to say,

> I know thy works, and charity, and service, and faith, and thy patience, and thy works; and the last to be more than the first. (v. 19)

The Lord gives Rome credit for a great deal that is good. Remember that from the seventh century to the present the Roman Catholic Church has done a great deal in the way of good works that cannot be overlooked. Roman Catholic nuns and monks have been ready to lay down their lives for the needy and the sick. Centuries before Luther, every hospital in Western Europe was simply a Roman Catholic monastery or convent. The Lord does not forget all of that. Where there is a bit of faith, His love takes note of it all. If there are hearts in the Church of Rome that, amid the superstition, reach out to the blessed Lord Himself, He meets them in grace and manifests His love to them. But having done this, He then puts His finger on the sore spot:

> Notwithstanding I have a few things against thee, because thou sufferest that woman Jezebel, which calleth herself a prophetess, to teach and to seduce my servants to commit fornication, and to eat things sacrificed unto idols. (v. 20)

To understand this verse well, we muin go back to Israel's history to the days of King Ahab. Jezebel was adept in the art of mixing. She undertook to unite the religion of Israel and the religion of Phoenicia. That is just what Romanism is— a mixture of heathenism, Christianity, and Judaism. It is not Christianity—yet there is in it quite a bit that is Christian. From where did its superstition and image worship come? It was all taken from heathenism under the plea that it would help to convert the pagans. The church became very accommodating. In the fourth, fifth, and sixth centuries, we find the church compromising with heathen rites and heathen ceremonies to such a degree that, by the seventh century, one could hardly tell heathen from Christian temples. The amalgamation is such that it is almost impossible to separate the one from the other. Go to a Roman Catholic church, and, after sitting through the whole ceremony, take your Bible and search it from one end to the other, and ask yourself, "Is there anything like that in the Book?" You will say, "No." From where does it come then? Go from there to a heathen temple. Observe its ritual, and you will say, "Yes, they are the same."

Romanism is Christianity, Judaism, and heathenism joined, and the Lord abhors the vile combination. Note two things that He holds against Rome: spiritual fornication and idolatry. The first is the union of the church and the work and "the friendship of the world is enmity against God" (see Rom. 8:7). Idolatry is the worship of images, which is strictly forbidden in the second commandment (Exod. 20:4–5). God gave her space to repent, and she repented not. Go back to the days of Savonarola in Italy, Wycliffe and Cranmer in England, John Knox in Scotland, Martin Luther in Germany, Zwingle in Switzerland, and Calvin in France—all of those mighty reformers God raised up throughout the world to call Rome to repent of her iniquity, but "she repented not."

Mark this: you could not transpose these churches. You could not put Thyatira in the place of Smyrna. It could not be said to the church in that early day, "I gave her space to repent, and she repented not"; but it is fully applicable to the Church of Rome. And, in our day, we have a lot of foolish Protestants who believe that the old Rome is now a harmless old pussycat sitting on the banks of the Tiber; she purrs so contentedly. They say, "We never understood Rome. What a pity we ever had that Reformation at all." And so efforts are being made to reunite the various great bodies of Christendom in one vast society headed by the pope. This is the avowed purpose of many leaders in the larger Protestant bodies.

What foolish people these Protestants are!—Protestants who have long ceased to protest against evil doctrine, forgetting the millions of lives that were sacrificed for the precious truth. Depend upon it: if the day ever comes that the pope gets into the saddle again, and gets control of the proposed union, it will only be at the expense of life if people will worship scripturally at all. But Protestant leaders are dazzled with the thought of a great united church and are hurrying us toward a union with Rome that Scripture shows clearly enough will yet take place. But, thank God, not until the church of Christ has been caught up to meet the Lord in the clouds, to be with Himself, according to His promise (John 14:2–3). God gave Rome space to repent. If she had had any desire to get right with Him, she would have repented in the sixteenth century.

Since the sixteenth century, she added to her blasphemies and errors the declaration of the absolute sinlessness of the Virgin Mary, lifting her to the position of a female God, and declared that she was caught up to heaven without dying and crowned queen of heaven.

At the Council of the Vatican less than seventy-five years ago, the Church of Rome produced another of her wretched dogmas—the infallibility of her popes. This dogma was so utterly without reason that many bishops said, "This is going too far. We know that popes have reversed each other over and over again." But Rome never repented; she has added sin upon sin to the heavy list that God had against her in the Middle Ages, and she will remain the same to the end. It behooves Protestants to keep clear of it all. God says that He is going to cast her into the Great Tribulation.

Ephesus is at an end; Smyrna was at an end about A.D. 312; and Pergamos is at an end. Thyatira begins in the seventh century, goes right on into the Great Tribulation, and manifests herself at last as Babylon the Great. Her children are to be judged; but wherever there is found a remnant who "have not known the depths of Satan," the Lord acknowledges them as His own, and exhorts them to hold fast what they have until He come. To the overcomer He promises what Rome has always sought—power over the nations. They will rule with Him when He comes again. Thus, the hope of the Second Coming of Christ is put before them and, henceforth, has a large place in each of these church letters.

Time has not permitted so full an exposition as I would have liked, but I trust enough has been brought before us to stir our hearts to search the Scriptures for ourselves and to study as never before this marvelous portion of God's Holy Word.

THE SEVEN CHURCHES (CONT.)

Revelation 3

None of you can have a keener sense than I of the cursory nature of these addresses. Time forbids going into that detail on all points that alone would enable one to give anything like a complete exposition of this marvelous portion of the Word of God. But if I can but whet your appetite for further study and start Christians searching the Word for themselves, and weighing, too, what others have written and published on this theme, I shall feel that these addresses have not been in vain.[1]

We now proceed to look at the next part in the marvelous series of this great annotated timetable of the church's history.

> And unto the angel of the church in Sardis write; These things saith he that hath the seven Spirits of God, and the seven stars; I know thy works, that thou hast a name that thou livest, and art dead. Be watchful, and strengthen the things which remain, that are ready to die: for I have not found thy works perfect before God. Remember therefore how thou hast received and heard, and hold fast, and repent. (vv. 1–3)

Sardis means "a remnant," or, "those who have escaped." This is surely very significant and tells its own story too plainly to be misunderstood. It brings before us, prophetically, the great State churches of the Reformation that escaped from Rome only to fall eventually (alas, that it should be so) into cold, lifeless formalism.

The first verse shows plainly that there is a measure of return to early principles. The Lord's introduction of Himself to this church is similar to that in the letter to Ephesus, and yet the difference is most marked. Here He is said to *have* the seven stars; there He was said to *hold* the seven stars in His right hand. It is, at least, the recognition that ministry belongs to Christ. Ministers are *Christ's* ministers—not the church's. Yet, even in the glorious days of the Reformation, many people did not fully apprehend the truth that ministers are to be controlled by and subject to Christ, without any human intermediary. Although the Protestant ministry is very different from the Romish hierarchy, human ordination unfortunately has done much to becloud a proper conception of the servant's responsibility to the Master.

The Lord declares solemnly, "I know thy works, that thou hast a name that thou livest, and art dead." How sad and solemn the indictment! One might well ask in amazement how such things can be after the blessing and revival of the Reformation. But when we remember that the State churches were, from the first, intended to include *all* of the population of a given country, who were supposed to be made members of the church and kingdom of Christ by baptism in infancy, one can readily understand why such churches, though, possibly, strictly orthodox, may yet be largely composed of persons who are still dead in trespasses and in sins. Nothing can be much sadder than vast congregations of people who are baptized, banded together as Christians, "taking the sacrament" of the Lord's Supper, zealous for church and Christianity, and yet largely devoid of personal, saving faith in Christ—trusting in forms, ceremonies, and what some people have called "birthright membership" rather than in new birth through the Word and the Spirit of God.

What is needed everywhere is a great revival of decided gospel preaching, pressing home on the consciences of men and women their lost condition, despite church membership, if they have not personally received the Lord Jesus Christ. The Word says, "Break up [the] fallow ground" (Jer. 4:3; Hos. 10:12); sow not among "thorns." We often hear people say that they would like to see more old-time conversions. Well, first there must firt be the old-time preaching of the exceeding sinfulness of sin, and the lost condition of all men by both nature and practice, until the old-time conviction will seize upon the souls of Christless men and women, and then the old-time gospel will be hailed as the only relief.

No wonder the Lord says to Protestantism, "Be watchful and strengthen the things which remain, that are ready to die; for I have not found thy works perfect before God." And He calls upon them to remember how they had received and heard, and to hold fast and repent. Now, surely, it must be plain to anyone who examines the Scripture carefully, that this message would in no sense have been as applicable to the Thyatira period as to the Sardis period. Such words would not have the same force when addressed to Rome as when addressed to the churches of the Reformation. What did these latter churches receive and hear? Clearly, they heard the great truths proclaimed so fearlessly in the days of the Reformation and embodied for the instruction of future generations in the creeds of the sixteenth and seventeenth centuries. And, may I say, I am not one of those who waste time denouncing creeds. *Credo* means "I believe." Any man who believes anything has a creed. All of the great creeds of Protestantism were but the carefully drawn-up declarations of the faith of those who had escaped from Romish superstition, who desired to make clear to their children what they recognized as the truth that they had received from God. We need not be surprised if we find in these creeds some statements that greater light and knowledge would lead us to refuse or revise, but I think we may say that there is not one of these symbols that does not hold within it every *fundamental* truth of the Word of God. Take the Augsburg Confession of the Lutherans, the Westminster Confession of the Presbyterians, the Thirty-nine Articles of the Church of England, and other creeds or confessions too numerous to mention. Every one of them insists on the true deity of Christ and the efficacy of His atoning work on Calvary's cross. All alike declare that salvation is only through *faith* apart from works.

Those creeds stand, I repeat, for the fundamental truths of Christianity, and it is not to any minister's credit today, if he is still attached to any such denomination to which I have referred, to stand up in the pulpits of such churches and say, "I have thrown the creed of the church overboard." When a man reaches that point, he either ought to be thrown out of the church whose principles he no longer believes or be honest enough to take himself out. One of the worst features of the current apostasy is that thousands of men occupy supposedly orthodox pulpits who would, if they could, destroy everything for which their respective denominations are understood to stand.

And so we may thank God for the truths contained in these creeds. On the other hand, we recognize that where the people submit to the Word of God no humanly drawn-up creed is needed. Nevertheless, it is in view of these very confessions, I am persuaded, that the Lord says, "Remember . . . how thou hast received and heard." He calls upon Protestants to remember the great truths committed to them at the Reformation and to hold them fast and repent for the slack way in which they have treated them in the past.

And now, for the second time in these letters, the Lord speaks of His approaching advent: "If therefore thou shalt not watch, I will come on thee as a thief, and thou shalt not know what hour I will come upon thee." How different this to the word in 1 Thessalonians 5:4. There, the apostle, speaking of the same wondrous advent, writes, "But ye, brethren, are not in darkness, that that day should overtake you as a thief." Evidently, therefore, the coming of the Lord should be the daily expectation of His own beloved people. It is only to the great mass of mere professors that His return will be as the coming of a thief, that is, as the unexpected and unlooked-for One, whose coming will spread dismay instead of gladness.

Blessed it is to know the declaration and promise of the Lord in verse 4. Even in Sardis He beholds a few names that have not defiled their garments, and such He declares shall walk with Him in white for they are worthy. His blood alone has made them so. There are thousands in Christendom who, though linked with much that is unscriptural and often almost undistinguishable from the masses are yet plainly discernible to His eye, for it is written, "The Lord knoweth them that are his." To these overcomers the promise is made that they shall be clothed in white raiment, nor will their names be blotted out of the Book of Life, when the thousands of names, representing a Christless profession, will be expunged from the records of those who profess to have life in the day of manifestation.

It is not a question of people who have been truly born of God losing that eternal life given them in Christ, for that, as many other Scriptures show, is an impossibility. In fact, were it otherwise, it would not be *eternal* life at all. But the Lord is referring to those who have a *name* to live but are *dead*. Their names are registered among those who profess to have life in Christ. In reality, they are, as Jude puts it, "twice dead"—first dead in trespasses and sins and then dead to their profession of life. So, in the day of manifestation, their names will be eliminated, and the only ones left are those who have proven by continuance in well-doing that they truly have life in Christ. Such will be confessed before the Father and the angels at the Lord's second coming.

The next in order is the letter to the church in Philadelphia, which means "brotherly love."

> And to the angel of the church in Philadelphia write; These things saith
> he that is holy, he that is true, he that hath the key of David, he that

openeth, and no man shutteth; and shutteth, and no man openeth; I know thy works: behold, I have set before thee an open door, and no man can shut it: for thou hast a little strength, and hast kept my word, and hast not denied my name. . . . Because thou hast kept the word of my patience, I also will keep thee from the hour of temptation, which shall come upon all the world, to try them that dwell upon the earth. (vv. 7–8, 10)

This, I believe, brings us to what we may call the revival period. Following the Reformation came a time when a cold, lifeless formalism seemed to settle over *all* Protestant Christendom—an era in which men were content simply to confess a creed and, as we have already mentioned, were supposed to be united to the church by baptism. But in the eighteenth and nineteenth centuries a great wave of blessing came over all of those lands where the Reformation had gone. God began to work afresh in mighty power. Marvelous awakenings occurred all over Northern Europe and the British Isles. A half century later, the same mighty power began to manifest itself in America. Spirit-filled servants of Christ went through these various countries like firebrands of the Lord, calling on sinners to repent and saints to awaken to their privileges. A little later, in the early part of the last century, God began in a very special way to arouse many of His people to a deeper sense of the value of His Word and its all-sufficiency for the guidance of His people in this scene. This led to the recognition of the fact that Christ Himself is the gathering center for His people; for His name's sake thousands of people left all human systems and began to meet in simplicity, seeking to be guided by the Word of God alone.

Now I do not mean to imply that we are to understand any special movement or association of believers to be in itself Philadelphia, but, just as Sardis sets forth State churches of the Reformation, so I believe that Philadelphia sets forth those in Protestantism who emphasize the authority of the Word of God and the preciousness of the name of Christ. For any particular company to claim to be Philadelphia is but detestable ecclesiastical pretension, and God has evidently blown upon all such conceit.

Notice what would secially mark those who seek to walk as Philadelphians. First is the very name of this church—"brotherly love," which implies that those contemplated here love as brethren. They are born of God, His love is shed abroad in their hearts by the Holy Spirit given unto them, and they are characterized by love to all who are Christ's. Alas, how little is this characteristic seen among many who make very loud pretensions to being the testimony of the

Lord today. There may be much high truth, a great pretension to divine ground, and maintaining of scriptural principles, but if this first mark of brotherly love be missing, depend upon it, you have not yet found Philadelphia.

Second, observe the character in which the Lord presents Himself to this church. "These things saith he that is holy, he that is true." This is, in itself, a challenge to separation from evil in life and error in doctrine. If we would walk in fellowship with the Holy One, we must remember the word, "Be ye holy; for I am holy" (1 Peter 1:16). And if we would enjoy communion with Him who is true, we must refuse Satan's lies and love and live the truth ourselves. Hence, it follows, as others put it, "separation from evil is God's principle of unity." Not, indeed, separation in a cold, pharisaic sense, but separation *to Christ* from that which is evil.

Next, the Lord speaks of Himself as "He that hath the key of David, he that openeth and no man shutteth; and shutteth, and no man openeth." In Isaiah 22:22, he who had the key of David was the treasurer of David's house. And the word used here is clearly a reference to that passage. There it is said of Eliakim, "The key of the house of David will I lay upon his shoulder; so he shall open, and none shall shut; and he shall shut, and none shall open." The rest of the passage shows that Eliakim was but a type of the Lord Jesus Christ, the one upon whom should be hung all of the glory of His Father's house. He, by His Spirit, opens the great treasure house of divine truth, and no one can shut it. On the other hand, where there is perversity of spirit and an unwillingness to wall in the truth, He shuts and no one can open. So He has said elsewhere, "If . . . the light that is in thee [become] darkness, how great is that darkness" (Matt. 6:23).

And it is blessed to realize that, while Christ is said to *have* the key of David, there is another sense in which we see that He *Himself is* the key; it is by the presentation of Himself to the souls of His people that He opens the treasures of His Word. Thus, Christ is the key to the Holy Scriptures, and no other is needed. To understand the Bible, you need only to know Christ.

Perhaps there is another sense in which we might apply the words regarding opening and shutting, that is, they may have an application to service. The Lord Himself opens the doors for those whom He sends forth, and He it is who closes them when He so wills. And this is one thing that Philadelphian believers, generally, have found. Acting on the truth that Christ is Son over His own house and that He has commanded His servants to go into all the world and preach the gospel to every creature, thousands of them have gone forth, in dependence on Him alone, not only in the homeland but also to lands beyond the seas, even among the heathen, without any organization or board behind them and have found the Lord Himself sufficient to meet every need and to open and close just as He will. "Faith can firmly trust him, come what may." I think the eighth verse emphasizes this second application. There He says, "I have set before thee an open door, and no man can shut it: for thou hast a little strength, and hast kept my word, and hast not denied my name."

Observe these important characteristics of Philadelphia. His Word is kept; His Name is confessed. The keeping of His Word involves a great deal more than just believing the Bible or reading and studying it. It implies *obedience* to the revealed will of the Lord. It is a blessed thing to realize that "All Scripture is given by inspiration of God, and is profitable . . . for reproof, for correction, for instruction in righteousness: that the man of God may be perfect, thoroughly furnished unto all good works" (2 Tim. 3:16–17). What immense scope is there here for faith to act upon! This blessed book of God marks out all of my path, and as long as I seek to walk in obedience, I will never be found in circumstances where this Book cannot guide me. And this, I believe, is what is involved in keeping His Word.

The denial of His Name is the increasing apostasy around us on every hand. Those who have not denied His Name refuse all fellowship with this God-dishonoring condition of things. Christ is to them more precious than everything else; even for the sake of service, they refuse to link themselves with that which dishonors or blasphemes that worthy name whereby they are called.

Significantly, wherever Philadelphian truth has been proclaimed, the Devil has raised up a counterfeit to draw people's hearts away from the truth, and so, in verse 9, the Lord speaks of those who will be manifested as the synagogue of Satan, "[who] say they are Jews, and are not, but do lie." The day will come when they will have to worship before the feet of those who are faithful to the Lord and shall know that He has loved them. Undoubtedly, the false Judaizing system is contemplated, whose advocates everywhere oppose the truth of grace and seek in every way to hinder the carrying out of the principles that we have been noticing as pleasing to the Lord. In their ignorance, these teachers give up the true Christian position, claiming to be the spiritual Israel, appropriating to themselves Jewish promises and Jewish hopes, and would put the consciences of Christians under the bondage of Jewish legalism, thus really doing Satan's work.

The promise of verse 10, like all of the promises to these different churches, is for every true child of God. "Because thou hast kept the word of my patience, I also will keep thee from the hour of temptation, which shall come upon all the world, to try them that dwell upon the earth." This is the Lord's own pledge to those who love His Name and seek to keep His word: they shall not be left down here to pass through the appalling Tribulation, which is just ahead of those who "dwell upon the earth." This expression is found frequently in the book of Revelation. It does not mean simply those who live in the world; a careful reading of the various passages in which this peculiar term is found will make manifest that "the earth dwellers" are in contrast to those whose citizenship is in heaven. They are persons who, while professing to be Christians, refuse the heavenly calling and prove by their earthly mindedness and worldly ways that they really belong to this world. All of their hopes and treasures are here, and the Lord has said, "Where your treasure is, there will your heart be also" (Matt. 6:21; Luke 12:34). The coming Great Tribulation will be, for them, a time of fearful trial.

The bulk of the book of Revelation deals with this hour of turmoil, as we shall demonstrate in later lectures. But when that hour comes the church of the current dispensation will have been caught up to meet the Lord according to the promise in 1 Thessalonians 4:13–18. And to this agrees the verse that follows in our chapter: "Behold, I come quickly: hold that fast which thou hast, that no man take thy crown." The Lord's return is the hope of every Christian heart. They long to see Him who loved them and gave Himself for them. At His return, they will be manifested before His judgment seat and be rewarded according to service here. Then He will give out the crowns for service in this day of His rejection. Observe that the warning is, "[Let] no man take thy *crown.*" It is not, "Let no man take thy *life*" or "thy *salvation.*" That is eternally secure in Christ. Being born of God, I cannot lose my salvation, but, if I am not a faithful servant, I may lose my *crown.*

The overcomer will be made a pillar in the temple of God, the God of our Lord Jesus Christ, and shall dwell in the Father's house to go no more out forever. Upon him will be written the name of God, the name of the Holy City, and Christ's new name. All that is involved in this is beyond our poor, finite comprehension, but it speaks of stability, security, fellowship, and intimacy with the Lord Himself, which, to the believer, will make heaven his blessed and eternal home.

Laodicea completes this septenary series and brings us, practically, to the last stage of the professing church's history on earth—the close of the current dispensation.

> And unto the angel of the church of the Laodiceans write; These things saith the Amen, the faithful and true witness, the beginning of the creation of God; I know thy works, that thou art neither cold nor hot: I would thou wert cold or hot. So then because thou art lukewarm, and neither cold nor hot, I will spue thee out of my mouth. (vv. 14–16)

Laodicea is a compound word meaning "the rights of the people." Could any other term more aptly set forth the condition of modern church affairs? It is the era of democratization in both the world and the church. The masses of the people are realizing their power as never before. The terrific slogan *vox populi, vox Dei* ("The voice of the people is the voice of God") is ringing through the world with clarion-like distinctness. Imperialism and every form of aristocratic government are disappearing—at least for the time being. The age of anarchy is almost upon us. Bolshevism is not confined to unhappy Russia; it is making tremendous progress in all Christendom. Statesmen and capitalists were never more anxious and nervous than now. In the Great War, we were told that our soldiers were fighting to make the world safe *for* democracy. In a little while, statesmen will be attempting to raise armies to make the world safe *from* democracy. The spirit of this ultrademocratic age has invaded a large portion of the professed church. The authority of God and His Word is rapidly being denied. The spirit of the age is the spirit of a large part of the church; hence, the striking correspondence between this letter to the Laodiceans and the latitudinarianism so prevalent about us.

In a day when faithful witnesses to God's truth are becoming fewer and fewer, the Lord addresses Himself to the church as the Amen (that is, the establisher of all of God's promises), the faithful and true Witness, who will maintain to the last what is of God, although the great majority of those who profess to follow Him are swept away by the apostasy. He reproves the church for its lukewarmness and indifference to Himself and the truth. He says, "Because thou art lukewarm, and neither cold nor hot, I am about to spue thee out of my mouth." There is neither burning zeal for His Word nor yet absolute repudiation of Christ and the Bible. Instead, there is a nauseating, lukewarm condition that is abhorrent to the Spirit of God. Lukewarm water is, in itself, an emetic; and this is the figure that the Lord here uses. He cannot tolerate such conditions much longer but will spew out the whole disgusting mass in judgment.

Meanwhile, the church continues in its pride and self-satisfaction, saying, "I am rich, and increased with goods, and have need of nothing," knowing not that, in His eyes, it is "miserable, and poor, and blind, and naked." Never were church dignitaries and carnally minded religious leaders more satisfied with themselves and their great work than today. They advocate anything and everything that will seem to increase the church's popularity. The rights of the people alone must be considered; the rights of the Lord Jesus Christ are not even thought of. We have come to a time when, in many places, it is easier to get on without Christ than with Him, easier to carry on religious programs without the Holy

Spirit than if He were working among us in mighty power. No wonder He says, "I counsel thee to buy of me gold tried in the fire [i.e., divine righteousness], that thou mayest be rich; and white raiment [i.e., practical righteousness], that thou mayest be clothed, . . . and anoint thine eyes with eyesalve [i.e., the anointing of the Holy Spirit], that thou mayest see." Yes, there is a lot of work and much fleshly energy and human effort being put forth to reclaim the world and make it a comfortable place in which for men to live apart from Christ, but the great things of God's truth are largely neglected, and myriad so-called church workers are utter strangers to the new birth, without which no one can see the kingdom of God.

And so we see the Lord standing at last outside the door of the professing church and saying so tenderly, "Behold, I stand at the door, and knock: if any man hear my voice, and open the door, I will come in to him, and will sup with him, and he with me." Ah, beloved friends, it is getting late in the dispensation, the night-shades are fast falling, and the Lord who, in the beginning, was in the midst of His church, stands *outside* that lukewarm system that calls itself by His name, and He knocks in vain for entrance! Yet, individuals here and there open to Him and find that His presence is more to them than all else that the earth or the professing church can afford.

And so we have come to the closing days of the current dispensation of grace. The Ephesus period passed away long ago, and the same is true of the Smyrna and Pergamos periods. Thyatira, which, as we have seen, speaks of Romanism and began properly when the pope was recognized as universal bishop, is with us still and will go on to the end. Sardis, which began centuries later, remains to the present, and it will remain until the Lord comes. Philadelphia, thank God, is also here, and, although it has but a little strength, it, too, will abide to the end. But Laodicea is more and more in evidence, and it seems to be swamping almost everything that is of God.

The next great event is the coming of the Lord Jesus Christ and our gathering together to Him. For this we wait, and our longing hearts cry, "Even so, come, Lord Jesus."

THE FIRST VISION OF HEAVEN

Revelation 4

A s we turn from chapter 3 to chapter 4, how different are the scenes! We are no longer occupied with either the professing church in the place of testimony or with events on the earth at all. But a door is opened in heaven, and, escorted by the beloved apostle John, if I may so speak, we are carried far above the shifting scenes of this poor world and permitted to gaze with awestruck eyes upon a scene of glory that is indescribable and to hear things that have been kept secret from the foundation of the world.

The opening verse begins the third great division of this book—"the things which shall be after these things," the stirring panorama of wonders, both heavenly and earthly, that must take place after the church's history is ended. From the close of chapter 3, we never see the church on earth again throughout the rest of this solemn book. We read of "saints," but they are distinct altogether from the church of the current dispensation. Israel comes into view, as does a great multitude of spared Gentiles who are saved out of the Great Tribulation, but there is no church, no body of Christ, no bride of the Lamb any more upon the earth!

The fact is patent enough for every careful reader to notice it. What is its explanation? Simply this, I believe: we must understand the Rapture of 1 Thessalonians 4:16–17 as transpiring between chapter 3 and chapter 4. Of this, the rapture of the apostle is the symbol. He sees the door opened in heaven. His attention is turned from earth to glory. He is, in spirit, caught up, and far above all of the mists of this lower scene, he beholds a "throne *set* in heaven" and a Throne-sitter upon it. The likeness of this august Being he cannot even attempt to portray. He ony tells us only that he beheld a Presence whose glory was like a jasper and a sardius.

The jasper of Revelation is not the opaque stone we know by that name today. It is later described as being as clear as crystal (21:11). It is probably the diamond, the most brilliant of all precious jewels. The other stone is blood-red and may really be the ruby. Thus, the two stones together give the idea of glory and sacrifice. Remembering that many of the first readers of the Revelation were converted Jews, we might ask, What would these stones suggest to them? Surely every instructed Hebrew would instantly recall that they were the first and last stones in the breastplate of the high priest (Exod. 28:17–20). As these stones bore the names of the tribes of Israel, arranged according to the births of the twelve patriarchs, the one would suggest at once the name Reuben, "Behold a Son," and the other Benjamin, "Son of my right hand." It is Christ enthroned, the Son about to reign in power who is before the Seer's vision. Round about the throne a rainbow, like an emerald, the stone of Judah ("praise") is seen, suggesting the perpetuity of the Noahic covenant, and God's unchanging goodness, despite all of man's failure, folly, and wickedness.

But now the fourth verse brings before us a sight never beheld in heaven on any previous occasion: twenty-four thrones (not merely "seats") surrounding the central throne, and upon them twenty-four elders were seated with victors' crowns (not diadems) upon their heads and clothed in priestly robes of purest white. Who are these favored ones gathered around the glorious central Being? I do not think we need be in any doubt as to their identity if we compare Scripture with Scripture and distrust our own imagination, which can but lead us astray.

In 1 Chronicles 24, we read of something very similar, and again I would remind you that many of John's first readers were Hebrews who would have been thoroughly familiar with the Old Testament. Can we question for a moment that every Jewish believer would instantly remember the twenty-four elders appointed by King David to represent the entire Levitical priesthood? He divided the priests into twenty-four courses, each course to serve for two weeks at a time in the temple that Solomon was to build. The same arrangement was in force when our Lord's forerunner was announced. Zacharias was "of the course of Abiah," the eighth in order (Luke 1:5).

The priests were many thousands in number; they could not all come together at one time, but *when the twenty-four elders met* in the temple precincts in Jerusalem, *the whole priestly house* was represented. And this is the explanation, I submit, of the symbol here. The elders in heaven represent the whole heavenly priesthood, that is, all of the redeemed who have died in the past or who shall be living at the Lord's return. In vision, they were seen, not as a multitudinous host of millions of saved worshipers but as just twenty-four elders, symbolizing the entire company. The church of the current age and Old Testament saints are alike included. All are priests. All worship. Twelve patriarchs were in Israel, and twelve apostles introduced the new dispensation. The two together would give the complete four and twenty.

Then, observe further: these people are not angels. They are redeemed men who have overcome in the conflict with Satan and the world because they wear victor's wreaths upon their brows. Angels are never said to be "crowned" nor have they known redemption.

Two kinds of crowns are mentioned in this book: the victor's crown and the ruler's diadem. The former is the word here used. It refers to the wreath of either laurel or pine that is bound about the brow of the victor in the Greek games. It is the same word as that so often used in the New Testament when reward for service is the theme. And now, note carefully that saints will never be crowned until the apostle Paul receives that crown of righteousness which the Lord revealed to him as his reward. In 2 Timothy 4:8, he says, "Henceforth there is laid up for me a crown of righteousness, which the Lord, the righteous judge, shall give me *at that day;* and not to me only, but *unto all them also* that love [or, have loved] His appearing." The expression *at that day* refers to the day of Christ, when He shall come for His own, and they all will be manifested before His judgment seat. He says, "Behold, I come quickly; and *my reward is with me,* to give every man according as his work shall be" (Rev. 22:12). Surely it follows then that no rewards are given until He returns for His saints; therefore, there can be no crowned elders in heaven until after the Rapture.

This, I believe, is a point of greatest importance today because many people are troubled by the thought that perhaps the Great Tribulation, with which so large a part of this book deals, has already begun. But all such fears are set at rest when the facts that I have been emphasizing are kept in mind. But because I want to dwell some more on this in the next lecture, I forbear further comment now. I only trust that it is clear to everyone that the elders are the *heavenly* saints surrounding the Lord in glory, God the Son sitting on the central throne.

Circumstances connected with that throne make clear that a dreadful storm is about to burst on that world below, from which they are viewed as having so lately come. Lightnings, thunderings, and voices tell of this storm, and as we continue our study of the book, we shall see more added from time to time as conditions become increasingly solemn.

Continuing the symbolism of the tabernacle, John sees seven lamps of fire burning before the throne, as the seven-branched lampstand burned just outside the veil before God's throne on earth—the ark of old. These lamps are said to be "the seven Spirits of God," a figure that we have already seen (in 1:4) sets forth, not seven distinct Spirits, but the one Holy Spirit in the sevenfold plenitude of His power.

The sea of glass of verse 5 reminds us of the sea of brass in Solomon's temple. *That* sea symbolized, like the laver, the Word of God because it contained the water used for priestly cleansing, and we are sanctified and cleansed by "the washing of water by the word." But *this* sea is *not* for cleansing, so it is as crystal, and later we find the martyred Tribulation saints *standing on it.* It is the Word of God still, but it is no longer needed for cleansing because desert experiences are viewed here forever passed. But the Word abides, stable and sure forevermore— a glassy sea filled with crystal—firm and glorious, on which the people of God can stand eternally.

It is well known that instead of four "beasts" connected with the throne we should read four *"living ones."* They are not beasts. The word is very different than that used in chapter 13. They are not created beings because they are in the midst of the throne, where only Deity can dwell, and they are linked with it round about. They represent the attributes of the living God. The lion is the well-known symbol of divine majesty. The young ox, the divine strength graciously serving man. The face of a man indicates intelligence and purpose; it tells us that Deity is no mere blind force, nor the "Great First Cause" or simply impersonal Law. The eagle suggests swiftness in detecting evil and executing judgment. Six-winged and full of eyes, the beasts speak of incessant activity and omniscience. "The eyes of the Lord are in every place, beholding the evil and the good." They cry, "Holy, holy, holy, Lord God Almighty, which was, and is, and is to come" because all of God's attributes glorify the Eternal Son.

The elders bow in worship at this announcement and cast their crowns at the feet of Him who sits upon the throne, adoring Him as Creator and saying, "Thou art worthy, O Lord, to received glory and honour, and power; for thou hast created all things, and for thy pleasure they are and were created" (v. 11). A higher note is struck in chapter 5, but the blessed truth is here proclaimed, that He who died on the cross is worshiped by all of the redeemed in heaven. There can be no mistake as to the Person. If John 1, Colossians 1, and Hebrews 1 are all carefully compared with this closing verse, they makes perfectly clear that it is Christ Jesus, the Son, who created all things. Without Him was nothing made. All things are *by* Him and *for* Him. So He it is who fills the throne and is the center of the worship here described.

In a day such as ours, when His glory as the Eternal Son is so often denied, when His true Deity, His virgin birth, His sinless humanity are alike flouted by apostate teachers as so much traditional lore to be rejected at will, how refreshing to the soul to turn from earth to heaven and contemplate the glory displayed there as His and the unhindered adoration of His own as they prostrate themselves before His throne. If He be not God, then heaven will be filled with idolaters because it is written, "Thou shalt worship the Lord thy God, and *him* only shalt thou serve" (Matt. 4:10; Luke 4:8).

But we need not for a moment enter such an "if." He is "over all God, blessed for ever" (Rom. 9:5; He is also Man. God the Son in grace was born of the Virgin, and He it is who fills the throne above. Nor will He ever abdicate that throne, own to Himself, and to reign over all of the earth as Son of man, sitting on the throne of His father David. Both thrones are His because all glory belongs to Him by the Father's firm decree. Thus shall all men eventually honor the Son even as they honor the Father.

I add a further word concerning the living creatures. In chapter 4, we see them linked peculiarly with the throne. In chapter 5, they are most particularly linked with the elders. We have suggested that they represent the divine attributes during the current age and before the Lamb takes the ministry. But "unto the angels hath he not put in subjection the [age] to come" (Heb. 2:5). In that day, God will work through His redeemed ones; hence, the living ones join in the new song, voicing the joy of the saints in whom the divine glory will be displayed. The living creatures of Ezekiel's vision and the cherubim on the mercy seat tell the same story.

THE SEVEN-SEALED BOOK

Revelation 5:1–6:8

Our subject in the previous lecture was Revelation chapter 4—the redeemed gathered around the throne of God and the Lamb in heaven. We noticed that the four and twenty elders, seen by John in vision sitting around the throne, represent all of the heavenly saints of this and past dispensations. I cannot reiterate, except to remind you that the symbol evidently is taken from the twenty-four elders of the priesthood of Israel. We can see how aptly the entire heavenly company would be represented by these heads of the Levitical priesthood. In heaven there is no special sacerdotal family; all of God's people are priests.

In the fifth chapter, we are still occupied with the same vision as in chapter 4, where we saw the Lord Jesus Christ worshiped as Creator. Here a higher glory is His—He is worshiped as Redeemer. "'Twas great to speak a world from nought; 'twas greater to redeem."

The first thing that attracts our attention is what is said of the seven-sealed book in the right hand of Him who sits on the throne. We have already seen in our review of chapter 4 that the *Son* is on that throne, but we must not forget that it is likewise the throne of God the Father. And so here we have in the Father's right hand a book written both within and on the back side, and it is sealed with seven seals. When we read of a "book," we must not think of a volume such as that with which we are familiar, but rather of a roll of parchment. The ancient books of Israel were generally sheepskin rolls, and when we are told that this book was sealed with seven seals, we are to understand that the book was rolled up to a certain point, and a seal was put upon the edge so that it could not be opened until that seal was broken. It was rolled up a little farther and another seal put on, and so on, until six seals were on the edge of the book and one seal was closing the entire scroll. When the first seal was opened, a certain portion of the book was exposed to view, and so with each seal following. When the seventh seal was broken, then the entire book would be unrolled.

What is this sealed book? I will again remind you of a principle that I want to keep before you in all of these lectures, and that is that it is never necessary in studying the book of Revelation to fall back on our own imagination about what a particular symbol means. *Every symbol is explained, or alluded to, somewhere else in the Bible.* Turn to Jeremiah 32. The prophet Jeremiah lived in a day just before the fall of Jerusalem under Nebuchadnezzar. He had been telling the people of Israel that they were going to be carried captives to Babylon. They would be in captivity for seventy years, but, at the end of that time, they would be restored and would build again the waste places (29:10). Hanameel, Jeremiah's cousin, who had a piece of ground, knew well that it was soon to be absolutely worthless, and he was anxious to get it off his hands and realize what he could from it. He decided to try to sell it to his prophet-cousin, who was in prison for the truth's sake at the time. The Lord said to Jeremiah, "Buy the field." He was commanded to accept it as though it were really worth having because the time was coming when it *would* be worth having, for just as surely as God's people were going down into Babylon, they were surely coming back again. That land would be worth far more in that day, and he would have it in his family.

So Jeremiah 32:8 says that Hanameel came and besought him to buy the field. Jeremiah acquiesced. The title deeds were made out, sealed, and hidden. Jeremiah purchased the land, but he was not going to enter into possession of it. He, too, was to be driven out—to be rejected and set to one side—but some day that sealed roll would be of great value when the restoration took place. He gave it to his secretary to hide with a view of making known to his heirs the location of the deed that was to give them the title to the land. The sealed book was the title deed to Jeremiah's inheritance, and when the people of Israel came back from Babylon a man could go into court and say, "This deed belongs to me. I am Jeremiah's heir. I have the right to break the seals and take the property."

With this illustration from the Old Testament before us, we have no difficulty in seeing what the seven-sealed book in Revelation means. The book that

John saw in the hand of Him that sat upon the throne is the title deed to this world; when God says, "Who is worthy to take the book and to loose the seals thereof?" it is just another way of saying, Who is the rightful heir? Who can say, "I have title to break those seals, title to claim that world, it belongs to me?" Who is worthy to take possession of that world and subject it to himself?

Adam, what about you? Wasn't that world given to you? When God created you and placed you in the Garden of Eden, did He not say that all of this was yours? Why do you not come forward, take this title deed, and claim your property? Adam says, "I forfeited my inheritance because of sin. It was mine, but I sinned it away. The Devil cheated me out of it, and I have no longer any title to it."

Is there any angel who can step up and take the book? No, not an angel among all of the serried ranks of heaven's hosts can say, "I have title to that world." Not a man in all of God's universe can say, "It is mine." And John says, "I wept much, because no one was found worthy." But as he was weeping, one of the elders said, "Weep not, the Lion of the tribe of Judah has prevailed to take the book, and to loose the seven seals thereof." And John looked for the Lion of the tribe of Judah, the majestic roaring King of Beasts, ready to spring upon the prey, but he beheld a Lamb.

Why, the Lamb *is* the Lion! The Lamb of God is the Lion of Judah's tribe. The lamb that speaks of innocence, meekness, gentleness, and sacrifice is the One who is to go forth as the mighty conqueror and claim this world as His own and drive all of His enemies from before His face. I like the translation of Weymouth here. He says, "I saw in the midst of the throne a lamb that looked as though it had been offered in sacrifice"—the Lamb in the very glory of God that will have through all eternity the marks of death upon His glorified body! It is right to sing as we sometimes do,

> I shall know Him, I shall know Him,
> As redeemed by His side I shall stand;
> I shall know Him, I shall know Him,
> By the print of the nails in His hand.

When He came forth from the tomb, the print of the nails was there. When John saw Him many years later in vision up there in glory, he saw a Lamb that looked as though it had once been offered in sacrifice. And when we get home to heaven, we will never make any mistake in identifying Him. We will never be found worshiping Gabriel instead of Christ; we will not mistake even so loving an apostle as John for his Lord. We will have only eyes for the Lamb upon whose body will be for all eternity the marks that tell of our redemption. Ah, what a sight that will be for God's beloved people—when we look upon His face, feel His gentle touch, behold the print of the nails in His hands and feet, and see the mark left by the Roman spear in His side!

The prophet Habakkuk describes Him as having "bright *beams* coming out of his side, and there was the hiding of his power" (Hab. 3:4, literal trans.). There, where the cruel spear pierced Him, is the hiding of His power.

> Oh, the Lamb, the bleeding Lamb,
>> The Lamb of Calvary;
> The Lamb that was slain, that liveth again,
>> To intercede for me.

Do you know this blessed Lamb of God? Are you acquainted with Him? Is He your own Savior? Have you cast yourself on His mercies?

It says that the Lamb in the midst of the throne had seven horns. Horns speak of power. In the Old Testament, we read of the "strong bulls of Bashan" (Ps. 22:12), of great heads, thick necks, and powerful horns. Israel would thus be accustomed to connect the thought of power with the horns. But it is not a mighty bull that is seen, but a lamb, and the diminutive form of the word, "a little lamb," with seven horns! Just as *horns* speak of power, *seven* speaks of perfection. Perfect power belongs to the Lamb of God. And we are told that He had seven eyes, which is interpreted as meaning seven Spirits of God sent forth into all the world, which we have connected with Isaiah 11:1–2. The Holy Spirit is the Spirit of Christ. "In him dwelleth all the fulness of the Godhead bodily" (Col. 2:9). All spiritual graces are His. He is anointed with the oil of gladness above His fellows, and He it is who gives the Holy Spirit to us.

He came and took the book out of the right hand of Him that sat upon the throne. What right had He thus to act? Because He went to the Cross in infinite grace to pay the great debt of sin, thus to redeem this forfeited inheritance and free it from Satan's domination. The Lamb has title to the book! The Lamb can claim the title deed to this world because when He died on Calvary's Cross He purchased the entire world to be His own—in which the glory of God is to be displayed through a thousand wondrous years. It was His because He created it. He gave it to man, but man forfeited it through sin. And the Lord Jesus Christ bought it all back when He hung on Golgotha's tree. But for nineteen hundred years, He has been waiting patiently up there in the glory until the appointed time for claiming His inheritance. So the book of the title deeds has been sealed.

In this interval, men have been having pretty much their own way down here; the Devil has been running things to suit himself. But in a little while, Christ is coming again. He is going to put everything right, but He will have to act in judgment to do so because the very world in which the Lord Jesus died is going to be the sphere in which the glory of God will be displayed, and that not only in the Millennium but also afterward in the new earth and the new heaven.

The moment that the Lamb takes the book, in verse 8, the four living ones and the four and twenty elders fall down before Him, every one of them having a harp and golden bowls full of odors, which are the prayers of saints. You know, I am very sentimental about the harp. I love it. I always think when I hear the harp being played that it is the instrument I am going to play in heaven. It is a figure, of course, but a very lovely one. "And they sang a new song, saying, thou art worthy to take the book, and to loose the seals thereof, for thou wast slain and hast redeemed to God, by thy blood, out of every kindred and tongue, and people, and nation, and hast made them unto our god a kingdom of priests, and they shall reign over the earth" (5:9–10, literal trans.). It is not merely of themselves they sing but of all of the redeemed; so the living ones, the divine attributes, join in it, too.

And note the great throng suggested by the words of the song. Far more people will be in heaven than will ever be lost in hell! All of the babes that died in infancy will be there. What a throng will fill that home! And oh, how wonderful the fellowship! We shall have the society of all of the pure and holy made pure by the blood of Jesus. But notice carefully what they sing up there. They ascribe their redemption entirely to the Lamb and His work. Those are the saints of God. Then you find another company in the next two verses, but they are angels. Notice that you have an inner circle composed of sinners who were redeemed. That will be the glory of heaven.

You often hear of the angels singing, but it is remarkable that when you go to the Bible there is only one place where you read of angels singing—in Job 38. The "morning stars" there are angels, and they sang together when this world in its pristine beauty sprang from God's hand. But that ancient song was stilled. Sin came in and marred that beautiful creation, and from the time that sin came in we never read again that angels sang. At the birth of our Lord Jesus a multitude of the heavenly hosts praised God, *saying,* "Glory to God in the highest" (Luke 2:14), but we do not read that they *sang.* It is *the redeemed* who sing, and they sing "a new song." It is the song of redemption. Will you be able to sing that song? Angels will praise the Lamb, truly, although it does not say that they will sing. Let me read the passage:

And I beheld, and I heard the voice of many angels round about the throne, and the [living ones] and the elders: and the number of them was ten thousand times ten thousand, and thousands of thousands; saying with a loud voice, Worthy is the Lamb that was slain to receive power, and riches, and wisdom, and strength, and honour, and glory, and blessing. (5:11–12)

What a host! You would think that God had enough without us. Old John Bunyan says, "Oh, this Lamb of God! He had a whole heaven to Himself, myriads of angels to do His pleasure, but this could not satisfy Him. He must have sinners to share it with Him!" If you are ever going to sing up there, you will have to start in down here. Can you say, "Thou wast slain, and hast redeemed *me* by thy blood"?

The angels stand in an outer circle. In other words, the angels stand off and look on and say, "The Lamb deserves all of the honor He is receiving." Then there is a third company, a third circle, embracing all creation. John looks throughout the universe, and he sees every creature extolling the Lamb. The day is coming when all created intelligences will join in saying, "Glory to the Lamb."

And now the Lamb, having taken the book, proceeds to open the seals. Here I want to pause for a moment in the course of the exposition. Many people have come to me since the Great World War began and said, "Don't you think that, perhaps, the Great Tribulation has already commenced? There have been events following one another in the last few years that so nearly answer to this opening part of the book of Revelation that one would be justified in believing that we are already in the throes of the Tribulation." My answer is that there can be no period of tribulation such as is depicted here until the Lamb breaks the seals of the seven-sealed book. But the Lamb does not break the first seal of this book until the redeemed are seen crowned in heaven, and no redeemed one will ever get his crown until they are taken up at the coming of the Lord Jesus Christ to the air and the setting up of the judgment seat. All of the crowns are going to be given out at the judgment seat of Christ before the Lamb takes the book and before the seals are broken.

A lady said to me, "But, dear brother, what tribulation could be worse?" Well, conditions are certainly terrible, but there has never been a war in which the organizations that profess to stand for righteousness have done so much for the soldiers, and the relatives, and the afflicted, as in this awful conflict. Consider the Red Cross, for instance. It was the spirit of sacrifice that caused people to start the society, and many of the founders of it were devoted to Christ; wherever the red cross was seen it was a reminder of the cross of Christ. There will be no Red Cross in the Great Tribulation. The cross of Christ will be so hated then that it will never be seen anywhere. Then look at the Y.M.C.A. I know all about the criticisms, and I have had to speak plainly myself, but the Y.M.C.A. movement was started by a man of God, and its original objective was to bring men to Christ. Much of their recent work is indeed open to just criticism; it is a shame that it has added to and detracted from its original purpose, yet we can thank God for the New Testament and the comforts it has brought to millions of men. Take the work of the Salvation Army. I have heard scores testify about the Salvation Army preaching the gospel of God in the trenches. Now think of a greater war than this (and it is in the future), a war in which there will be no Salvation Army, no Y.M.C.A., no Red Cross, no Bible societies, and no Christian workers—absolutely no spiritual ministry of any kind to alleviate the awful conditions that will then prevail. The thought is unspeakably terrible, but such a war is predicted in this Book.

But, I repeat, that tribulation time cannot begin until the redeemed are gathered around the Lord in the glory and crowned there. And it cannot be emphasized too much that no saints in heaven now have crowns. The apostle says, "Henceforth there is laid up for me a crown of righteousness, which the Lord . . . shall give [to] me at that day: and not to me only, but unto all them also that love his appearing" (2 Tim. 4:8). "That day" when the saints are gathered around the judgment seat of Christ is the day when they will get their crowns.

Well, then, after the church has gone, what is going to take place in the world? When I get to this chapter, I always like to view it thus: we are in heaven already, the Rapture having already taken place. Look at it with me from that standpoint. Let us suppose that last night, while things were going on in the ordinary way, suddenly a heartening shout was heard from the glory, and every redeemed one responded to the trump of God. In a moment, the graves were opened, and in every place where the believing dead were resting, their bodies were raised, and the living saints were changed. We found ourselves caught away, and we entered with Him into the Father's house, gathered around the throne, and fell down to worship. We will say that we have had twenty-four hours in heaven. O sinner, you wouldn't be there. It is *saved* people about whom I am talking. At first, our hearts would just be too full of Christ to think of anything else. But He Himself stirs us at last to think of what He is about to do. We say to ourselves, *What is going to be the next thing in that world we have left behind?* We look down to that poor scene where we lived yesterday. Men are going on much as they were before, only in great excitement. Look at the streets of the great cities. We can see the newsboys shouting, "Extra! Extra! A great number of people have disappeared!" There is a rush to get the newspapers to find out all about this strange event. Throngs are crowding the popular churches to hear the Rev. Dr. Ananias and his like give their explanation of the great disappearance of so many people.

I believe there will be a lot of churchgoing for a little while after the rapture of God's people; they will be crowding into the churches as never before. I think I see the Rev. Mr. Smooth-things standing in his pulpit, with pale, wan face as he looks at scores of parishioners whom he hasn't seen for many years, and thinking, *Now, I see I have got to explain to these people. I have been telling them for twenty years that this talk of the Second Coming is false.*

People who believed in the Second Coming were looked upon as idiotic ranters who didn't know what they were talking about. I think I hear mutterings down in the congregation: "We trusted our souls to you. You had been to the colleges, seminaries, and universities; read a whole library of books; and we believed you when you told us that the old idea of salvation by the blood of Christ was all worn out and that we could save ourselves by culture. We believed you when you said that Christ's second coming was only a fantastic notion. Now explain *this* to us."

Another person cries, "What about my grandmother? She believed in her Bible to the last. She was reading just the other day, 'In an hour when ye think not, the Son of Man cometh.' Now Grandmother is gone, and I am here. Now, Doctor, explain all of this."

Oh, there are going to be some wonderful meetings after the Lord has come! There is that world seething with corruption and men's hearts failing them for fear. Christian statesmen will have gone; Christian businessmen and people of all ranks who knew Christ will have disappeared. Cities and communities will be in turmoil. What are they going to do? Let's look at the Book and see.

> And I saw when the Lamb opened one of the seals, and I heard, as it were the noise of thunder, one of the four beasts saying, Come and see. And I saw, and behold a white horse: and he that sat on him had a bow; and a crown was given unto him: and he went forth conquering, and to conquer. (6:1–2)

We behold the Lamb as He breaks the first seal, and John hears a noise as of thunder. Thunder speaks of a coming storm, although the scene seems peaceful enough. What is this? A warrior comes forth on a white horse, and a bow is in his hand. A bow speaks of distant warfare. Horses, as in Zechariah 1, symbolize providential movements. This rider on the white horse evidently pictures man's last effort to bring in a reign of order and peace while Christ is still rejected. It will be the world's greatest attempt to pull things together after the church is gone. It will be the Devil's cunning scheme for bringing in a mock millennium without Christ. How long will it last?

> And when he had opened the second seal, I heard the second beast say, Come[!] . . . And there went out another horse that was red: and power was given to him that sat thereon to take peace from the earth, and that they should kill one another: and there was given unto him a great sword. (6:3–4)

He opens the second seal, and a red horse appears. Anarchy, a bloody warfare! "When they shall say, Peace and safety, sudden destruction cometh upon them." The first effort, down in the world we are supposed to have left, will be to bring in universal peace apart from Christ, but it will end in universal, bloody warfare greater far than has ever been known. The rider on the blood-red horse has a sword; it speaks of warfare of a different type altogether from that of the bow: man wrestling with man and nation with nation. Internal strife, class wars, civil wars—the breaking up of all established order—is here set forth.

> And when he had opened the third seal, I heard the third beast say, Come[!] . . . And I beheld, and lo a black horse; and he that sat on him had a pair of balances in his hand. And I heard a voice in the midst of the four beasts say, A measure of wheat for a penny, and three measures of barley for a penny; and see thou hurt not the oil and the wine. (6:5–6)

Very naturally, when he had opened the third seal, a black horse appears, with his rider holding a pair of balances. We have that which inevitably follows world-wide war—worldwide famine. I don't wonder that people think they have seen all of this in the last four years: an effort to bring in universal peace, but almost universal war and famine in many parts of the world. But, by and by, it is going to be all over the world. We know a little better now what this means than when these things were first opened up by men of God. We have had our food sold to us by measure, and we have known much of the high cost of living, but, in this coming day, conditions will be so dreadful that it will be a measure of wheat for a *denarius,* or three measures of barley for the same amount. The word translated "measure" means just enough wheat to make a man one meal, and the *denarius* was a full day's wages. Enough food for one meal for a whole day's wages! That is, if one is going to eat wheat. Now, if they will take barley, they will get three meals for a day's work. What hard conditions! We thought war prices were exorbitant, but they are going to be unprecedented in those days of the Tribulation.

"But see thou hurt not the oil and the wine." The oil and the wine are put in contrast with the wheat and the barley. The wheat and barley are the food of the poor, almost out of reach, but the food of the rich, or the luxuries, are not touched.

> And when he had opened the fourth seal, I heard the voice of the fourth beast say, Come[!] . . . And I looked, and behold a pale horse: and his name that sat on him was Death, and Hell followed with him. And power was given unto them over the fourth part of the earth, to kill with sword, and with hunger, and with death, and with the beasts of the earth. (6:7–8)

And now he opens the fourth seal, and a pale horse ridden by Death appears. The word rendered *pale* means green, chrome. A better translation would be a *livid* horse, in the sense of being the color of a corpse. Of what is it the picture? Of pestilence, which always follows war and famine. We have known something of that in this last year, but the complete fulfillment awaits a not far-distant day.[1]

THE FIFTH AND SIXTH SEALS

Revelation 6:9–17

B efore examining what is written concerning the breaking of the fifth and sixth seals, it is necessary to say something as to God's dispensational dealings with His earthly people Israel and to endeavor to show how the book we are studying links with the older prophecy of Daniel.

For fifteen hundred years before the Cross, God was dealing in covenant relationship with this one people whom He had chosen to be peculiarly His own in accordance with His promise to Abraham, Isaac, and Jacob. He separated them to Himself, giving them the land of Canaan as their inheritance as long as they remained faithful to Him as their unseen King. He gave them His holy Law and declared that if they obeyed His voice they would be the head of all nations and His witnesses to the ends of the earth. On the other hand, He warned them, if they were disobedient to Him, if they did not keep His testimonies, if they broke His commandments, and if they turned to the false gods of the surrounding nations, He would no longer protect them from their enemies but would give them up to desolation and scattering until they judged themselves and turned from their sins, when He would remember His covenant with their fathers, restore them to their own land, and fulfill all of His promises.

They completely broke down under every test and, in accordance with His

Word, ten tribes were carried away by the king of Assyria, and a little later, the remaining two tribes were deported to Babylon, where they remained in bondage for seventy years. Upon the expiration of this prophetic period, they were permitted to return to their own land that they might be there to welcome their promised Messiah when He would be manifested. Only a remnant of the Jews availed themselves of this privilege, and it was their descendants who were living in Palestine when the Lord Jesus Christ appeared in the fullness of time, only to be rejected by the very nation that had waited for Him so long.

The time of His coming had been very definitely foretold in the book of Daniel. The ninth chapter tells us that a heavenly messenger brought the word to the prophet that God had appointed seventy weeks to His people and their holy city. These weeks are not to be understood as weeks of days but sevens of years. The term *weeks* might better be simply rendered *sevens*. Seventy times seven years would be 490 years. It is an appointed period in the course of time and has to do especially with the Jews and Jerusalem.

This period was divided into three parts: 7 weeks, or 49 years, in which the streets and the wall of the city were to be rebuilt; 62 weeks, or 434 years, immediately following the completion of this work unto the appearing and cutting off of Messiah the Prince; and then one final week, or 7 years, to complete the cycle, at the end of which the King would be reigning in the Holy City and all prophecy fulfilled by the establishment of the kingdom so long foretold. The starting point is clearly defined as "The going forth of [a] commandment to restore and to build Jerusalem" (Dan. 9:25), which is the decree of Artaxerxes as recorded in Nehemiah 2. During the next forty-nine years, the city was rebuilt. Then, 434 years later, our Lord rode into Jerusalem and was acclaimed by the multitudes as King, the Son of David, but a few days later was rejected and crucified. Thus, Messiah was cut off and had nothing.

What, then, of the last week? Has it been fulfilled? It has not. When His Son was cast out, God cast off the nation, and that week will not be fulfilled until a future day, when He takes up Israel again.

The angel-revealer said to Daniel, "Until the *end* shall be war; desolations are determined" (9:26). This gives the whole history of Palestine for the past nineteen hundred years. It has been a great battleground and a scene of almost unparalleled desolation because Israel knew not the time of their visitation. Their times are not in progress now. God is doing another work. While the Jews are blinded, in part, and are wanderers over the face of the earth, He is gathering out the church, the body of Christ, a heavenly company, who will reign with Christ when He establishes His kingdom of righteousness upon the earth. The last week of seven years cannot begin to run until the Jews are again in the land, and Jerusalem becomes the Jewish capital, after the church has been caught up to meet the Lord in the air. The majority of the book of Revelation deals with this last week. Only when this fact is seen does everything become plain and the prophecy becomes intelligible.

The church began on the Day of Pentecost, when the Holy Spirit, sent by Christ glorified, came upon the disciples, although the full truth of this wonderful mystery was not made known until Saul of Tarsus became Paul the Apostle. To him, and through him to us, was made known the truth of the current dispensation. The church of Christ is one, although men who take His name and claim to be His followers have become sadly divided and have formed many systems, often embracing saved and unsaved alike. But God's church consists only of those who are born of the Spirit, and all such are by the same Spirit baptized into "the body of Christ"—the church. This special work will cease at the return of the Lord in the air, which is the first stage of His second coming. The second stage will be when He comes to the earth in manifested glory to reign. The seventieth or last week of Daniel comes in between these two momentous events. The Lord spoke of this period as the "end of the age" in Matthew 24, and He divides it into two parts, "the beginning of sorrows" and "the Great Tribulation."

A careful comparison of our Lord's great prophecy with the portion of Revelation that we have before us, will, I believe, make plain that the first six seals answer to the first half of the week—"the beginning of sorrows" (Matt. 24:8) whereas from the opening of the seventh seal we are introduced to the Great Tribulation itself with all of its attendant horrors. His warning about false Christs, implying false hopes of a lasting peace, corresponds to the first seal. His declaration that wars and rumors of wars will follow fits perfectly with the second seal. In like manner, His solemn warnings of famine and pestilence find their counterparts in the third and fourth seals.

The Lord then foretells a time when His followers shall be ruthlessly slain and when it will be all one's life is worth to confess His name. This brings us to the breaking of the fifth seal, when John saw under the altar the souls of those who had been beheaded for the Word of God and the testimony of the Lord.

> And when he had opened the fifth seal, I saw under the altar the souls of
> them that were slain for the word of God, and for the testimony which
> they held: and they cried with a loud voice, saying, How long, O Lord,
> holy and true, dost thou not judge and avenge our blood on them that

dwell on the earth? And white robes were given unto every one of them; and it was said unto them, that they should rest yet for a little season, until their fellowservants also and their brethren, that should be killed as they were, should be fulfilled. (vv. 9–11)

Who are these martyred saints, and to what dispensation do they belong? They cannot belong to the church because, as we have already seen, that is represented by the throned and crowned elders in heaven before the first seal is broken. But Romans 11 makes clear that after the fullness of the Gentiles has come in, that is, after the current dispensation has come to an end and the church has been removed to heaven, the blindness will pass away from Israel, and they will realize their true condition and their sin in rejecting their Messiah. Then they shall call upon Him for deliverance.

Thus, a new company of saints will be formed upon the earth, altogether different from the current heavenly company. Many of these Jewish believers will be martyred by the satanic hosts of the last days, and these are they who are seen as having been sacrificed and their souls poured out at the bottom of the altar. They cry for vengeance on their adversaries, for this is fully in keeping with the dispensation of judgment to which they belong whereas it would be thoroughly contrary to the grace of the current gospel dispensation.

God's people are taught of His Spirit to pray according to the ruling principle of the specific time in which their lot is cast. This accounts for what often disturbs and even shocks sensitive souls—the so-called imprecatory psalms. They cannot understand the cries for vengeance that seem so opposed to the grace of God as now made known. And it is no wonder that they are troubled and hesitate to take such words upon their lips; they do not belong to us at all. But they will be exactly suited to the remnant of Israel, suffering for Jehovah's sake but with no clear knowledge of an accomplished redemption—waiting for their Messiah to appear and overthrow the last great Gentile confederation, which, as we shall see when we come to chapter 13, will be bent upon their absolute extermination.

To these souls under the altar, invoking the judgment of God upon their merciless adversaries, white robes are given, and they are told that they must wait a little season until the Time of Jacob's Trouble is ended and they are joined by their brethren who are yet to be slain, as the hatred to God and His Christ rises ever higher until the Lord Jesus shall be revealed from heaven in flaming fire, taking vengeance on those that know not God, as we read in 2 Thessalonians 1.

The opening of the sixth seal gives a marvelous symbolic picture, of such grave import that I must give it to you in its entirety. John says,

And I beheld when he had opened the sixth seal, and, lo, there was a great earthquake; and the sun became black as sackcloth of hair, and the moon became as blood; and the stars of heaven fell unto the earth, even as a fig tree casteth her untimely figs, when she is shaken of a mighty wind. And the heaven departed as a scroll when it is rolled together; and every mountain and island were moved out of their places. And the kings of the earth, and the great men, and the rich men, and the chief captains, and the mighty men, and every bondman, and every free man, hid themselves in the dens and in the rocks of the mountains; and said to the mountains and rocks, Fall on us, and hide us from the face of him that sitteth on the throne, and from the wrath of the Lamb: for the great day of his wrath is come; and who shall be able to stand? (vv. 12–17)

It should be evident from the rest of the book that we are not to take this as a literal earthquake, although our Lord's words in Matthew 24 show us that there will be such phenomena in divers places and terrific in character as the end draws near. Already, perhaps we have had, in the past two decades, some noteworthy reminders and warnings in the many horrors of this nature that shocked the civilized world, but they are apparently so easily forgotten within a very short time. But the earthquake of the sixth seal is of a different character altogether. It cannot be merely literal because the actual islands, mountains, and seas, together with the cities of the nations, are still seen to be in existence long after this vision has had its fulfillment. Rather, it sets forth the complete breaking up of society as now constituted, the destruction of the boasted civilization of our present day. Looked at from this standpoint, we have abundant Old Testament Scripture to throw light upon it and to make plain its awful portents.

We shall be helped, too, if we remember that in the very beginning of the book we are told that the Lord sent and "signified it unto his servant John." That is, He made it known by signs or symbols. If we keep these in mind, we shall be preserved from taking literally what God meant us to take symbolically, and so we shall be more likely to get the mind of the Spirit regarding the future of both Christendom and Judaism, the two spheres with which this book especially deals.

Therefore, it is not a worldwide, literal earthquake that the sixth seal introduces but rather the destruction of the current order—political, social, and ecclesiastical order reduced to chaos, the breaking down of all authority, and the breaking up of all established and apparently permanent institutions.

We may see, I believe, a foreshadowing of this destruction in what has so lately taken place in Russia—the overturning of the throne, the blotting out of the Romanoff Dynasty, the wrecking of all industrial and social order, the fearful orgies of fanatical Bolshevism, blood-red anarchy everywhere holding sway, and making wild promises of liberty while destroying every safeguard against the unrestrained brutality of beastlike men. Take as but one horrible instance the attempted abolition of marriage (that which God Himself instituted at the very beginning of human history for the sanctity and blessing of His creatures) and the substitution of the degrading custom of forcing all women to be common property, taken by whoever may desire them, and all children born in these abominable conditions to be taken from their parents and reared as children of the State. Natural affection at once receives its death-blow and all restraint on man's animal propensities is at an end. Another event that has shocked the world has been the overturning of Russia's State Church. It is true that it had become unspeakably corrupt, but in their wild desire to destroy it, the Soviet government has declared war on all that bears a religious name, whether human or divine. "No God and no church" is the cry ringing through the unhappy land, and who can foretell what the dreaded future has in store?

Many people in the past century thought that they saw the French Revolution portrayed in this sixth seal, and it was indeed but an earlier sample of the same conditions we have been considering. So was the breakup of the Roman Empire in the fifth, sixth, and seventh centuries. But none of these cataclysms, stupendous as they were, met fully the requirements of the prophecy because the church of the First-born is still here, and the gospel of the grace of God is still being proclaimed to a guilty world. But we have already seen that when the seals are broken, the church will be with Christ, waiting for the moment when He will descend to take His world kingdom and establish His authority in righteousness.

But we must now proceed to look at the passage in detail that we may better grasp its true import.

The sun, we are told, became as black as sackcloth of hair. The sun, the source of light and life for this planet, speaks of supreme authority, and is the well-known type of the Lord Himself. "Unto you that fear my name shall the Sun of righteousness arise with healing in his wings" (Mal. 4:2). Such is Malachi's declaration concerning the coming of Christ the second time. Now, Christendom acknowledges, at least nominally, His lordship. We even date our letters A.D., *anno Domini.* We speak of Him as our Lord and profess to receive our governments from His hand. But soon He will be entirely rejected and His Word utterly despised. Thus will the sun be blotted out from the heavens, and God will seem to have been dethroned.

Naturally enough, this will mean the complete destruction of all derived authority, so we next read, "the moon became as blood." The moon gets all of its light from the sun, just as "the powers that be are ordained of God" (Rom. 13:1) and are appointed by Him for man's blessing. But, all government having been thrown down, the lurid glare of anarchy will take its place, at leasdt for a time.

The stars falling from heaven indicate, I take it, the downfall and apostasy of great religious leaders, the bright lights in the ecclesiastical heavens. In Daniel, those who turn many to righteousness shine as the stars. In the first part of our book, the stars are said to be the messengers of the churches. So it would seem clear that we are to understand the symbol in the same sense here. After the true church has been caught up to meet the Lord in the air, a vast host of unconverted ecclesiastics will be left behind—thousands of church dignitaries, both Protestant and Romanist, who, though looked upon as guides in things spiritual, shall be manifested as utterly bereft of divine life; professional clergymen who, despite their pretensions and exalted calling, are simply natural men intruding into spiritual things, like the Philistines of old, who dwelt in the land of Canaan and gave their name, Palestine, to the whole thing as though it belonged of right to them, while all the time they were unwarranted intruders of Egyptian descent. These are the stars who will be hurled from their places of power and eminence in that awful day of the wrath of the Lamb, and who, apostatizing from the vestiges of Christianity, will soon become leaders in the worship of Antichrist.

Thus, the heavens, the ecclesiastical powers of every description, will depart as a scroll when it is rolled up. The whole fabric of Christendom will be wound up as something obsolete. Recently, leaders of religious thought, as they are called, have been questioning the *finality* of the Christian religion and declaring that out of the chaotic conditions brought about by the war shall arise a new religious conception altogether, superseding that of "the Nazarene" and resulting in the worship of humanity—a new conception of God as immanent in all men and found only within the heart of man. Such teachers are undoubtedly correct as to their expectation and for this so-called Christian Science, the New Thought, the New Theology, Theosophy, and kindred cults (all founded on the same basic philosophy) are preparing the world. But as long as the Holy Spirit is here on earth, dwelling in the church of God, the full development of this mystery of iniquity is checked. But as soon as He goes up with the church, however, the whole profession that is left will be destroyed, and from its ruins will arise the final satanic masterpiece of the last days.

The destruction of all organized religion, however, will but intensify the frightful conditions of that dreadful time. Men, drunk with their sham liberty and rejoicing in the triumph of a blatant, God-defying demagoguery, will for a brief period turn this earth into a great madhouse. The vile orgies of those days will be indescribable, until there shall dawn upon multitudes the realization that the Lamb of God whom they had rejected and whose gentle rule they had spurned has in some way visited their sins upon their own heads. Then we have depicted what someone has called "the greatest prayer meeting of all history," when "the kings of the earth, and the great men, and the rich men, and the chief captains, and the mighty men, and [the bond and the free]" shall hide themselves in the dens and in the rocks of the mountains, crying out in their sore distress for mountains and the rocks to cover them and hide them from the face of Him that sits upon the throne and from the wrath of the Lamb, "for," they will cry as with one voice, "the great day of his wrath is come, and who shall be able to stand?"

Yet, we read of no repentance, no true turning back to God or trusting His Christ—just an awful realization that it is the rejected Lamb with whom they have to do, and whose wrath they would fain escape. They are like those of whom Jeremiah prophesied who will cry in that day of the fierce anger of the Lord, "The harvest is [passed], the summer is ended, and we are not saved" (Jer. 8:20).

Notice the solemnity of the expression "The wrath of the Lamb." We are not accustomed to couple the thought of wrath, or indignation, with the *Lamb*, which has ever been the accepted symbol of gentleness. But a terrible truth is involved in it nevertheless because if the grace of the Lamb of God be rejected, His indignation and wrath must be faced. It cannot be otherwise. It is part of eternal righteousness to do so. God Himself will not and, in accordance with the holiness of His nature, cannot have it otherwise. As we read elsewhere, "He cannot deny himself" (2 Tim. 2:13).

> Hear the just law, the judgment of the skies:
> He that hates truth must be the dupe of lies:
> And he who *will* be cheated to the last,
> Delusions strong as hell must bind him fast.
> —Cowper

For such there can be nothing in reserve but a certain fearful looking for of judgment and fiery indignation that shall devour the adversaries, and this of a much sorer character than that which befell those who despised Moses' Law because they now defy God revealed in grace, who has come out to man in the person of His Son. For such there must be "the wrath of the Lamb."

> Grace like this despised, brings judgment
> Measured by the wrath He bore.

But the *wrath of God* is even a deeper and more intense form of judgment, which will be poured out upon the earth from the "seven vials [or bowls] of the wrath of God" and under which the Christ-rejecter must abide for eternity because it is written, "He that believeth not the Son shall not see life, but the wrath of God abideth on him." Note the hopelessness of the condition here depicted. Abiding wrath precludes any thought of either annihilation or restoration, and it tells us that the results of refusing the matchless grace of God are eternal because that which "*abides*" is unending.

But I must bring this address to a close, and, as I do so, I would again remind you that this sixth seal brings us to the end of the first part of that last unfulfilled week of the ninth chapter of Daniel. It divides into two parts, and the Lord Himself defines the first part as "the beginning of sorrows," while He designates the last part as "the Great Tribulation." This time is introduced for us in the book of Revelation by the breaking of the seventh seal, and that will come before us after the great parenthesis of the seventh chapter.

The wrath of *the Lamb* is visited upon the nations in the beginning of sorrows; the wrath of *God* will be their portion in the Great Tribulation. May He grant, in His mercy, that none who hear these words may enter into either the one or the other. Grace is still reigning through righteousness, and a just God waits in loving kindness to be the justifier of everyone who believes in Jesus (see Rom. 3:26).

THE 144,000 AND THE GREAT MULTITUDE OF GENTILES

Revelation 7

I n our last address, we were occupied with the first half of the seventieth week, yet future, of Daniel's prophecy: "the beginning of sorrows," when "the wrath of the Lamb" will be poured out on guilty Christendom and apostate Judaism. Now we find that before the Lord gave John the vision of the opening of the seventh seal (which introduces the Great Tribulation in all of its intensity), we have this parenthetic seventh chapter in which are recorded two important visions. In the first vision, John sees 144,000 Israelites sealed by an angel, and in the second vision, he beholds a great multitude of Gentiles led in triumph by the Lamb who is in the midst of the throne, taking possession of the millennial earth.

I am sure that many of my hearers have often been perplexed by conflicting theories regarding the 144,000. The way in which so many unscriptural and often positively heretical sects arrogate to themselves this title would be amusing if it were not so sad. You are perhaps aware that the Seventh-Day Adventists apply it to the faithful of their communion, who will be found observing the Jewish Sabbath at the Lord's return. They suppose that these people will be raptured when the Lord descends and that judgment will be poured out upon the rest of the church. Then we have the followers of the late Pastor Russell who teach that the 144,000 include only the "overcomers" of their persuasion who continue faithful to the end, following the teaching of the system commonly called "Millennial Dawnism." That very absurd and weird cult known as the "Flying Roll" claims the same thing, only with them, the 144,000 are those who will have their blood so cleansed that they cannot die but will have immortal life on this earth! Besides these are many other sects whose leaders consider that their own peculiar followers will be the 144,000 sealed ones at the time of the end. All of these views, however, overlook a very simple fact that, if observed, would save them from their folly. That is, the 144,000 are composed of twelve thousand people from each tribe of the children of Israel. Not a Gentile is among them, nor is there confusion as to tribe. Whenever I meet people who tell me they belong to the 144,000, I always ask them, "Which tribe, please?" and they are invariably put to confusion for lack of an answer.

Now let us look carefully at the three opening verses.

> And after these things I saw four angels standing on the four corners of the earth, holding the four winds of the earth, that the wind should not blow on the earth, nor on the sea, nor on any tree. And I saw another angel ascending from the east, having the seal of the living God: and he cried with a loud voice to the four angels, to whom it was given to hurt the earth and the sea, saying, Hurt not the earth neither the sea, nor the trees, till we have sealed the servants of our God in their foreheads. (vv. 1–3)

John tells us that he saw "four angels [four is the world number] standing on the four corners of the earth, holding the four winds of heaven that the wind should not blow on the earth, nor on the sea, nor on any tree." In Daniel's vision, as recorded in the seventh chapter of his prophecy, he beholds "the four winds of heaven" striving upon the great sea; as a result, you have the various world empires coming forth like wild beasts from beneath the restless waves. Here we have the angels holding back these four winds until a certain event takes place. It is very evident that they are restraining the last wild beast from making his appearance. In chapter 13, the beast with seven heads and ten horns, the Roman Empire in its last form, comes forth from the sea, symbolizing the nations in unrest. This is the great federation of nations that God's Word predicts for the very near future—a federation of satanic origin that will not be developed until after the church is gone, and even then certain events must transpire before it assumes its final diabolical form.

Verses 2 and 3 make clear what this event is that must first take place. John sees another angel ascending from the east, having the seal of the living God: "And he cried with a loud voice to the four angels, to whom it was given to hurt the earth and the sea, saying, Hurt not the earth, neither the sea nor the trees, till we have sealed the servants of our God in their foreheads." The point is, you see, that God has chosen a remnant of Israel to inherit the kingdom under the Son of Man, which is so soon to be established. Before the final form of the Roman Empire is fully developed, these people are sealed, marked out for God's protecting care, so that all of the power of the Beast and all of the hatred of his ally the Antichrist will not be able to destroy them and thus prevent the carrying out of God's purpose.

Verses 4–8 leave no doubt whatsoever as to the identity of these sealed ones. John "heard the number of them [that] were sealed: and there were sealed a hundred and [forty-four] thousand of all the tribes of the children of Israel."

As you go over the last half, note that the tribe of Dan is absent; instead, you have two tribes from Joseph—Manasseh and Ephraim. Ephraim, however, bears Joseph's name. Why is Dan omitted from the twelve, and the twelfth made up in another way? I cannot positively tell you. The rabbis used to say that the false Messiah (the Antichrist) would arise from Dan, and they based the supposition on Jacob's words in Genesis 49:17: "Dan shall be a serpent by the way, an adder in the path, that biteth the horse heels, so that his rider shall fall backward." We note from the historical record, in the book of Judges, that Dan was the first tribe to go into idolatry, and it would not be a matter of surprise if Dan would be the leader in the last great idolatry—the worship of Antichrist. But we may leave this where faith leaves every other difficulty—resting in the infinite wisdom of God and knowing that He has revealed all that is necessary for us to know in the current age.

The rest of the chapter, from verse 9, brings before us an entirely different company. John says,

> After this I beheld, and, lo, a great multitude which no man could number, of all nations, and kindreds, and people, and tongues, stood before the throne, and before the Lamb, clothed with white robes, and palms in their hands; and cried with a loud voice, saying, Salvation to our God which sitteth upon the throne, and unto the Lamb. And all the angels stood round about the throne, and about the elders and the four beasts,

and fell before the throne on their faces, and worshipped God, saying, Amen: Blessing, and glory, and wisdom, and thanksgiving, and honour, and power, and might, be unto our God for ever and ever. Amen. And one of the elders answered, saying unto me, What are these which are arrayed in white robes? and whence came they? And I said unto him, Sir, thou knowest. And he said to me, These are they which came out of great tribulation [*literally*, the tribulation, the great one], and have washed their robes, and made them white in the blood of the Lamb. Therefore are they before the throne of God, and serve him day and night in his temple: and he that sitteth on the throne shall dwell among them [or, spread his tabernacle over them]. They shall hunger no more, neither thirst any more; neither shall the sun light on them, nor any heat. For the Lamb which is in the midst of the throne shall feed [or, shepherd] them, and shall lead them unto living fountains of waters: and God shall wipe away all tears from their eyes.

It seems very strange that some people have taught that in this great multitude we have the raptured church; hence, they have supposed that the Lord would not come for His church until the middle of the tribulation period. But a careful study of the passage makes very evident, it seems to me, that we are here gazing upon an earthly, not a heavenly, company. This great multitude embraces the Gentile nations who will enter into millennial blessing. It is the great ingathering of the coming dispensation, when from all nations, kindreds, peoples, and tongues, a vast throng from all parts of the earth will be redeemed to God by the blood of the Lamb and will enter into the earthly kingdom of our Lord. During the dark days of the Great Tribulation, they will heed the testimony that will be carried to the ends of the earth by Jewish missionaries, "the wise among the people" (see Dan. 12), who shall instruct many in righteousness. They are identical, I take it, to the "sheep" of Matthew 25, who are placed on the right hand of the Son of Man when He comes in His glory and all of His holy angels with Him, and who inherit the kingdom prepared for them from the foundation of the earth.

They are said in verse 14 to "come out of the great tribulation," to have washed their robes and made them white in the blood of the Lamb, but they are nowhere said to be taken away to heaven. Quite the contrary, they are in a scene where it is necessary that the Lamb should feed them, lead them, and spread His tabernacle over them. Verse 15 tells us plainly, "Therefore are they before the throne of God, and [minister before] him day and night in his temple," that is,

I take it, the millennial temple, which is to be built in the land in that coming day. There will be no day and night in heaven. The expression can only refer, in this connection, to the temple on earth. Then we read, "He that sitteth on the throne shall [spread his tabernacle over] them." The reference is undoubtedly to the Lord's covering His people when He led them of old through the wilderness. The pillar of cloud by day and the pillar of fire by night not only guided them through the scene but also sheltered them from the fierce rays of the desert sun. Thus will He protect and shield His redeemed ones in the age to come.

We are also told that "they shall hunger no more, neither thirst any more; neither shall the sun light on them, nor any heat, for the Lamb which is in the midst of the throne shall [shepherd] them, and shall lead them unto living fountains of waters: and God shall wipe away all tears from their eyes." It is probably because people have not realized the blessedness of the millennial day that these verses are made to refer to heaven, but they are at one with the predictions of Isaiah and others of the prophets regarding the blessing that the saved nations shall enjoy when the Lamb Himself reigns. The struggle for daily bread will be over—they shall hunger no more; the often vain effort to quench their thirst will be at an end—they shall thirst no more. Even the unpleasant and disagreeable things with which men have been afflicted because of the way sin has jarred God's creation will be at an end. The sun shall not light upon them, nor any heat.

In that day, all of the saved of the nations will be able to take up, in the fullest sense, the beautiful words of the psalmist, into which we but feebly enter now: "The LORD is my shepherd; I shall not want. He maketh me to lie down in green pastures: he leadeth me beside the still waters. He restoreth my soul: he leadeth me in the paths of righteousness for his name's sake" (Ps. 23:1–3).

Although it is true that the church of God will be in a far better scene, while our hope is heavenly, not earthly, yet we can indeed rejoice and our hearts may well swell with gladness to think of the blessing awaiting the earth and its inhabitants. And God has surely promised it, and He will fulfill all that He has caused to be written by His holy prophets in the sacred Scriptures because "the scripture cannot be broken" (John 10:35).

What a long, dreary night with what frightful disturbing nightmares, if I may so speak, has this world known since sin, with all of its attendant evils, came in to wreck man's hopes of joy and gladness! But how precious to know that evil shall not always have the upper hand; that a time is coming, aye, and is very near, when the curse will be lifted, the desert shall rejoice and blossom like the rose; even the lower creation will be changed and revert to former habits before sin entered; "the lion shall eat straw like the ox" (Isa. 11:7); the little child need not fear the most savage of beasts because they shall not hurt nor destroy in that day. Then government will be righteously regulated; abuses of every kind will be stopped, and for a thousand glorious years our Lord Himself shall reign in righteousness.

But there is one thing I wish especially to press upon both saved and unsaved, and that is this: whether in dispensations past, in the present age, in the period of judgment just before this world, or in that glorious millennial age, everyone who is saved at all will be saved through the precious blood of Christ. God has never had any other way of reconciling man to Himself than through the blood of His Son. In Old Testament times, men were saved, if I may so say, on credit. The Lord Jesus Christ had already pledged Himself to pay the fearful debt with His own most precious blood, and all who, in every dispensation, admitted their guilt and believed the record that God had given, were justified by faith on the basis of the work that Christ was yet to accomplish. That work having now been completed, God has manifested His righteousness in passing over these sins done aforetime in the days of His forbearance, and now He shows Himself to be just and the justifier of him that believeth in Jesus. If you admit your sin, dear unsaved one, if you confess your guilt and put your heart's trust in that blessed One, who on Calvary's Cross gave Himself for you, then you will be justified and accepted with God in all of the value of that precious blood. In the coming hour of tribulation, the 144,000 of Israel, and all of the Gentiles who receive their message, will be saved in exactly the same way—but saved for *earth,* not for heaven. To the very end of the Millennium, that precious blood will still have the same cleansing efficacy, and the last soul who trusts in Christ will have an unimpeachable standing before the throne of God through its infinite value.

So all blessing for time and eternity rests upon the Cross of Christ, and the reason the nations have missed their way in the past nineteen hundred years and are struggling in vain for peace and a government in righteousness is that they have ignored the blood of that Cross, where, alone, peace was made, in relation to both time and eternity.

And now, in closing, let me emphasize one thing that I believe needs to be emphasized in these days. I have run across the error in many recent books on the coming of the Lord that after the rapture of the church will be a great revival, an unprecedented spiritual awakening in Christendom, when vast numbers of people who have been undecided during the current dispensation of grace will turn to the Lord. It is being widely taught that these people will form the great multitude of which we have been speaking. Let me say that I have searched my

Bible diligently for any confirmation of such teaching, but I fail to find it. On the contrary, we are distinctly told in 2 Thessalonians 2:11 that God is going to give up those who, during the present age, receive not the love of the truth that they might be saved; they will be given up to hardness of heart and perversity of spirit. We read in verses 11–12, "And for this cause God shall send them strong delusion, that they should believe a lie: that they all might be damned who believed not the truth, but had pleasure in unrighteousness." Now, there is no intimation here that people who refuse the gospel in this dispensation will have another opportunity to be saved if they are still living when the dispensation of judgment begins. A careful reading of the entire passage will show that the time referred to is when the mystery of iniquity is fully developed and the Wicked One is revealed—that is, the Man of Sin. In that age, the Holy Spirit will have been withdrawn. He will go up with the church at the Lord's return to the air.

This is not to say that the Holy Spirit will not act afterward, during the tribulation period, but His operations will be similar to His activities in Old Testament times. From heaven, He will influence the hearts of men, opening the eyes of the remnant of Israel, and, through them, reach, as we have seen, an innumerable multitude of Gentiles. But there is no promise that He will operate for blessing on the hearts of those who have had the opportunity to be saved but have refused it. They will be given up to the strong delusion of the last days. They will believe the lie of the Antichrist and thus go into judgment because they deliberately refused the truth when it was offered to them, choosing instead error and sin.

It is a very solemn thing to harden the heart against God and His message of grace. Pharaoh tried it and is the standing example of what strong delusion really means. He hardened himself against the message that Moses brought, and afterward God Himself confirmed him in his course. Light rejected brings abiding night. Darkness may be natural; in this all are born. It may be willful; in this men deliberately choose darkness in place of light. It may be, and alas, often is, judicial; in this men are given up to darkness because of their own perversity. So we read in Jeremiah 13:16, "Give glory to the LORD your God, before he cause darkness, and before your feet stumble upon the dark mountains, and, while ye look for light, he turn it into the shadow of death, and make it gross darkness."

No man need be lost for lack of light. He who will follow the slightest gleam that God gives may be sure of increasing light, light sufficient to lead him to the knowledge of sins forgiven. But, I repeat, light rejected brings night! Therefore, let me plead with anyone who has not closed with God's offer of grace in Christ Jesus, to receive now the gift of His love and thus be assured of a place with

Christ in that coming day. If the Lord should descend from heaven to call His church away, the doom of you who have heard the gospel and are rejecting it, abiding in your sins, will be eternally sealed.

Among the heathen nations, where the gospel has not yet been fully proclaimed—in the waste places and the neglected parts of the world, where the grace of God is as yet unknown—a vast number will be found to receive the message of the Israelitish remnant as they flee from Antichrist's persecutions and proclaim to all the world the gospel of the kingdom. But you will not be numbered among them if the coming of the Lord finds you still unsaved. You will be in exactly the same condition of soul and position of condemnation before God as if you had died in your sins. Jesus said, "When once the master of the house [has] risen up, and . . . shut the door" (Luke 13:25)—who is there that shall open it? The five foolish virgins who were left outside when the Bridegroom came knocked in vain for admittance later. They picture those who will be on the wrong side of the door, which is closed for all eternity.

Yet, strangely enough, certain teachers have used this very parable of the ten virgins to bolster their unsound theory of a second chance for Christ-rejecters after the Savior calls His church away. According to them, the foolish virgins are supposed to represent persons afterward gathered in but who miss the heavenly blessing. Other teachers have based *on* this parable the equally unscriptural hypothesis that only the more spiritual saints will be caught up at the Rapture, and the weaker ones will be left behind to be purified during the Great Tribulation. This is a virtual denial of the truth of the one body, the unity of the body of Christ. The weakest member of that body is as dear to the Head as is the strongest member, and all who are Christ's will have their part in the Rapture, regardless of their stage of development in the Christian life. It is the perfection of the work of redemption that gives title to any of the promises of God; it is not as a reward for service or merit.

THE BREAKING OF
THE SEVENTH SEAL

Revelation 8

I am to speak to you tonight on the breaking of the seventh seal, which opens fully the book of title deed to this world—the roll that was put into the hands of the Lord Jesus by the Father after the church, represented by the glorified elders, was seen around the throne in heaven.

First, let me make a few remarks, which I think have not previously been made in the course of these lectures, regarding the structure of the book of Revelation. The main body of the book is divided into four sevens: the *letters* to the seven churches of Asia, then the seven *seals,* then the seven *trumpets,* and farther on the seven *vials* of the wrath of God.

In connection with these last three sevens something is very striking. We have, first, six seals opened, then a parenthesis that takes up chapter 7. In chapter 8, the seventh seal is opened, and the book as a whole is open to view.

We find that this seventh seal includes the seven trumpets. Six trumpets are sounded, and there is again a parenthetical portion, including chapter 10 and chapter 11 to verse 14. At the conclusion of this parenthesis, the seventh trumpet brings us to the end of all things.

Chronologically, we are as far along when we reach 11:18 as when we reach the Great White Throne in chapter 20 because the seventh trumpet introduces the world kingdom of our God and His Christ and continues to the time when the dead shall be judged. So you see that we really have a duplication, in measure, of prophetic truth from this point. That is, from chapter 4 to the end of chapter 11 truth is presented in orderly sequence—a prophetic outline of the things that shall take place from after the rapture of the church to the end of time.

Then, beginning with chapter 12, God seems to turn the roll over that we may view the other side, and He gives us a second view of the events but especially in relation to Israel. We have details that bring before us the great actors for good and evil in the last days—the woman clothed with the sun; the Manchild, Christ, who is to rule the nations with a rod of iron; Michael, who is the archangel; the dragon, who is that old serpent, the Devil; and the coming world confederacy and its blasphemous head; the lamb-like Beast, who I believe is the Antichrist, who looks like a lamb but speaks like a dragon—the counterfeit of the Lamb of God. There follows a parenthetical portion in chapter 14 that brings vividly before us once more the final issues.

Then, in chapters 15–16, we have the vials, or bowls, of the wrath of God. Once more, you will notice, we have the same structure that has engaged our attention in connection with the seals and the trumpets: we have six bowls and then a parenthesis. In this instance, the parenthesis occupies only one verse (16:15). Immediately following this, the seventh bowl of the wrath of God is outpoured, bringing us on to the doom of Babylon, which is described in detail through chapters 17 and 18. Then, in chapter 19, we have the Lord's descent to the earth, accompanied by the armies of heaven, to establish His millennial kingdom and reign for a thousand years. At the close of this event, the final judgment takes place; the heavens and the earth as we now know them, with all of the works of man, will be destroyed, and new heavens and a new earth shall be brought in, where God will be all in all throughout an eternity of bliss. On the other hand, the wicked—those who have persistently rejected the Lord Jesus Christ, both before and since the Cross, and the millennial dispensation of righteousness—all who have rejected the message of God will be cast into the lake of fire.

I have searched this Book of God through and through repeatedly to find one ray of hope for men and women who leave this world rejecting Christ, and I have never been able to find it. I have looked into all kinds of theories, and I have read hundreds of volumes, some depicting the annihilation of all of the wicked dead and some, like the wild dream of the so-called "Pastor Russell," promising a second chance after death, but I have never found one statement in all of the books, no statement based upon the Word of God, to give the slightest hope to the Christ-rejecter. This is the only world in which God is offering salvation to Christless men; if you refuse the message of His grace now, if you deliberately steel your heart against the convicting power of the Holy Spirit and you die in your sins, go down to a Christless grave, you will be *Christless for all eternity!* I think the most awful picture the Bible gives us of the doom of the lost is in the epistle of Jude, which forms such a fitting preface to the book of Revelation. Jude speaks of those who make light of God's salvation and who follow after unrighteousness, as "wandering stars, *to whom is reserved the blackness of darkness for ever*" (Jude 13). I cannot see the least hope for a Christless soul in that figure.

I remember how, when I was a mere boy in my home in Canada, night after night, a blazing comet appeared in the skies, and I heard older people telling that this particular "night wonder" had not been seen for something like three hundred years. I asked in amazement where it had been, and for the first time in my young life I came up against the wonder of infinite space. I was told that that comet had been driving on with tremendous velocity millions and millions of miles away from the sun for one hundred and fifty years, and that one hundred and fifty years ago it had gradually begun to come back toward the sun, and that was why it was then visible. In a few weeks, it passed out of sight, to appear to us no more for another three hundred years. I can recall pondering what would happen if that comet went off on a tangent (although I do not suppose that I knew either that word or its meaning then), and never came back! And, my friend, this is the appalling picture that Jude presents in the passage to which I refer. Those who turn the grace of God into lasciviousness—those who despise the boundless mercy He has bestowed upon them in His blessed Son, and persist in refusing His goodness, continuing in their sins—will be driven away from the Sun of Righteousness into the outer darkness and will drive on, and on, and on, throughout eternity, nevermore to find their way back into the presence of God. He is giving a little space now for repentance, but the day of His grace will be over when He rises to shake terribly the earth. And how are you treating His offer of mercy?

But we return to our chapter.

And when he had opened the seventh seal, there was silence in heaven about the space of half an hour. (8:1)

First, notice the opening verse. We are told that when the Lamb had opened the seventh seal, there was silence in heaven about the space of half an hour. May we not say that it is the "calm before the coming storm," the most awful storm that shall ever break over this poor world? Some of you have lived in regions where thunderstorms are common, and you have often, no doubt, noted on a hot summer day the clouds suddenly gathering in the heavens, becoming heavier and darker every moment. You have heard the thunder reverberating in the skies, peal after peal, with ever-increasing intensity. You have observed the lightning flashes striking terror into many a heart. Then, suddenly, all became still; there seemed to be not even a breath of wind to move the leaves upon the trees. Yet, there was an overcast, threatening sky that cuased the fowls to run for a hiding place and the cattle to move uneasily; all nature is expectant. A few moments pass, then vivid flashes of lightning cause us to shrink back, dreading to be stricken. Crash upon crash follow, and the windows of the heavens seem to be opened— the storm pouring down in a deluge!

We have something similar to this here. We saw in chapters 4 and 5 the saints gathered around the throne of God and of the Lamb, and we noted that from the throne proceeded thunder and lightning. As the seals were broken one after another, judgment followed judgment in quick succession upon the poor world from which God had gathered His beloved people. But even the crashing under the sixth seal is not the climax. In heaven lies the mystery of God's dealing with this world and the judgments yet to fall upon it. But when the last seal is broken, it will be clearly manifested then just what side God takes in all of the affairs of earth. He will judge according to the holiness of His character and the righteousness of His throne. The seventh seal, as we have before noted, introduces the final drama of the Great Tribulation. No wonder there is silence in heaven for half an hour before that seal is broken!

It is as though all heaven is waiting in breathless expectation. We seem to hear the questions: What will the Lamb do next? What will be God's next move toward judging and reclaiming that rebellious world? The verses that follow give the answers. John says,

> And I saw the seven angels which stood before God; and to them were given seven trumpets. And another angel came and stood at the altar, having a golden censer; and there was given unto him much incense, that he should offer it with the prayers of all saints upon the golden altar which was before the throne. And the smoke of the incense, which came with the prayers of the saints, ascended up before God out of the

angel's hand. And the angel took the censer, and filled it with fire of the altar, and cast it into the earth: and there were voices, and thunderings, and lightnings, and an earthquake. (vv. 2–5)

Careful readers of the Bible will connect the seven trumpets with the fall of Jericho, that great city just across the Jordan that barred the progress of the people of Israel into the Promised Land, the city that fell with the blast of God alone. The priests of Israel were given the trumpets of judgment, and for seven days they marched about the city blowing the trumpets; seven times on the seventh day they did so, and at the seventh blast the walls fell down flat. Jericho is a type of this current world in its estrangement from God, with enmity to the people of God. Jericho fell at the sound of seven trumpets, and the world, as you and I know it, is going to fall at the sound of the seven trumpets of doom, blown by these angels of judgment.

The seal is broken, the book is fully unrolled, and the seven angels appear to whom are given seven trumpets. And as these angel messengers stand by, waiting one after the other to herald with a trumpet blast the coming judgments, we are told that another angel came and stood to officiate at the golden altar. He is seen offering incense; therefore, he is an angel-priest. Who is this angel-priest? I think you will agree that he can be no created angel. Scripture never speaks of any created angel offering incense with the prayers of saints to make them acceptable to God. The Church of Rome says that, but nowhere in the Bible do you get anything of the kind. Throughout the Old Testament, the preincarnate Christ is again and again presented as the Angel of Jehovah. He was the angel who appeared to Abraham; He was the angel who guided the children of Israel; and He was the angel who wrestled with Jacob and put his thigh out of joint by the brook at Peniel. He was the angel who appeared to Moses in the mount when the prophet prayed that he might behold God; He was the angel who appeared to Joshua to lead the people of Israel against their foes in the land of Canaan; and He was the angel of Jehovah again and again manifesting Himself throughout the entire dispensation. In the book of Zechariah, He is the angel-advocate who stands to plead for Joshua, the high priest. So we again find Him in the book of Revelation presented as an angel-priest who still has a people on earth for whom to plead. They are not members of the church of God, but, as we saw in connection with the fifth seal and the parenthetical portion of chapter 7, the one hundred and forty-four thousand, a remnant who will be taken out of Israel after the church of God will be called home.

The Word of God is very clear on all of this. Romans 11 pictures the Gentiles as having been grafted into Israel's olive tree of promise (Rom. 11:17). And the Holy Spirit goes on in that chapter to make plain that when the Gentile church becomes apostate, God is going to reject it and turn back to Israel. In the tribulation period, they will again be grafted into their own olive tree. They will be the witnessing remnant of that awful time and the Lord Jesus will make intercession for them in heaven, as He now does for His church. He will not be indifferent to their sorrows and perplexities in those days of unparalleled tribulation, but He will, as the faithful High Priest, bear His people on His heart and on His shoulders, even as Aaron of old bore the names of the twelve tribes on the breastplate and on the onyx stones set in the brooches of gold upon his shoulders. So we see Him pictured by this angel-priest, offering incense at the golden altar in the very presence of God.

Now, the Jews bewail their desolation and cry out in anguish of heart year after year at the most solemn of their set times, "Woe unto us, for we have no Mediator!" But when their eyes are opened and grace begins to operate in their souls, they will know the blessedness of priestly intercession on the part of their once-rejected Messiah, whom they will learn to identify with the Angel of the Covenant of old. They will search their Bibles, doubtless read the book of Hebrews, and study the four gospels, and they will see the truth. They will look upon Him whom they pierced, they will repent and mourn, as described in Zechariah 12:10–14, and God will receive Israel and make her His messenger to the nations. We are not surprised, therefore, when we get this look into glory and see the Lord Jesus as the Angel-priest.

He has a golden censer. Is it not a blessed thing to think that Israel will have such an Intercessor in the coming day? We are told that the smoke of the incense is the prayers of the saints—those suffering saints on the earth. The angel took the censer, filled it with the fire of the altar, and emptied it upon the earth. Here is the answer to the cry of His afflicted ones down in that scene of tribulation. The prayers went up to the Father, and judgment came down, "and there were thunderings, lightnings and an earthquake." The final storm breaks at last!

> The first angel sounded, and there followed hail and fire mingled with blood, and they were cast upon the earth: and the third part of trees was burnt up, and all green grass was burnt up. (v. 7)

I cannot explain the symbol fully, but I think I can see a hint of the awful time that is before the people of Christendom who have refused the gospel. Do you remember that the grass is used as a symbol of man (see Isa. 40:6)? Grass trampled beneath the foot is the picture of man in his frailty and weakness. What about the tree? It is but another picture of man, but rising up in his pride and independence of God. You remember how Nebuchadnezzar is likened unto a great tree and how the rulers in Israel were spoken of as great cedars. John the Baptist said, "Now the ax is laid to the root of the trees. Every tree that beareth not good fruit is hewn down and cast into the fire." Grass is man in his weakness, man in his littleness; the tree is man in his dignity, in his greatness, in his independence—man lifting himself up against God. So the first angel's trumpet distinctly indicates a fiery judgment upon that part of the human race that has rejected the gospel now so freely proclaimed. It is an appalling picture, but, remember, the reality is far worse than the picture!

This is followed by another fearful portent that has to do especially, I believe, with the judgment of the great world church that has borne sway over the consciences of so many people and enslaved so many nations.

> And the second angel sounded, and as it were a great mountain burning with fire was cast into the sea: and the third part of the sea became blood; and the third part of the creatures which were in the sea, and had life, died; and the third part of the ships were destroyed. (vv. 8–9)

I direct your attention to Jeremiah 51:25, where we have the same symbol— a great mountain cast into the sea. I have already said that every symbol in the book of Revelation was explained somewhere else in the Bible. Now here in the Old Testament a great mountain burning with fire is the symbol of Babylon, literal Babylon. In the New Testament, this great destroying mountain burning with fire that is cast into the sea and brought to an end under the judgment of God in this coming day is evidently spiritual Babylon. Babylon of old was the fountainhead of idolatry. Every idolatrous system has had its root in Babylon. Spiritual Babylon is the direct successor of literal Babylon. The direct communication between the mystic religions of the old Babylon and spiritual Babylon of today is so marked that, if anyone attempts to make a study of it, he is perfectly astonished to find where many of the ritual services used in "Christian" churches sprang from. In the coming day, when the second angel's trumpet sounds, Babylon will be cast into the great sea of the nations. That is, in the day of God's wrath, the false church will be utterly destroyed by the people over whom she once tyrannized. Of this, we shall learn more when we come to chapter 18.

The third angel follows. We read,

And the third angel sounded, and there fell a great star from heaven, burning as it were a lamp, and it fell upon the third part of the rivers, and upon the mountains of waters; and the name of the star is called Wormwood: and the third part of the waters became wormwood; and many men died of the waters, because they were made bitter. (vv. 10–11)

A great star falls from heaven. Stars in the prophetic Scriptures are religious dignitaries. They that turn many to righteousness are to shine as the stars forever and ever, and the symbol is used again and again in the Bible for persons occupying places of importance in the spiritual, or religious world, as we say. Here we have a star whose influence over man is so great that when he falls the third part of men are poisoned because of the evil influence of this apostate leader.

Who is this star? Although I do not want to try to prophesy, let me give you a suggestion. Who occupies the highest place in the church in the minds of millions of professing Christian people? Many would say the pope. Can you imagine what might be the effect on vast numbers of people if tomorrow the newspapers came out with an "Extra" something like this: "The pope declares that Christianity is all a sham, that religion is just a fraud!"? Can you imagine the effect that would have? Tens of thousands of people would say, "Well, the man we looked upon as the head of the church, as infallible, as the authoritative voice on all matters of a religious nature, has denied it all. Now, whom can we trust, and what can we believe?" Leo X did this privately. Suppose that a future pope did it openly. I do not say that certainly it will be so. I am just giving you a hint of what might be. Do we not see the same thing on a small scale today? When a professing Christian leader gives up that for which he has once stood, it has a tremendous influence for evil upon people of lesser influence and lesser knowledge. And after the true church is gone, I gather from this symbol that one of the greatest "lights" in the false system left behind will openly apostatize, and his teachings will become as wormwood, poisoning and embittering, to his deluded followers.

The darkness deepens when the fourth trumpet sounds.

And the fourth angel sounded, and the third part of the sun was smitten, and the third part of the moon, and the third part of the stars; so as the third part of them was darkened, and the day shone not for a third part of it, and the night likewise. And I beheld, and heard an angel flying through the midst of heaven, saying with a loud voice, Woe, woe,

woe, to the [inhabitants] of the earth by reason of the other voices of the trumpet of the three angels, which are yet to sound! (vv. 12–13)

Again, I do not attempt to tell you exactly what this symbolizes, but evidently light is being withdrawn rapidly. The third part of the sky is smitten. The third part of the moon and stars are darkened. What does it mean? Well, you know what the Lord Jesus says to the individual, "If the light that is in thee be darkened, how great is that darkness." "Light obeyed increaseth light—light resisted bringeth night." Do you know why so many people in Christendom are going into what they call Christian Science, Theosophy, Spiritualism, and so-called New Theology? Do you know why so few people ever get out of them? Because they have had the opportunity to receive light from God, but they have rejected it, and it is written in the Word that "God shall send them strong delusion that they should believe a lie, that they all might be damned who obeyed not the truth but had pleasure in unrighteousness" (2 Thess. 2:11–12). When God presents His truth to people, responsibility comes with it. When God presents Christ to them, tremendous responsibility is put upon them. If you hear the message and reject Christ, do not be surprised if you are caught in one of these unholy ideas of the present day; perhaps you will never be delivered from it until you wake up in a lost eternity.

The thirteenth verse introduces very solemnly the three trumpets yet to follow, which are distinguished from the four upon which we have already commented as "woe" trumpets. They speak of a more intensified form of judgment than any previously portrayed. These will occupy us in our next lecture. I only desire now to call your attention to the expression *the inhabiters of the earth*. We find frequently in this book a similar term: "Them that dwell upon the earth." Upon these the heaviest judgments fall. They are not merely they that live here upon earth, but they form a distinctive class. They are the people who have rejected the heavenly calling. When God offered them full and free salvation through the death of His beloved Son, they turned away from Him because to have closed with Christ would have meant to give up their worldly desires and love of sin; therefore, they become the "dwellers on the earth."

THE FIRST AND SECOND "WOE" TRUMPETS

Revelation 9

We are to be occupied this evening with the fifth and sixth trumpets, known respectively as the first and second *woes*. The added designation of these trumpets implies a solemnity and a tearfulness beyond anything we have previously considered. That we may have all the details clearly before us, I will quote the text in full as we proceed with the address.

> And the fifth angel sounded, and I saw a star fall from heaven unto the earth: and to him was given the key to the bottomless pit. And he opened the bottomless pit; and there arose a smoke out of the pit, as the smoke of a great furnace; and the sun and the air were darkened by reason of the smoke of the pit. (vv. 1–2)

In place of "I saw a star fall from heaven," we should read, "I saw a star *fallen* from heaven." The reference, I take it, is undoubtedly to that apostate leader referred to under the third trumpet. There, we read of a great star that fell from heaven burning like a lamp and, falling upon the third part of the rivers and fountains of waters, poisoned them so that men drinking of them died, the waters being made bitter.

Under this fifth trumpet, we have the development of the apostasy, of which this leader is evidently the head. He opens the bottomless pit, using a "key." We have been made familiar, in the Gospels, with the thought of the key where Christ commits to Peter the keys of the kingdom of heaven, and you will remember our Lord's words to the lawyers, "Ye have taken away the key of knowledge" (Luke 11:52). From these Scriptures, it is clear that a key implies a system of teaching and possibly ritual observances connected with it. With this hint, we can readily understand what follows.

This arch-apostate—by a system of erroneous teaching, damnable heresies, and denying the Lord that bought them—opens the bottomless pit, from whence issues a blinding smoke as the smoke of a great furnace and so intense that the sun and the air become darkened because of the smoke of the pit. It is the strong delusion, to which we have had occasion to refer frequently in the course of these addresses. Although 2 Thessalonians says that "God shall *send* . . . strong delusion" (2:11), we here learn that He sends it by permitting this satanic envoy to delude the nations.

Darkening of the sun by means of these Stygian fumes implies the blotting out, from before men's eyes or minds, the supreme source of light. Their whole spiritual sky will be made dark by the false system with which they will be deluded. The air is particularly Satan's realm. He is called "the prince of the power of the air" (Eph. 2:2). The darkening of the air implies the control of this realm by satanic agencies. I do not think we will be far wrong if we identify with this coming delusion the occult systems of gnostic origin, so largely prevailing and so rapidly spreading today. These systems, as we have before noticed, are a unit in denying (in any true sense) the personality of God and in asserting the divinity of humanity. They reproduce, in some form or other, the primeval lie, "Ye shall be as Elohim." This is the very essence of New Thought, New Theology, Eddyism, Spiritism, Theosophy, and other offshoots of these evil systems. After the restraining power of the Holy Spirit has been removed, they will spread like locusts over all the earth, having tremendous power over the minds of men. This is what the third verse indicates: "And there came out of the smoke locusts upon the earth: and unto them was given power, as the scorpions of the earth have power."

Anyone familiar with the locust plagues of the East will understand at once the figure here used. Travelers have told us how the locusts appear in swarms so vast that they seem like great clouds, actually shutting out the sun and filling the whole air. They devour everything before them. Falling upon a green field, they leave it within a few minutes as bare as though no vegetation had been there at all. They are the dread of Oriental husbandmen, who are utterly powerless to combat them. They aptly typify or symbolize the spiritual plague of the last days. The symbol of the locusts is coupled with that of the scorpion because of the torment these evil teachings eventually bring to those who accept them.

That we do not have any merely literal plague of locusts in view here the next verses make evident:

> And it was commanded them that they should not hurt the grass of the earth, neither any green thing, neither any tree; but only those men which have not the seal of God in their foreheads. And to them it was given that they should not kill them, but that they should be tormented five months: and their torment was as the torment of a scorpion, when he striketh a man. (vv. 4–5)

Literal locusts would do the very thing which these are commanded *not* to do. The grass of the earth, green things, trees of all descriptions, are here distinctly protected from their power. This verse seems to be rather in the way of explanation than a continuation of the symbol; otherwise, we might think of the grass and trees as representing mankind. But it would seem that the apostle here expounds rather than continues the description of his vision that we may not be misled by a literal application. The locusts' power is expended upon those men who do not have the seal of God in their foreheads. They are tormented by them for five months, a torment akin to that of a scorpion when he strikes a man. We have already seen that those bearing the seal of God are the remnant of Israel. These alone in Christendom and Judaism will be preserved from the strong delusion of that day. Our Lord Himself limits Satan's power in the same way, when, referring to this very period and the plague of false teaching, He says, "If it were possible, they would deceive the very elect." Thank God, it is not possible because the seal of the living God in the current dispensation is the indwelling Holy Spirit given to guide into all truth, and in that coming dispensation of judgment the same Holy Spirit will illumine the minds of those who repent in Israel, and thus preserve them from this satanic delusion.

For the rest, so great will be the distress caused by these evil teachings when men fully give themselves up to them that, "In those days shall men seek death, and shall not find it; and shall desire to die, and death shall flee from them" (v. 6).

Anyone who has ever sought to give spiritual help to persons awakening in measure from the delusions of Eddyism, or Spiritism, or in fact any other satanic system, will understand at once the condition of mind here depicted. I shall never forget the almost insane glare of the eye and the hopeless wail in the voice of a poor woman who, after having been under spiritualistic influences for a number of years, at last began dimly to apprehend the dreadful character of the system that had been enslaving her. Only through much prayer and earnest holding on to God on her behalf was she delivered, but she told me on one occasion that she had suffered all of the torments of the damned during the year and a half when she was seeking deliverance from demon control.

A few years ago, I was laboring among the Mormons in Utah, where I learned of a most pitiable case. A family who had accepted the Mormon delusion and emigrated from Great Britain to Utah, after practicing the heathenish rites of Joseph Smith's abominable system for thirty years, were at last awakened to the untrustworthiness of it all by the perfidious conduct of certain eminent church leaders. As a result, they renounced the entire system and were left, if one may so speak, without religious convictions of any kind. A few months later, the wife and mother was dying. She tossed upon her bed in the greatest agony of mind, moaning in her distress and despair, afraid to meet God in her sins. A minister of the gospel was urged by some friends to call and see her, although much against the will of the family, and finally gained admittance to the dying woman's room. He sought faithfully to present the precious truth of gospel God's Holy Word, but though for a time she seemed to listen eagerly, she turned from him at the very last, crying out, "Oh! sir, after one has been fooled by one religion all her life, it is too late to trust another in the hour of death." And so, in great agony, she passed away, as far as he could tell, into a hopeless eternity.

Oh! I would that I had the power to impress upon men and women everywhere the dreadful responsibility they assume when they tamper with these unholy teachings that already have escaped from the bottomless pit and that even now have for many souls darkened the air and blotted out the light of the sun. No torture can compare with spiritual torment, and the only remedy is that perfect love alone displayed in Calvary's Cross that casteth out all fear. In the days to which our chapter refers, those who have rejected the grace of God will never again hear that precious gospel, and so they are left to cry out in their anguish, seeking death but finding it not.

In verses 7–12, we have a highly symbolic description of this delusion, which I wish to examine in detail, so I quote the passage in full.

And the shapes of the locusts were like unto horses prepared unto battle; and on their heads were as it were crowns like gold, and their faces were as the faces of men. And they had hair as the hair of women, and their teeth were as the teeth of lions. And they had breastplates, as it were breastplates of iron; and the sound of their wings was as the sound of chariots of many horses running to battle. And they had tails like unto scorpions, and there were stings in their tails: and their power was to hurt men five months. And they had a king over them, which is the angel of the bottomless pit, whose name in the Hebrew tongue is Abaddon, but in the Greek tongue hath his name Apollyon. One woe is past; and, behold, there come two woes more hereafter.

The shapes of the locusts, we are told, are like unto horses prepared unto battle, thus symbolizing their rapid progress and apparently providential irresistibility in obtaining sway over those who are unprepared to do battle with them. "Upon their heads were crowns like gold"—because apostasy during that time of delusion will seem to carry all before it triumphantly, driving from Christendom the last vestige of orthodoxy. Our Lord Jesus asked the solemn question in view of His second advent, "When the Son of man cometh, shall he find faith on the earth?" (Luke 18:8). The "coming of the Son of man" (Matt. 24:27, 37, 39) refers not to the rapture, but to the *appearing in glory;* at that time it will, for the moment, seem as though all true faith has been driven from the prophetic earth; nevertheless, there will arise by the power of God's Word, from the distant parts of the world, a vast company, as we have seen, who will not have bowed the knee to this latter-day Baal.

We are next told "their faces were as the faces of men, and they had hair as the hair of women, and their teeth were as the teeth of lions." Three symbols here intermingle, all of which are very evidently found in the occult systems to which we have referred. Faces as of men would seem to imply intelligence, and these evil teachers make a great appeal to human reason and ridicule the truth of God as a system of cunningly devised fables, whereas actually they themselves follow but sophistical and illogical theories. Their appeal is to human intelligence, to the mind rather than to the heart and conscience, to which Scripture appeals. Moreover, they are characterized by intense seductiveness and attractive fancies, typified by "the hair of women." A woman's hair, we are told in Scripture, is her glory. In the Song of Solomon 7:5, following the marginal reading, we are told, "[Thy] head upon thee is like Carmel, and the hair of [thy] head like purple; the king is held in the [tresses]." How many people have been turned aside from the path of duty by natural attractions, grossly misused for the purpose of accomplishing unholy ends.

But as seductive and apparently rational as these systems are when they are first presented, they prove at last to have teeth like the teeth of lions, tearing to pieces those who put their trust in them. In verse 9 we read, "And they had breastplates, as it were breastplates of iron; and the sound of their wings was as the sound of chariots of many horses running to battle." These iron breastplates utterly destroy all conscience, or, rather, render them impervious to the shafts of truth, so that the conscience is never reached; while the wings, whose sound is as that of myriads of chariots rushing to battle, would speak of the swiftness with which they conquer those who have turned from the truth and had pleasure in unrighteousness.

Verse 10 again emphasizes the scorpion-like torment they produce. "And they had tails like unto scorpions, and there were stings in their tails: and their power was to hurt men five months." What a mercy that their power is thus limited. I see no reason why we should not understand the five months literally. For a very limited time, this apostate leader and his emissaries will be permitted to dominate those who would not have Christ the Lord to reign over them. In His place, Satan himself is worshiped as Abaddon and Apollyon. "And they had a king over them, which is the angel of the bottomless pit, whose name in the Hebrew tongue is Abaddon, but in the Greek tongue hath his name Apollyon" (v. 11). This can only refer to the Devil himself. He alone is the angel of the bottomless pit. So it is made evident at last that the "God within," to which men are turning today, is none other than Satan, the great archenemy, who has been plotting man's destruction from the very beginning. Self-worshipers are devil worshipers, and in some instances already this has been avowed by the followers of current apostasy. This, then, is the first "woe." "One woe is past; and, behold, there come two woes more hereafter" (v. 12).

We next read,

And the sixth angel sounded, and I heard a voice from the four horns of the golden altar which is before God, saying to the sixth angel which had the trumpet, Loose the four angels which are bound in the great river Euphrates. And the four angels were loosed, which were prepared for an hour, and a day and a month, and a year, for to slay the third part of men. (vv. 13–15)

This is evidently something very different from that at which we have already been looking. It seems to be the result, however, of the previous woe. That is, it shows us what the effect upon the world when Satan worship becomes everywhere prevalent in what was once called Christendom. It will bring about a tremendous conflict, setting nation against nation and man against man, until the third part of men will be destroyed.

I think we have had a remarkable illustration of this in the great conflict from which we have so lately emerged. Who can deny that it was the direct result of rationalistic "Kultur," and the denial of the authority of the Word of God? If education without Christ could save, Germany should have been the most blessed nation on the face of the earth because there education seemed to have reached its highest point—but with what dire results, not only to that nation but also to a large part of the human race! German philosophy had poisoned the world. The colleges and universities of almost every civilized land drank greedily from the poisoned streams of Teutonic philosophies and infidel hypotheses, and it is only now that we are beginning to awaken to the baleful effects of such folly. I have no doubt that Satan himself would have restrained men from rushing into such bloody conflict had it been possible. What I mean is this: he was seeking to entrap men with his specious theories and unholy philosophies, and the Great War of 1914 was an almost unforeseen result of those very ideas. The nations were thrown into confusion by the teachings they had imbibed. The war was like a great explosion that could no longer be prevented.

These considerations will help us, I think, to understand the second "woe." In chapter 7, we saw the four angels restrained from letting loose the four winds of the earth upon the great sea of the nations. Here, a voice from the four horns of the golden altar that is before God, in response, undoubtedly, to the angel-priest's intercession in 8:3, cries out to the angel that had the sixth trumpet, "Loose the four angels which are bound in the great river Euphrates." These angels are evidently at the present time restraining the great Asiatic hordes from pouring themselves upon the Land of Palestine and Europe. The Euphrates formed the eastern limit of the Roman Empire, and thus was the barrier, as it were, between the East and the West. We are told that the four angels were prepared, not exactly—as our Authorized Version reads—for an hour, and a day, and a month, and a year, but for *the* hour, day, month, and year." That is, there is a definite moment in the mind of God at which this awful power is to be let loose. Until that hour strikes, not all of the evil machinations of men and not all of the ambitions of nations can bring about the conflict here predicted. But when that hour does strike, no astute statesman's policy, no treaties, and no world federation movements can prevent the dire catastrophe predicted.

Two hundred thousand thousand horsemen are hurled upon western Asia and Europe. They seem like unearthly warriors, with breastplates of fire, jacinth, and brimstone. The horses' heads seem as the heads of lions because of the unspeakable ferocity of these Asiatic hordes while fire, smoke, and brimstone seem to issue from their mouths, telling of the satanic character of this dire invasion. The result will be a third part of men killed by the fire, the smoke, and the brimstone that issue from their mouths. When we recall the millions who have perished as the direct or indirect result of the recent war and pestilence, we can see how a greater war in the future may well tend to almost depopulate the earth, destroying one-third of the prophetic earth, which is identical with the limits of the old Roman Empire. In verse 19, we read, "For their power is in their mouth, and in their tails: for their tails were like unto serpents, and had heads, and with them they do hurt." Isaiah 9:15 helps us to understand both this passage and verse 10: "The prophet that teacheth lies, he is the tail." Whether it be the occult woe of the fifth trumpet or the carnage woe of the sixth trumpet, in each case lying prophets are the leaders in each movement and are responsible for the mental, spiritual, and physical harm accomplished.

It is a solemn thing to realize that even judgments such as these will have no effect in leading men back to God or to repentance. Punishment does not of itself lead men to repentance. Verses 20–21 say, "The rest of the men which were not killed by these plagues yet repented not of the works of their hands, that they should not worship devils, and idols of gold, and silver, and brass, and stone, and of wood: which neither can see, nor hear, nor walk: neither repented they of their murders, nor of their sorceries, nor of their fornication, nor of their thefts." This is in accordance with the general testimony of Scripture, which nowhere intimates that punishment produces penitence. The Restorationist and Universalist teachers deny this and insist that all punishment, whether in time or eternity, is with a view to the final salvation of the delinquent and that eventually all men will learn by judgment, if they refused to learn by grace, and will turn to God for salvation. But both here and later in this same book of Revelation, we find that the heaviest judgments of God, falling on guilty men, do not soften the stony, rebellious hearts; rather, men become hardened in their sins and are more blasphemous and God-defiant when judgment is poured out upon them than they were before.

In eternity, God will not permit open defiance of His will. Our Lord Jesus tells us that in hell there will be not only "weeping" because of suffering but also "gnashing of teeth," which expresses not manifest opposition but the angry defiance of the heart of man, which will be filled with hatred toward God but will be powerless to oppose His government openly. If the Cross of Christ, with its marvelous exhibition of holy love, will not reconcile men to God, punishment will never avail to win their hearts either.

LECTURE 11

EATING THE LITTLE OPEN BOOK

Revelation 10

We will look this evening at the first part of the parenthetical portion that comes between the sixth and seventh trumpets. We have already noticed that similar parentheses are between the sixth and seventh seals and the sixth and seventh vials. This is an evidence of divine order not to be overlooked. The seventh trumpet ushers in the millennial kingdom and continues to the close of the course of time and the establishment of the Great White Throne for the judgment of the wicked dead. But before this consummation is brought to our attention, we are given fuller instruction regarding the place that Israel has in the mind of God in connection with these future events.

This tenth chapter contains truth largely of a moral character; therefore, one is likely, in studying the book, to pass over it without very careful attention. It does not seem, at first sight, to have to do with any of the great movements that we have been considering in connection with either Israel or the Gentiles. But just as in the first chapter of the book of Daniel we have set before us, in the history of the three Hebrew youths who refused to be denied with the king's meat, the moral condition suited to instruction in the things of God, so in this tenth chapter we find the Lord dealing in a very special way with His beloved apostle John that he may be the better prepared to unfold the great mysteries lying just beyond us in the rest of this solemn book. And in the Lord's preparation of His servant John, we get great moral principles that should speak to our own hearts, and, if laid hold of aright, fit us the better to serve the living and true God while we wait for His Son from heaven. In verses 1–3, we read,

> And I saw another mighty angel come down from heaven, clothed with a cloud: and a rainbow was upon his head, and his face was as it were the sun, and his feet as pillars of fire: and he had in his hand a little book open: and he set his right foot upon the sea, and his left foot on the earth, and cried with a loud voice, as when a lion roareth: and when he had cried, seven thunders uttered their voices.

This mighty angel can surely be no other than that same glorious Angel of the Covenant whom we have already beheld standing at the golden altar officiating as the Angel-priest of the heavenly sanctuary. Of no created angel could such glorious things be said as those that John here mentions in connection with this wondrous being.

The reason our Lord is brought before us in this angelic character is that in this portion of the book of Revelation we are dealing largely with Israel, the earthly people before their Messiah has been revealed to them. Therefore, it is but natural that He should take toward them the same position that He occupied in Old Testament times. A fuller revelation they will receive when He descends in glory, and they behold the marks of His passion and cry out in amazement, "What are those wounds in thy hands?" Then He will answer, "Those with which I was wounded in the house of my friends." At last, the full truth will burst upon them that the crucified Nazarene and the Angel of the Covenant are identical, and "they shall look upon him whom they have pierced, and shall mourn for him, as one mourneth for his only son, and . . . as one [who] is in bitterness for his firstborn" (Zech. 12:10). This will be, for Judah and Jerusalem, the true day of atonement, when they will afflict their souls as they realize the enormity of their sin in rejecting their divine Savior, and the merits of His atoning work shall be applied to their hearts and consciences. Then will they be able to cry out in the full assurance of faith, "He was wounded for our transgressions, he was bruised for our iniquities: the chastisement of our peace was upon him; and with his stripes we are healed" (Isa. 53:5). But until that moment of His full manifestation, He is to them the Angel of the Covenant—an uncreated angel, therefore—Jehovah's fellow; for, as we have intimated above, to no created angel could this description be rightly applied. He comes down from heaven, clothed not merely with *a* cloud but *the* cloud, as it should read, and the cloud is the symbol of the divine glory.

The cloud is the chariot in which He led His people of old through the wilderness all of the way from Egypt to the Land of Promise. We are expressly told that in that cloud was the Angel of the Covenant. It is the uncreated cloud of glory that dwelt between the cherubim in the tabernacle above the mercy seat. When Solomon built the temple and dedicated it to Jehovah, He came in the cloud, dwelling in it as His house. When, nearly five centuries afterward, Ezekiel was called upon to declare the desolation of that once-holy house, he beheld the cloud lifted up from the most holy place, tarrying a moment over the door of the sanctuary, and then departing and hanging above the city wall as though loath to give up the place where His glory had so long been manifested. Slowly, the cloud moved over to the adjoining mountain on the east, that is, the Mount of Olives, and then up into the heavens.

Thus, the visible manifestation of Jehovah's presence had disappeared from Israel because of their sins. That cloud never returned to the land of Palestine until our Lord Jesus Christ went up into the holy mount, which we commonly call the Mount of Transfiguration, where Peter, James, and John had a vision of the coming kingdom—"the power and coming of our Lord Jesus Christ" (2 Peter 1:16). There, they saw Him transfigured and talking with Moses and Elijah—Moses representing the saints who have died and will be raised again at our Lord's return, and Elijah picturing those who shall be caught up at Christ's coming without dying.

Peter, overwhelmed by such an abundant revelation and knowing not what to say, cried, "Lord, it is good for us to be here: . . . [and] let us make . . . three tabernacles; one for thee, and one for Moses, and one for Elias" (Matt. 17:4). And while he thus spoke, there came a "cloud and overshadowed them" (v. 5). This was the Father's way of showing them that He would have no mortal man, however holy and devoted, put on the same level with His beloved Son. After Christ had died on the Cross and was raised from the dead by omnipotent power, He led His disciples out to the Mount of Olives nigh unto Bethany and, with hands uplifted in blessing, was parted from them, and they beheld Him going up, until the cloud received Him out of their sight. When He returns again, we shall behold Him on the cloud, and every eye shall see Him. So here, when John says, "I saw [a] mighty angel . . . clothed with [the] cloud," we may understand at once that this angel can be no creature but is Himself the Creator of all things, our Lord Jesus Christ, clothed with the sign of the divine majesty.

Observe, in the next place, that the rainbow that was round about the throne of God in chapter 4 is now seen wrapped, as it were, about the head of this mighty angel. It seems to speak of His coming to confirm the covenant made of old with Noah after the world had been destroyed by a flood. Another evidence that it is a divine person who is here brought before us, is found in the next clause: "His face was as it were the sun." It is the same face that Saul of Tarsus saw when he was marching along the Damascus turnpike, his heart filled with hatred against the Lord Jesus and burning with rage against His followers. Stricken to the earth, he saw a light above the brightness of the sun, and in that glorious light he beheld the once-crucified Christ of God and heard Him ask in tenderest accents, "Saul, Saul, why persecutest thou me?" When He comes again, it will be as the Sun of Righteousness.

"His feet," we are told, "[were] as pillars of fire," thus linking Him with the same wondrous Being described in chapter 1, of whom we read that "his feet [were] like unto fine brass, as if they burned in a furnace" (v. 15). This is also the same Being that Daniel saw and describes in similar terms in his seventh chapter.

We are next told that He had in His hand "a little book open." People have offered various speculations as to what this book might be, but it seems to me that it could be none other than the very book that we have had before us heretofore. It is the title deed to the earth, the seals of which have been broken, one after the other, until the entire scroll is seen unrolled. The Lord descends with all of the evidences of divine majesty and, with this title deed in His hand, He sets His right foot upon the sea and His left foot upon the earth, as indicative of taking possession of His own inheritance—the inheritance that He, as Man on earth, had redeemed with His own precious blood.

His voice is the voice of the conqueror—"He cried as a lion roareth"—because the Angel and the Lion of Judah's tribe are one and the same. When He had cried, seven thunders uttered their voices. The thunder, we noticed earlier, speaks of judgment, and John says, "When the seven thunders had uttered their voices, I was about to write: and I heard a voice from heaven saying unto me, Seal up those things which the seven thunders uttered, and write them not." As Mediator of the new covenant, He seals up the utterance of the seven thunders. It is not necessary for us to know *what* they uttered. They speak of judgment that is due wayward man, but He Himself has borne the judgment, and those who trust in Him need never know its dreadful secrets.

Let us love, and sing, and wonder,
Let us praise the Savior's name;

He has hushed the law's loud thunder,
He has quenched Mount Sinai's flame.
He has bought us with His blood;
He has brought us home to God.

Have you ever noticed how inquisitive people often are regarding those things that the wisdom of God has purposely kept from them? In the Old Testament dispensation, the Law was hidden in the ark, covered with the mercy seat; yet, the men of Bethshemesh foolishly looked into the ark and were smitten in judgment. So some things are hidden from the people of God in all dispensations, and He would have us leave them with Himself. "The secret things belong unto the LORD our God: but the things [that] are revealed [are] for us and . . . our children" (Deut. 29:29). Alas, it is only too natural for man to pass over the precious revealed truth that would be for his sanctification and blessing and to occupy himself with hidden things that are not given for him now to know and that, if it had been for his blessing to know, God would have revealed them. I am often asked, "What do you suppose was written in the flying roll of Zechariah's vision?" (see Zech. 5:1–2). I only know what the Word has said. "What were the unspeakable things that Paul heard when he was caught up into the third heaven?" (see 2 Cor. 12:4). If *Paul* could not utter them, how could *we?* And so many people have puzzled over the things that the seven thunders uttered, but faith rests in the fact that John was commanded *not* to write them.

And the angel which I saw stand upon the sea and upon the earth lifted up his hand to heaven, and sware by him that liveth for ever and ever, who created heaven, and the things that therein are, and the earth, and the things that therein are, and the sea, and the things which are therein, that there should be time no longer: but in the days of the voice of the seventh angel, when he shall begin to sound, the mystery of God should be finished, as he hath declared to his servants the prophets. (vv. 5–7)

It is important here to notice the difference between the last clause of verse 6 as found in the Authorized Version and in any critical translation. Instead of reading, "That there should be time no longer," read, "That there should be no longer delay." Because of the erroneous translation given in our generally correct and excellent English version, many people have been misled into supposing that this vision brings us to the end of time, whereas, the context makes very plain that such is not the case. The vision is distinctly premillennial. The point is that the hour of accomplishment has almost struck, and God will not delay the completion of His plans and the fulfillment of His promises. "A short work will the Lord make upon the earth" (Rom. 9:28). The Angel swears by Him who lives forever and ever (that is, by Jehovah Himself, the Creator of all things), that nothing shall cause any more delay. But in the days when the seventh angel sounds, the mystery of God, that is, the mystery of God's long tolerance of evil, will be finished. Everything will then be made plain. The mystery of retribution, the mystery of predestination, and the mystery of the great struggle between light and darkness and good and evil—all of that will be explained then. There will be no more secrets in God's ways and dealings, and man need no longer question; the dispensations of faith will have come to an end, and the dispensation of sight will have dawned.

Are you often troubled by questions about God's purpose, His counsels, His judgments, or His apparently strange dealings with you and with the world? To the man who has not the secret of the Lord, His ways may seem contradictory. Learn from this Scripture to wait patiently until God Himself makes everything clear in the days of the voice of the seventh angel.

In the second part of the chapter, we are occupied with a very different line of things. We are now to read of an experience that the apostle John had and into which God would have every student of His Word enter. He tells us,

> And the voice which I heard from heaven spake unto me again, and said, Go and take the little book which is open in the hand of the angel which standeth upon the sea and upon the earth. And I went unto the angel, and said unto him, Give me the little book. And he said unto me, Take it, and eat it up; and it shall make thy belly bitter, but it shall be in thy mouth sweet as honey. And I took the little book out of the angel's hand, and ate it up; and it was in my mouth sweet as honey: and as soon as I had eaten it, my belly was bitter. (vv. 8–10)

Now what are we to understand by this? You will, at once, recall that a similar experience was given to the prophet Ezekiel (Ezek. 3). He, too, was called upon to "eat the book." And the lesson in both instances is the same. It is only as we feed upon and digest the Word of God that we ourselves are nourished and built up in the truth of our most holy faith and are in a right condition of soul to use that Word for the help and instruction of others. David said, "Thy word have I hid in mine heart, that I might not sin against thee" (Ps. 119:11). And again, "Thou desirest truth in the [inmost] parts: and in the hidden parts thou [wouldst] make him to know wisdom" (Ps. 51:6). This, I take it, is what John's experience illustrates. He was commanded to eat the little book that was in the angel's hand, that is, to *meditate* upon it, to make it thoroughly his own.

Someone has said that meditation, in these busy days of ours, is a lost art. Would to God it were restored and that His people, generally, were more given literally to feed upon His truth. It is not only that God would have John and Ezekiel eat the book but also that He wants *you* to eat it. He has given it to you who believe on His Son to be the food of your own souls and to make you fit to serve Him in this scene. And remember that this is just as true of the prophetic books as it is of every other portion of the Word of God. In both of the instances cited, however, it is particularly the prophetic word that is in view. Lay hold of dispensational truth, of prophetic teaching, in this very practical way, and it must have a most beneficial effect upon your inner man.

John tells us that when the book was in his mouth it was very sweet, but when he had eaten it his inward parts were made bitter. This is most instructive. There is no sweeter portion in all Scripture than that which God has revealed concerning the manifestation of His blessed Son. Prophetic truth is generally sweet and attractive to those whose interest is just being awakened in it. But, if follow up, if they really eat the book, it leads to self-judgment and to separation from evil, and this task will always be bitter because not one of us readily takes the place in which God's Word would put him during this period of Christ's rejection. So the point here is that God's truth makes demands upon people.

And you who are following these studies with me will soon find this out if you have not already done so. If you conscientiously undertake to walk in the revealed truth, you, too, will know something of its bitterness. You cannot enjoy things that you used to enjoy if you receive the prophetic testimony and walk in the power of what is there revealed. As the great divine program unfolds before your mind, it may be very interesting, and, in this sense, the book is sweet; but, as great divine principles enter your hearts, and you realize more and more the call to strangership in this Satan-controlled scene, the truth becomes bitter indeed, and it makes demands upon you. How many a soul has greatly enjoyed his first taste of instruction as to the second coming of the Lord Jesus Christ! It was all so new, so wonderful, and so different than the platitudes perchance that he had been hearing as he sat under the ministry of some cold semiworldling who was posing as a minister of Christ. But as this truth got a grip upon him, as it entered into his innermost being, he found that it made demands from which he shrank, and it required of him what at first he felt he could not give. It was bitter, truly; yet, it is not always the sweet things that are best for us. We need the bitter as well as the sweet, and every soul who has walked in the truth, as God has revealed it to him, has found, at last, the blessedness of obedience. "To obey is better than sacrifice, and to hearken than the fat of rams" (1 Sam. 15:22).

It is a very sad thing indeed when truth is simply held in the intellect with no particular bearing upon the life. The apostle John tells us, speaking of the second coming of the Lord, "Every man that hath this hope in him purifieth himself, even as he is pure" (1 John 3:3). It is a truth that should affect the believer at every angle of his life. Anyone who *really* believes it cannot afterward live for self or for the world. If one professes to hold the second coming of Christ and yet lives like the world, it but evidences the fact that, whatever he may hold mentally, the truth of the Lord's coming *does not hold him*. That truth believed makes carnal Christians spiritual, it makes worldly people heavenly, it makes covetous people generous, and it makes careless people earnest. I want to be very frank with you. If you do not desire to let this truth have its sway over your lives, it might be better to cease studying this book of Revelation right here because all of God's truth has been made known for the obedience of faith. And I am certain that these truths are either going to change the lives of some people completely or harden them in their waywardness and be the means of searing their consciences as with a hot iron.

After the apostle had eaten the book, the angel said unto him, "Thou must prophesy again before many peoples, and nations, and tongues, and kings" (v. 11). This passage is of importance in connection with the further opening of the book. The Lord says to John, "Thou must prophesy *again*." It is not that he is to go to other peoples and nations and so forth to prophesy. Rather, he is to prophesy regarding these nations, to the same servants of God to whom he has already been giving the Word. The point is that, when the seventh trumpet sounds (of which we shall read in the next chapter), the current outline of prophecy comes to a close because, as we mentioned earlier, the seventh trumpet carries us right on to the great day of judgment at the end of time. But in the last verse of the eleventh chapter (which properly belongs to chap. 12), John begins once more to prophesy concerning nations, kings, tongues, and people, and this second great outline culminates in the new heaven and new earth. Remember that the roll that was seen in the hand of Him that sat upon the throne, the seals of which were broken by the Lamb, was written on two sides. As the book was unrolled, John would see clearly what was written on the inside, and this, I take it, is the outline we have already had before us. But, beginning with chapter 12, the roll is, so to speak, reversed, and we see what was written on the other side. That is, God confirms the former outline and fills in details that are omitted there, so that we have a clearer and fuller understanding of the great events yet to take place in the world where our Lord was crucified.

If this fact is seen clearly, the book becomes plain; otherwise, there is confusion. Some people try to make everything chronological with their scheme of interpretation. The trumpets not only follow the seals, which is quite correct, but also these interpreters go on to make the vials, or bowls of wrath, follow the trumpets, and this necessarily puts chapter 12 and the rapture of the man-child far over into the seventieth week, whereas, as we shall see when we reach that point, chapter 12 and chapter 4 fit together chronologically. As of old God gave Pharaoh two dreams, the one confirming the other, so here the message is duplicated, if I may so say, that we may know the certainty of the words of truth wherein we are being instructed.

THE TWO WITNESSES AND THE SEVENTH TRUMPET

Revelation 11

In the first thirteen verses of this eleventh chapter, which we are now to consider, we have the rest of the parenthesis that has occupied us in our study of chapter 10. The careful student of the Word of God will, upon reading this portion, immediately recall the measuring of Jerusalem in Zechariah 2 and the measuring of the millennial temple in Ezekiel 40. In this same book of Revelation, we also read of the measuring of the Holy City, the New Jerusalem, in chapter 21. In the opening verses of our current section, John says,

> And there was given me a reed like unto a rod: and the angel stood, saying, Rise, and measure the temple of God, and the altar, and them that worship therein. But the court which is without the temple leave out, and measure it not; for it is given unto the Gentiles: and the holy city shall they tread under foot forty and two months. (vv. 1–2)

The vision clearly involves Jerusalem and the future temple in the last days. I think we may say that throughout the Bible when God speaks of measuring anything the thought is implied that He is marking it off as that which belongs to Himself. When one purchases a piece of ground or is about to take possession of a property, it is very common to measure it and mark off its lines. In Zechariah 2, we are told that the prophet beheld a man with a measuring line in his hand, to whom he put the question, "Whither goest thou?" and the answer was, "To measure Jerusalem, to see what is the breadth thereof, and what is the length thereof" (Zech. 2:2). And in the fourth verse, the angel who is interpreting the visions for Zechariah says to another angel, "Run, speak to this young man, saying, Jerusalem shall be inhabited as towns without walls for the multitude of men and cattle therein: for I, saith the LORD, will be unto her a wall of fire round about, and will be the glory in the midst of her" (vv. 4–5).

Then, in the rest of the chapter, we have a very distinct prophecy of the future deliverance of God's earthly people from all of their foes, when they will be brought from the land of the north and from all parts of the world where they have been carried in the days of their captivity. This will not be fully accomplished until the Lord Jesus Himself has appeared in glory because verse 8 reads, "Thus saith the LORD of hosts; *After the glory* hath he sent me unto the nations which spoiled you: for he that toucheth you toucheth the apple of his eye. For, behold, I will shake my hand upon them, and they shall be a spoil to their servants: and ye shall know that the LORD of hosts hath sent me" (vv. 8–9). The daughter of Zion is then called upon to rejoice because Jehovah Himself will dwell in the midst of her. "And many nations shall be joined to the LORD in that day, and shall be [his] people" (v. 11), and He will dwell in the midst of them, and they shall know that the Lord of hosts hath sent His prophet unto them. "And the Lord shall inherit Judah his portion in the holy land, and shall choose Jerusalem again" (v. 12). This is the sure Word of God.

Clearly, it is this very restoration that God had in mind when He gave to John the vision of this eleventh chapter. The angel calls upon him to "Rise, and measure the temple of God, and the altar, and them that worship therein." That is, once more God owns a witnessing company, a worshiping people in Jerusalem, and observe that this is in the days of the Great Tribulation before the complete fulfillment of Zechariah's prophecy because the glory will not yet have appeared. Therefore, he is instructed to leave out the court that is outside the temple, and measure it not because it is still to be given to the Gentiles, "and the holy city shall they tread under foot forty and two months"; that is, for the last three and a half years of the final seven that compose Daniel's seventieth week, which, as we have seen, has not yet been fulfilled, nor can be until Jerusalem and the people of the Jews are again owned by God as His own.

It is very evident that already God is overruling events with a view to this restoration. The marvelous deliverance of Jerusalem in December 1917, when the Turkish flag was hauled down after practically 1,260 years of misrule and oppression and the banners of the Entente Allies were raised in its place, was preparing the way for this very thing. It was indeed a most important event, fraught with greater meaning than millions of people dreamed, when General Allenby received from the Turkish governor of Jerusalem the surrender of the Holy City. And it is well known that General (now Lord) Allenby, to whom God gave this great victory over the Turkish Army, was knowledgeable of the truth of the second coming of our Lord Jesus Christ. This event clearly was ordered of God in view of the promised restoration of Israel to the land. It was one of His hidden purposes when He permitted the world war. The surrender of the Holy City, without the firing of a shot, as the airplanes of the allied forces circled about over the ancient capital of the land of Palestine, was undoubtedly in answer to the prayers of thousands of the people of God who could not bear to think of the representative of a so-called Christian nation shelling the city where our Savior taught and died and that must ever be sacred in the eyes of both Jews and Christians.

When the armies of the Allies entered through the Jaffa Gate with Allenby walking in before his troops, Arabs, Jews, and Christians alike recognized the fact that the hour had struck for God to open the way for the fulfillment of many prophecies of bygone ages, as recorded in His Word. Many stories have been told of this event, some of which have not been substantiated, but even allowing for a large percentage of unverified tales, evidently the whole civilized world saw in it a most extraordinary event, and it was undoubtedly the turning point of the entire conflict because in eleven months afterward the armistice was signed.

Zionism from that time took on new and remarkable vigor, and money has been pouring into its coffers to transplant the poor of the flock from the lands of the north and the country where they have suffered so much to their own ancient patrimony. Alas! they little realize to what they are going back! Their hopes are high and their jubilation is great, but Scripture makes very plain that they have before them the bitterest experiences they have ever known, and these they are to endure right in their own land. Although the Turkish power no longer holds Jerusalem, it is still subject to the Gentiles, and it will be until the Lord Himself returns in person for its complete deliverance. He declared that from the days of Titus Jerusalem should be "trodden down of the Gentiles, until the times of the Gentiles be fulfilled" (Luke 21:24).

The expression *the times of the Gentiles* refers to the entire period of Gentile supremacy, beginning with the day when God gave Judah into the hand of Nebuchadnezzar, king of Babylon, and continuing to the time when the Stone from heaven shall smite the image on its feet; that is, when the Lord Jesus Christ, at His second coming in judgment, shall destroy all Gentile dominion, and His own kingdom shall supersede every other.

The last three and a half years, designated here so definitely as forty and two months, will be the worst of this entire period of Gentile treading down. So dreadful will be the tribulation of those days, our Lord has told us, that except they be shortened, no flesh would be saved. And the center of all of this tribulation will be the land of Palestine itself. But during this time and immediately preceding it God will not leave Himself without witness. So we read,

> I will give power unto my two witnesses, and they shall prophesy a thousand two hundred and threescore days, clothed in sackcloth. These are the two olive trees and the two candlesticks standing before the God of the earth. (vv. 3–4)

I speak somewhat diffidently here, but it seems clear to me that the twelve hundred and sixty days of these verses refers to the first half of the week, during which God will have a witnessing remnant in Jerusalem, testifying to the near coming of the kingdom and calling upon all Israel to repent in view of that time of the restitution of all things spoken of by the prophets.

I do not know that we need to limit the witnesses to two individuals. Two is the number of testimony, and we need to remember that we are dealing here with symbols, not necessarily the literal personalities. Therefore, the two witnesses might well symbolize the witnessing remnant of Judah as a whole. But I would not be dogmatic because it might be the mind of God to send two individuals, as here described, to herald the near coming of His Son. The fourth verse again links the prophecy with Zechariah 4:3: "And two olive trees by it, one upon the right side of the bowl, and the other upon the left side thereof." There, the two olive trees are priesthood and prophetic testimony, keeping the candlestick shining for God. Here the olive trees are said to be two candlesticks, but the thought, I take it, is the same. It is worship and testimony in that time when Jacob's trouble is just beginning.

These witnesses are "immortal until their work is done" because we are told that "if any man will hurt them, fire proceedeth out of their mouth, and devoureth their enemies: and if any man will hurt them, he must in this manner be killed"— that is, if any man wills or desires to hurt them, he is cut off in judgment.

We next learn that "these have power to shut heaven, [so] that it rain not in the days of their prophecy: and have power over waters to turn them to blood, and to smite the earth with all plagues, as often as they will" (v. 6). It is a testimony in the power and spirit of both Elijah and of Moses. Hence, some people have concluded that the two witnesses will be Moses and Elijah, sent back to earth before the coming of the Lord Jesus Christ. I admit the possibility of this, although it does not seem to me probable; but just as John the Baptist came of old in the spirit and power of Elijah—and, to those who would receive it, he was Elijah which was to come—so these witnesses, whether actually two people only or in reality a much larger company thus symbolized, will be in the spirit and power both of the prophet who came to restore Israel to the true God and the great prophet who first led them out of Egypt.

Nothing can interfere with their witnessbearing until they shall have finished their testimony. Then "the beast that ascendeth out of the bottomless pit [of whom we shall learn more when we come to study chap. 13] shall make war against them, and shall overcome them, and kill them." They will be the objects of the bitter enmity of the vile head of the coming revived Roman Empire, or Western Federation of Nations, who will not tolerate any worship but that which is offered to himself. He, therefore, will destroy them, "and their dead bodies shall lie in the street of the great city, which spiritually is called Sodom and Egypt, where also our Lord was crucified" (v. 8). It is Jerusalem, God's holy city, that, through apostasy culminating in the worship of the Antichrist and the Beast, shall sink at last to the level of Sodom, from which Lot was saved only by fire, and Egypt, out of which Israel of old was delivered by Jehovah. Through the unbelieving Jews "the name of God [has been] blasphemed among the Gentiles" (Rev. 2:24); by them the Lord of glory was crucified, and wrath shall come upon them to the uttermost.

In verses 9–10, we have the sad picture of joy among the nations because this last testimony for God on earth has been destroyed. We see the whole apostate world—Christendom and Judaism alike—congratulating one another that there is no longer any voice raised to question their apostasy and wickedness.

> And they of the people and kindreds and tongues and nations shall see their dead bodies three days and an half, and shall not suffer their dead bodies to be put in graves. And they that dwell upon the earth shall rejoice over them, and make merry, and shall send gifts one to another; because these two prophets tormented them that dwelt upon the earth. (vv. 9–10)

In the present time of our Lord's rejection and His session at God's right hand, Christendom, in the very manner here depicted, pretends to observe Christ's coming to earth. Having crucified the Lord of glory, the nations join in celebrating what is called "His birthday," sending gifts one to another. In that coming day, in the same way, they will make merry and manifest their delight because the last voice on His behalf has been silenced, and they will rejoice over the dead bodies of His witnesses. What a solemn scene it shall be—civilized people making merry in that awful day when the wrath of God is just about to be poured out in all of its fullness upon that guilty, guilty world. For three and a half days it will seem as though Satan were triumphant and everything that is of God is overthrown!

> And after three days and a half the Spirit of life from God entered into them, and they stood upon their feet; and great fear fell upon them which saw them. And they heard a great voice from heaven saying unto them, Come up hither. And they ascended up to heaven in a cloud; and their enemies beheld them. (vv. 11–12)

It is another rapture—another cohort of the first resurrection—taking place in the midst of that final week. These martyrs, who had sealed their testimony with their blood, are raised in power and caught up to be with their still-rejected Lord. Like Himself, they shall ascend to heaven in a cloud, but, unlike their Master, their enemies will behold them. It would seem as though this visible rapture will have some effect upon those remaining in Jerusalem because in verse 13 we learn, "The same hour was there a great earthquake, and the tenth part of the city fell, and in the earthquake were slain of men seven thousand: and the remnant were affrighted, and gave glory to the God of heaven." Observe that He is still the God of heaven, but in a little while He will be manifested as the God of the whole earth, as verse 4 has already intimated. This is the first time that we read of anyone during that period of tribulation giving glory to God, but whether this implies any true turning of heart to Himself on the part of some, I dare not attempt to say. All that this Scripture says is that "the remnant were affrighted," and this in itself does not necessarily imply that there is any true conscience work.

With this great earthquake the second woe is past, and we are told, "Behold, the third woe cometh quickly." This third woe is none other than the seventh and last of the trumpets, which ushers in the world kingdom of our God and His Christ. It is a woe to only His enemies; it is a cause of great rejoicing to all who love His name, in view of creation's deliverance from bondage to sin.

And the seventh angel sounded; and there were great voices in heaven, saying, The kingdoms of this world are become the kingdoms of our Lord, and of his Christ; and he shall reign for ever and ever. And the four and twenty elders, which sat before God on their [thrones], fell upon their faces, and worshipped God, saying, We give thee thanks, O Lord God Almighty, which art, and wast, and art to come; because thou hast taken to thee thy great power, and hast reigned. And the nations were angry, and thy wrath is come, and the time of the dead, that they should be judged, and that thou shouldest give reward unto thy servants the prophets, and to the saints, and them that fear thy name, small and great; and shouldest destroy them which destroy the earth. (vv. 15–18)

I purposely refrained from reading the last verse because it properly belongs to the next chapter. What we have before us completes the current prophetic series. The seventh angel's trumpet brings in Christ's long awaited and glorious kingdom. Upon its proclamation, the saints in heaven, as symbolized by the four and twenty elders, will fall before God on their faces, worshiping Him and giving Him thanks—He, the everlasting Jehovah—because He has taken to Himself His great power to reign.

The eighteenth verse covers the entire Millennium and carries us on to the judgment of the wicked dead, to the end of time because to the Lord Jesus Christ all judgment has been committed. And we need to remember that the entire Millennium is a period of judgment. First, it is judgment upon the angry nations when the wrath of God is poured out upon them at the beginning of the Millennium; it is judgment for His own servants who shall be rewarded in that glorious kingdom according to their faithfulness during Christ's rejection; and it is judgment upon the wicked dead who, at the Great White Throne, will answer for the deeds done in the body and be dealt with accordingly. Those who have arrogated to themselves the right to judge and destroy others will then be judged and destroyed themselves when the great moral Governor of the universe, who has kept Himself hidden so long, will be fully manifested. So the seventh angel's trumpet brings us now to the end of the first prophetic outline. That is, chapter 11:18 carries us as far along chronologically as 20:11–15.

And now may I press upon everyone here the importance of being prepared for the near coming of the Lord Jesus Christ, in view of the remarkable manner in which Palestine, the Jews, the nations of Christendom, and the professed church of God are even now being prepared for the very experiences we have been attempting to describe? These things are not "cunningly devised fables" (2 Peter 1:16) but stern realities, and anyone who has his eyes opened and understands something of the teaching of the prophetic Word can see clearly that we are very near the end of the current dispensation.

I remember on one occasion speaking in the city of San Jose, California, before a group of more than forty ministers about the second advent of our Lord. Many of them ridiculed the idea; only four declared themselves as believing in it. Most of them were noncommittal, having no definite convictions either for or against my theme. One dear old minister seemed to resent the thought of the Lord's coming as a future event, declaring that, to him, Christ came when, some forty years earlier, he had been converted to God. But I was invited to return a week later, and for an hour and a half we had a most animated debate on the subject. Finally, one clergyman declared that he thought the personal coming of the Lord Jesus was an absolute absurdity. He did not believe that He existed as a distinct personality, clothed with a resurrected body; His resurrection was entirely spiritual, and, to quote him, "He only exists today as part of the all-pervading spirit of the universe. Therefore," exclaimed he, dramatically, "I believe, my brethren, in no apocalyptic coming of Jesus. I never expect to see Him in a body, but I believe in the ever-coming Christ. He is coming in the clouds, but they are not literal clouds. He comes in the clouds of affliction, in the political clouds, in the war clouds, in the clouds of sorrow and distress, but a personal premillennial advent is, in my judgment, an utter impossibility."

This statement brought to his feet the minister who had somewhat opposed me at the previous meeting, and he cried in distress, "Do I understand, Doctor, that I shall never see my Lord who saved me by His death upon the Cross?"

"I think not," was the reply.

"Have I then," exclaimed the other, "been wrong all these years as I have sung,

> I shall know Him, I shall know Him,
> As redeemed by His side I shall stand;
> I shall know Him, I shall know Him
> By the print of the nails in His hand?"

"Oh!" replied the other, "that's all very well as poetical license, but I don't think you should take it literally."

"Brethren," cried the aged minister as the tears burst from his eyes, "I take back what I said last week. I find that I agree with this brother, who has been speaking to us on the coming of the Lord, far more than I thought I did. I look to see the personal coming of my Savior. I shall never be satisfied until I behold the King in His beauty. But I have always supposed that He would not come until the day of judgment; but as I think it over, it seems to me that, after all, that is what my brother believes; only he thinks the day of judgment will be a thousand years long. And, Doctor," he continued, turning to the minister who had presented such unscriptural and unholy views, "I am afraid, if there are many in the church like you, it will take a thousand years to put things right."

My friends, this is indeed what I would impress upon you and what the seventh angel's trumpet so clearly intimates. The day of judgment *will* be a thousand years long. The judgment seat of Christ takes place in the heavens immediately after the rapture of the church. The judgment of the living nations referred to in Matthew 25 will take place upon the earth when the Son of Man shall come in His glory, and all His holy angels with Him, to establish His kingdom over all the world. That thousand years will be the reign of righteousness, when He shall rule all nations with a rod of iron and judge unsparingly everything that ventures to lift itself up against His authority—all that refuses to be subject to His dominion. And at the close, He will judge all of the wicked dead, who shall be raised for that very purpose, and cast them into the lake of fire because they have rejected His grace. And, in view of all of this, I plead with you who are outside of Christ, "Agree with thine adversary quickly, whiles thou art in the way with him" (Matt. 5:25). In other words, come to God in Christ Jesus now and have your case settled out of court because if you first meet God in that solemn hour of judgment, you will be forever beyond the reach of mercy.

For all who trust in the Lord Jesus now, there will be no judgment in that solemn day because He has said, "Verily, verily, I say unto you, he that heareth my word, and believeth on him that sent me, hath everlasting life, and [cometh not into judgment, RV]; but is passed from death unto life" (John 5:24). How sweet and precious the promise here given to every believer in the Lord Jesus Christ!

Observe that all such people possess eternal life *now.* It is not that they are looking forward to receiving eternal life in the day of judgment or at the coming of the Lord—although they will enter into life then, that is, they will become participants in that scene where eternal life is fully revealed. But they have that life *now* by virtue of having received Christ because "he that hath the Son hath life" (1 John 5:12). Therefore, they shall not come into judgment. They will be called to appear at the judgment seat of Christ to give an account of their service for the Lord. Because His grace saved them, they shall never be called into judgment for their sins, and that for the best of all possible reasons—because those sins have already been judged upon the person of the Lord Jesus Christ when He died on Calvary's Cross, where He bore the condemnation of all who would put their trust in Him. Such have already passed from death unto life and enjoy even now the earnest of the coming glory.

THE WOMAN AND THE MAN-CHILD

Revelation 12

With this address, we begin our study of a very distinct part of the Book, embracing Revelation chapters 12–14, which form a connected outline of events. The first two of these chapters bring before us "the great actors for good and evil in the last days," to use the very striking language of another,[1] whereas chapter 14 gives us the consummation—the Lamb on Mount Zion, returned to bless the remnant of Israel, and through them the world, and the final judgments relating to the preparation for the actual setting up of the kingdom.

I think I may say without exaggeration that I have read or carefully examined several hundred books purporting to expound the Revelation. I have learned to look upon this twelfth chapter as the crucial test regarding the correct prophetic outline. If the interpreters are wrong as to the woman and the man-child, it necessarily follows that they will be wrong as to many things connected with them. Therefore, I ask your particular attention as we endeavor to see what light Scripture itself throws upon this remarkable vision.

As I indicated in the previous address, we should begin to read from verse 19 of chapter 11 because this is the commencement of the third great division of the book.

> And the temple of God was opened in heaven, and there was seen in his temple the ark of his testament: and there were lightnings, and voices, and thunderings, and an earthquake, and great hail.

It might be good here to draw attention to the several "openings" in their order. In 4:1, we read, "A door was opened in heaven," which introduces the third division of the book and shows us the saints in heaven around the throne of God and the judgments that follow the taking of the seven-sealed book.

In 11:19, we have, "The temple of God was opened in heaven," and there is seen in the temple the ark of the covenant, which at once calls to mind God's covenant with His earthly people Israel and shows us that although the lightnings, voices, thunderings, earthquake, and great hail that followed the opening of the temple speak of fearful judgments to be poured out upon the prophetic earth, God will remember His covenant with Israel and preserve the remnant safely through it all.

In 15:5, this thought is intensified in connection with the coming forth of the seven angels that have the seven last plagues. There we read, "After that I looked, and, behold, the temple of the tabernacle of the testimony in heaven was opened," and from that temple the seven angels went forth. The fact that the testimony is thus mentioned again emphasizes God's protecting care of His earthly people.

The fourth "opening" is in chapter 19:11: "And I saw heaven opened, and behold a white horse; and he that sat thereon was called Faithful and True, and in righteousness he doth judge and make war." The chapter goes on to describe, in highly symbolic form, the Lord's appearing in open judgment. These four openings are of deep significance and help greatly to an understanding of the book. The first "opening" we have already considered. The second "opening" is to occupy us tonight and for several more evenings. The third "opening" introduces the seven last plagues, in which is filled up the wrath of God. And the fourth "opening" ushers in the glorious millennial kingdom.

Now let us note carefully the vision of chapter 12:1–6. I read the first four verses:

> And there appeared a great wonder in heaven; a woman clothed with the sun, and the moon under her feet, and upon her head a crown of

twelve stars: and she being with child cried, travailing in birth, and pained to be delivered. And there appeared another wonder in heaven; and behold a great red dragon, having seven heads and ten horns, and seven crowns upon his heads. And his tail drew the third part of the stars of heaven, and did cast them to the earth: and the dragon stood before the woman which was ready to be delivered, for to devour her child as soon as it was born.

It is a divinely given picture, in which God is throwing His own white light upon events that otherwise would be incomprehensible to His creatures. A woman appears arrayed with the sun and the moon beneath her feet, and upon her head is a crown of twelve stars. She cries out in anguish, travailing in birth, until she is delivered of a man-child. This man-child is distinctly said to be the one who is to rule all of the nations with a rod of iron. The woman has a terrible, a most vindictive adversary—a great red dragon with seven heads and ten horns, and upon his heads are seven diadems. Notice that the word rendered "crown" in the Authorized Version is not the word we have already had before us in this book— the crowns on the heads of the elders in heaven. Theirs was a victor's *wreath,* but the dragon wears the imperial *diadem.* His is a reigning crown because he is "the prince of this world," acting, as we shall see shortly, through the Roman Empire. His tail, we are told, "drew a third part of the stars of heaven, and did cast them down to the earth."

In the vision, John beheld him standing before the woman, waiting for her deliverance, that he might devour her child immediately upon its birth. But he was thwarted in his malignant intentions because the child was caught up unto God and to His throne, and the woman, the mother, then fled into the wilderness, where God Himself had prepared a place for her that she might be kept in security and nourished for 1,260 days.

Now, first, who or what are we to understand this woman to represent? Many people tell us that she is the church. Others, and their number I notice of late is increasing, insist that she represents, rather, some system of teaching. Roman Catholic expositors have seen in her the Virgin Mary, and they suppose the whole scene to depict her assumption into heaven and her glory as its queen.

Throughout the Christian era, there has been no shortage of people who have arrogated the vision to themselves, as for instance, Johanna Southcott, who declared herself to be the bride of Christ and deceived many a century or so ago. Or, in our own day, Mrs. Mary Baker Glover Patterson Eddy, who very modestly conceived and gave forth the thought that the woman was a highly symbolic picture of—herself! And the man-child represented that which she brought forth—Christian Science; whereas, the dragon was "mortal mind," endeavoring to destroy her new religion! With such theories as these two, however, I need not take up the time of sane people.

The first view I mentioned is one that needs careful examination. In doing this, let us first inquire who, or what, the man-child symbolizes. If we allow Scripture itself to answer, we find that both a person and a company of people answer to this description. In Psalm 2, Jehovah says to Messiah, "Thou art my Son; this day have I begotten thee. Ask of me, and I shall give thee the nations for thine inheritance, and the uttermost parts of the earth for thy possession. Thou shalt break them with a rod of iron; thou shalt dash them in pieces like a potter's vessel" (vv. 7–9). This, clearly enough, is our Lord Jesus Christ, who is soon to reign over all the earth, and undoubtedly He is primarily the Man-child who is to rule the nations with a rod of iron, and He is the special object of Satan's malignity. But we have already seen in Revelation 2:26–28 that when He reigns He will not reign alone; His promise to the faithful overcomers in the church period is, "And he that overcometh, and keepeth my works unto the end, to him will I give power over the nations: and he shall rule them with a rod of iron; as the vessels of a potter shall they be broken to shivers: even as I received of my Father. And I will give him the morning star."

Is there then any incongruity in understanding the man-child to represent both Christ Jesus our Lord and His church? Surely not, for He is the Head of the body, the church, which is the fullness, or completion, of Himself, so that the title "the Christ" is applied to both head and body viewed as one in 1 Corinthians 12:12, where we read, "For as the body is one, and hath many members, and all the members of that one body, being many, are one body: so also is Christ." It reads literally, "the Christ." We may then, on the authority of Scripture itself, safely affirm that the man-child represents the one New Man who is to rule the nations with a rod of iron—Christ, the Head, and the church, His body. If this be so, then it is impossible for the woman to symbolize the church.

But some people (and not a few) tell us that only the strong spiritual members of the church are designated in Scripture as overcomers, and that the woman pictures the church as a whole whereas the man-child symbolizes the overcoming part of the church who, they say, will be raptured before the Great Tribulation while the rest of the church will be purified through that time of trouble. But Scripture definitely determines the untruthfulness of this contention, for we are told distinctly, "This is the victory that overcometh the world, even our faith. Who is he that overcometh the world, but he that believeth that Jesus is the Son of God? (1 John 5:4–5). An overcomer is one who has personal faith in Christ, and in this sense every believer overcomes. Those who do not are proven not to have real faith and are simply professors, not possessors. This theory to which I refer denies the unity of the body of Christ; it fails to recognize the intimate relation existing between the head and all of its members.

But who, then, is this star-crowned, sun-robed woman, who has the moon beneath her feet? First, let me ask, "Is there any other place in Scripture where we have the sun, moon, and twelve stars brought together similarly?"

You will at once recall Joseph's dream. He beheld the sun, moon, and eleven stars making obeisance to him. He himself was the twelfth star. His father rightly saw in this a picture of all twelve tribes of Israel. And this was a hint worth considering. But, again, we are distinctly told concerning our Lord Jesus that it was of Israel "as concerning the flesh that Christ came" (Rom. 9:5). And it is of Israel that Isaiah is singing when he exclaims, "Unto us a Child is born, unto us a Son is given: and the government shall be upon his shoulder: and his name shall be called Wonderful, Counsellor, The mighty God, The everlasting Father, The Prince of Peace" (Isa. 9:6). *Israel* is the mother of whom, as concerning the flesh, Christ came. The church did not birth Christ. He founded the church. He, as the last Adam, slept in death that the church might be taken from His wounded side. But He did come from Israel. Over and over again in the Old Testament that nation is depicted as being in travail-pain, waiting for His appearing.

Turn to Micah 5:2 and Isaiah 66:7–8. Comparing these Scriptures with the one before us, we see that "before [Israel] travailed, she brought forth." That is, Christ Himself personally was actually born before the time of her great period of anguish in the days of the coming tribulation, but it will be during that time of trouble that He will be born in the consciousness of the nation and that they will realize that He belongs to them—that He is Israel's Son. The twelve stars upon her head may well speak of her twelve patriarchs and her twelve tribes. The moon beneath her feet speaks of the reflected glory of the old covenant, and the sun in which she is enwrapped tells of the new covenant glory in which she appears before God. At Christ's actual birth, Satan put into operation the power of the Roman Empire through Herod, its puppet in Jerusalem, to seek His destruction. But He was preserved from Herod's efforts when the young children of Bethlehem were destroyed, and although He was crucified by a Roman governor and under Roman authority, He was raised from the dead by the glory of the Father and caught up to God and to His throne.

Now I apprehend that in the vision before us this is in view, but there is more than that because we have seen that the man-child symbolizes both Head and body—the complete Christ. Therefore, as in other prophecies, the entire current dispensation is passed over in silence, and the church is represented in its Head, caught up with Christ. Immediately after this, Satan, again acting through the Roman Empire, which is to be revived in the last days, turns upon the woman, Israel, and seeks to vent his wrath and indignation against her. But God prepares a place for her, and she is hidden in the wilderness—possibly the wilderness of the peoples, as Ezekiel (20:35) so graphically puts it. There she will be protected during the 1,260 days, which, as we have already seen, seem to refer to the first half of the seventieth week—"the beginning of sorrows" (Matt. 24:8).

In the next section of the chapter, verses 7–12, our attention is turned from earth to heaven; it is a future great conflict that will occur in the heavenly places.

> And there was war in heaven: Michael and his angels fought against the dragon; and the dragon fought and his angels, and prevailed not; neither was their place found any more in heaven. And the great dragon was cast out, that old serpent, called the Devil, and Satan, which deceiveth the whole world: he was cast out into the earth, and his angels were cast out with him. And I heard a loud voice saying in heaven, Now is come salvation, and strength, and the kingdom of our God, and the power of his Christ: for the accuser of our brethren is cast down, which accused them before our God day and night. And they overcame him by the blood of the Lamb, and by the word of their testimony; and they loved not their lives unto the death. Therefore rejoice, ye heavens, and ye that dwell in them. Woe to the inhabiters of the earth and of the sea! for the devil is come down unto you, having great wrath, because he knoweth that he hath but a short time.

A third actor in these stirring scenes is now introduced—Michael, the leader of the heavenly hosts. But he is no stranger to the reverent student of the Word of God. We have already made his acquaintance in the book of Daniel, and we know him as the great angelic prince, the archangel, who is particularly charged with the care of Daniel's people; and Daniel's people, we have seen, are symbolized by the woman whom we have been considering. When our Lord Jesus Christ returns for His church, we are told that the voice of the archangel will be heard from heaven, together with the shout of the Lord and the trump of God. Michael's voice will awaken, or call together, all of those of Israel who have died in the previous dispensation and will have their part in the first resurrection. Together with the church and the saints of previous ages, they will enter into the Father's house. Their passage through the air and enthronement in glory would seem to be the signal for the driving out of Satan and his hosts from the upper air, where they have been permitted to maintain their hold during the past five thousand years. Satan is called the prince of the power of the air. Believers are told that their conflict is with wicked spirits in heavenly places. These evil hosts are continually endeavoring, by deception, to keep Christians from enjoying their current portion in Christ, but when the church is caught up, they will be driven ignominiously from what we might call the "outer court of heaven" and cast down upon the earth. The great dragon, the energizing spirit of the old Roman Empire, and the one who is to be the energizing spirit of the same empire when it is revived, is to be cast down. In verse 9, that there might be no possibility of mistake, he is distinctly designated as "[the] old serpent, called the Devil, and Satan, [the deceiver of] the whole [earth]."

When he and his accursed followers are hurled from the heavens, a voice of praise is heard above, celebrating the full salvation of God's redeemed and the establishment in power of the kingdom of our God and the authority of His Christ because the accuser of our brethren, who accused them before our God day and night, has been cast down. This is no new thought; he appeared in this way in the days of Job, accusing that righteous man before the Lord. Zechariah also beheld him, in vision, accusing Joshua, the high priest. God has permitted him to act as the great prosecuting attorney, if I may so put it, at the High Court of the Universe, but no charge that he has ever brought against those redeemed to God by the precious blood of Christ has ever stood because that infinite sacrifice has fully availed to meet them all. Well may we sing,

> I hear the accuser roar
> Of ills that I have done;
> I know them all, and thousands more,
> Jehovah findeth none.

Or, as a verse of another beautiful hymn puts it,

> Though the restless foe accuses,
> Sins recounting like a flood;
> Every charge our God refuses—
> Christ has answered with His blood.

Christ is our advocate, and it is Satan's malicious accusations that call for His constant advocacy on our behalf. As a result of this, the Holy Spirit applies to the hearts of the saints on earth the truth of God in divine power, practically cleansing their ways. And so it is said, "They overcame him because of the blood of the Lamb, and because of the word of their testimony; they loved not their life even unto death" (v. 11 RV).

Satan's casting down will be the signal then for great rejoicing in the heavens, where the Old and New Testament saints will have been caught up. But it also will be the signal of great sorrow upon the earth because the Devil will have come down in great wrath, knowing that his time is short. He has ever been the hater of all who belong to Christ and will seek for any on earth who own His name in that day utterly to destroy them. This is what is brought before us in verses 13–17:

> And when the dragon saw that he was cast unto the earth, he persecuted the woman which brought forth the man child. And to the woman were given two wings of a great eagle, that she might fly into the wilderness, into her place, where she is nourished for a time, and times, and half a time, from the face of the serpent. And the serpent cast out of his mouth water as a flood after the woman, that he might cause her to be carried away of the flood. And the earth helped the woman, and the earth opened her mouth, and swallowed up the flood which the dragon cast out of his mouth. And the dragon was wroth with the woman, and went to make war with the remnant of her seed, which keep the commandments of God, and have the testimony of Jesus Christ.

The explanation is plain in view of what we have already had before us. The dragon will at once turn all of his energies against Israel, but God has pledged Himself to preserve her through the Great Tribulation. And so, we are told, there were given to the woman not merely two wings of a great eagle but, more emphatically, the two wings of the great eagle that she might fly into the wilderness, into her place, to be nourished by God for a time, and times, and half a time from the face of the serpent. That is, for the last three and a half years of the tribulation period. "A time" indicates a year; "times," two years; and "half a time," six months. This is the same as the forty-two months of the previous chapter. As to the expression "the two wings of the great eagle," God says regarding Israel, "I [bore] you on eagles' wings, and brought you unto myself" (Exod. 19:4). He who delivered them from Egypt and cared for them in the wilderness will, in that coming day, deliver them from the wrath of the dragon and protect them in the wilderness of the peoples, from which they will afterward come up in great numbers to dwell in their own land.

In vain the serpent casts out of his mouth water as of a great river, hoping that he might cause her to be carried away by the stream. He would seek to ruin her by that which comes forth from his mouth—evil teachings, I take it, in contrast to the water of life given by our Lord Jesus Christ. We may get the idea of this if we recall the fact that today myriad Jews are being carried away by that satanic flood from the mouth of the dragon known as Christian Science. So, in the days of the Great Tribulation, Satan will try to swamp and destroy Israel as a nation by the evil teachings that he will spread through the world. But even the earth itself will help the woman, opening her mouth and swallowing up the river that the dragon sends forth. That is, when Israel is driven out among all of the nations, as I take it, she will be so shocked and horrified by the evil results of these satanic teachings that they will themselves be preserved from them. Just as of old a sojourn in Babylon, the fountain-head of idolatry, cured Judah, for the time being, of her own idolatrous tendencies, so Israel's experiences among the Gentiles in the last days will be used of God to preserve her from the evil river in which the dragon would drown her.

Unable to destroy the nation as such, he makes a special effort to ruin the rest of her seed, or the remnant that keep the commandments of God and the testimony of Jesus. These, I take it, are those who remain in the land, as pictured by the two witnesses, and there maintain a testimony for God against all of the persecutions of the Antichrist. How the Devil will seek to destroy these people the next chapter will tell us.

THE COMING "FEDERATION OF NATIONS"

Revelation 13:1–10

A federation of nations! How much this phrase is on the lips of politicians and persons interested in national affairs today! It was far otherwise just a few years ago. When teachers of prophecy declared that the Word of God predicted just such a federation as that in which men are now deeply interested, they met with ridicule. They were openly declared to be dreamers, giving rein to foolish imaginations and proclaiming something that could never be fulfilled. But the Great War and new conditions have changed the viewpoint of these cavilers considerably in the last few years. Now there are people who hold the confederacy of nations to be the one solution to the difficulties everywhere confronting statesmen, and many people consider that it will be the panacea for all reconstruction perils. Just what will come of it all, while the church still remains on earth, one would not attempt to prophesy. But after the church is gone, there will, indeed, be a great confederacy of the nations that have sprung out of the old Roman Empire. It will be satanic in origin and character and will, in fact, be the Devil's last card, if I may borrow such an expression, before he is obliged to admit his complete defeat. It is with this that the portion of Scripture before us deals.

In our last lecture, we noted that the enmity of Satan will be turned against God's earthly people Israel in a special manner after the church has been caught up to meet the Lord in the air. In conclusion, I said that we would see tonight just what form that enmity will take. And in properly placing what now comes before us, let me emphasize the necessity of remembering that, throughout this portion of the book of Revelation, we have in view a time of solemn and momentous import after the first resurrection and translation of the saints at the Rapture and before the appearing of the Lord Jesus Christ in glory as the long-awaited Messiah of Israel, who is to sit upon the throne of His father David, and the Son of Man, who is to reign in righteousness over all of the earth. If there is confusion as to this, nothing will be clear.

It is not hard to imagine something of the condition in which this world will be found after all real Christians have been snatched away to be with the Lord, especially when we realize that many people in high places—rulers, governors, and other political leaders—are at heart Christian men. Perhaps, I should hardly say "many." In contrast to those who are unsaved and indifferent to the claims of Christ, they may be few indeed because Scripture tells us that "not many mighty, not many noble, are called" (1 Cor. 1:26). You will remember that Lady Huntington, that earnest, devoted woman who lived in the days of Whitefield and the Wesleys, and who was such a help in spreading the gospel, used to say that she was just going to heaven by an *M*. Had the word been "Not any noble," there would have been no hope for her, but the *M* included her.

But certainly there are *some* people in high places who truly know the Lord and who would be caught away with the church at His coming. Their removal would be like the breaking of a dike, permitting the rushing waters of anarchy and Bolshevism to sweep over every land. Think how evil will then be intensified. To what frightful lengths unsaved men will go in their efforts to bring about a millennium without Christ! Regardless of whether carnal men realize it, the true Christians are the light of the world and the salt of the earth. Let every Christian suddenly be taken away from this scene, and you will have gross darkness covering the earth. With the preservative power of righteousness gone, the masses of men will be given up to corruption and violence. Read the account of the days before the Flood, and you will have some sense of the chaotic condition that will prevail. Even now, we see lawlessness spreading everywhere in the world, and it is only with the greatest difficulty that the vile thing called Sovietism is kept from gaining a foothold, even in this land of liberty. And behind it all is a satanic effort to destroy all faith in God and His Word and to substitute in its place evil systems that can result in only eternal ruin to those who follow them.

In our day, although the enemy comes in like a flood, the Spirit of God is here to lift up a standard against him. The Word of God tells us that the mystery of lawlessness is already at work, but during this dispensation there is one who hinders the full development of evil—the Holy Spirit. But when He is taken out of the world, that is, when the Holy Spirit takes the church up to meet the Lord in the air, then the last hindrance to the power of evil will be gone. No longer will there be any restraint on the machinations of the Devil. In the heavens, the saints will be presented before the judgment seat of Christ, and, as we have seen, Satan will appear for the last time as the prosecuting attorney against them before God, as he has done day and night for so many centuries. But he will be utterly cast out of heaven and will come down to the earth, having great wrath, because he knows that his time is short. In Israel alone will he find a testimony for God in that day, and against that people he will turn all of his malice and will undertake to work for their ruin through human government when it has utterly cast off God.

You will recall how, in the book of Daniel, we are told that Nebuchadnezzar had a dream of a great image, which, I think everyone will agree, sets forth "the times of the Gentiles." By this term is meant the period during which the Jews are scattered among the Gentiles, the times in which the nations hold authority over the land of Palestine. These Gentile times began with Nebuchadnezzar, the head of gold. He is so represented in the image. Following this comes the rule of the Medes and the Persians, depicted by the silver breast and arms, and that, in turn, was succeeded by the Greco-Macedonian Empire, set forth by the brazen torso of the image. The last world empire is the kingdom of iron, the Roman. But Daniel goes on to show that the Roman Empire would take on a very peculiar form in the time of the end. In the feet of the image you have an attempt to amalgamate that which cannot be amalgamated, iron and clay. It is a picture of man's attempt to amalgamate the iron of imperialism with the potter's clay of social democracy.

If you ask me where we are in the course of time, as far as it is represented in this image, I should say, unhesitatingly, that we have reached the feet of the image. We see, even now, the great nations of Europe making a tremendous attempt to amalgamate the iron and the clay. And the troubles of recent years have been, largely, the result of this attempt. Great national leaders are at their wits' end, trying to save something of imperialism while still obliged to bow to the demands of the people for a government of a democratic character. But it is impossible to mix the two. The one must, of necessity, destroy the other. And the Scripture that we now have before us makes plain that, at last, the imperial power is going to triumph in measure. Men will grow weary of the constant conflict, which has been so prolonged because whatever optimistic statesmen still may say, God's Word shows that the confusion will grow worse and worse. And we need not be surprised if, even before the church is taken away, instead of raising armies "to make the world safe *for* democracy," it may become necessary to conscript the young manhood of our nation in an attempt to save the world *from* democracy. The people will soon attempt to take everything into their own hands, thus jeopardizing all property rights. This is a condition that cannot forever be tolerated, and out of it all will rise, eventually, after the church has been caught up to meet the Lord, one man who will combine in himself the statesmanship of a caesar, the military genius of a Napoleon, and the personal attractiveness of a Chesterfield. This man will head a combination of ten powers, formed, as before mentioned, from the nations that have sprung out of the old Roman Empire. When they have cast off all allegiance to God and His Word, he will through this confederacy, for a time at least, dominate the world.

As we've already intimated, Daniel pictures this final phase of things by the ten toes of the image. Of old, the Roman Empire was divided into the Eastern and Western parts, which is symbolized by the two legs of the great image, but it was united under one central authority until disintegration began.

In Daniel's seventh chapter, we have the same thing pictured differently. The man of God himself had a vision of the times of the Gentiles. He saw in them nothing beautiful or grand, but the four great empires were represented as four ravenous beasts, watching to spring one upon the other—beasts so dreadful that nothing on earth fully answers to the description of the wild creatures there depicted. The Babylonian Empire was symbolized by a lion with the wings of an eagle—a hybrid, formed from a beast of the earth and fowls of the air. The Medo-Persian dominion appeared as a bear, lifting itself up on one side. It had between its teeth three ribs dripping with blood, representing probably the three chief cities of the Babylonian Empire, which were sacked by the Medes and the Persians under Cyrus. The Grecian, or Alexandrian, Empire was pictured as a leopard with four heads and with four wings of a fowl upon his back. The four heads, of course, set forth the fourfold division of this Greco-Macedonian Empire after Alexander's death. Finally, Daniel tells us that the fourth beast was dreadful and terrible and had great iron teeth, and it brake in pieces and devoured all that came in its way. He gives no exact description of it. He adds, however, that it had ten horns.

Now that last beast clearly answers to the iron legs of the image, the Roman power, and the ten horns to the ten toes, which set forth the last form in which it will appear. I think there can be no doubt whatsoever that it is this last dreadful beast that is fully delineated for us in our present chapter. It is the Roman power that was in existence when the Lord was born and was responsible for His death upon the Cross because the Jews had no power at all unless it were ratified by Pilate, as representing Caesar. Therefore, the Roman Empire, of which Pontius Pilate was the official representative, crucified the Lord of glory. It is true that Pilate simply gave the sentence that the Jews desired, and therefore they are responsible for killing their Messiah, but the Roman procurator must face that clause, repeated over and over again through the centuries in the recitation of the Apostles' Creed, "He was crucified under Pontius Pilate." Pilate can never get away from that fact; it shall stand against his record forever.

We have already seen in the twelfth chapter that the great red dragon that had seven heads and ten horns represents Rome energized by Satan seeking to destroy the Man-child. Here, in chapter 13, we have Rome in the time of the end. The empire revived, it is summoned from the sea of the nations by the Devil himself because verse 1 should read, according to the best manuscripts, *"He* stood upon the sands of the sea," that is, Satan, the dragon. And it is he who summons the wild beast to rise up out of the waters, "having seven heads and ten horns, and upon his horns ten crowns, and upon his heads the names of blasphemy." This is imperial Rome revived, as the ten *crowns* declare.

After the death of the Lord Jesus Christ, the Roman Empire continued in existence for something like five hundred years, although it was divided into the Eastern and Western parts, which, until the end of its history, held together more or less loosely. It was finally destroyed by the invaders from the north and the east. Although the Empire as such was broken in pieces, Roman principles prevailed throughout the greater part of Europe and became the basis of the civilization that we now know. Our American system of jurisprudence is founded upon that of Rome. In the recent world war, the Entente Allies, and America too, were all representatives of the old Roman Empire, with the exception, of course, of Japan, China, and other heathen nations. On the other side we saw joined the very same powers (the Goths, the Vandals, and the Huns) that, in the fourth, fifth, and sixth centuries, hurled themselves upon the Roman Empire and destroyed it. Surely, it was a most singular thing and almost unexplainable for those who do not read their Bibles, that in the twentieth century the same great divisions were maintained as existed in the closing days of Roman domination. But we may see from this how readily that Roman Empire will be revived through a great international movement—a confederation, offensive and defensive, of all of the Latin or Latinized nations. One of the great agencies that shall have much to do in bringing this about will be the Roman Church, whose power is increasing continually, even in the very lands where the Reformation, at one time, would have made this impossible.

It was the boast of the Roman conquerors that they never destroyed a civilization, but absorbed into their own great commonwealth everything that was best of the various nations that they subjugated. And we cannot but be reminded of this fact as we read the second verse: "And the beast which I saw was like unto a leopard, and his feet were as the feet of a bear, and his mouth as the mouth of a lion: and the dragon gave him his power, and his seat, and great authority."

Observe how, in these few words, we have distinctly set forth the fact that the last phase of the Roman Empire will be linked with all that has gone before. In Rome, you have the leopard of Greece, the bear of Persia, and the lion of Babylon. Thus, you have incorporated into this last great confederacy the chief elements of every civilization that has left a great mark upon the world. Everything that man has been able to build up and has learned to value throughout the centuries will be apparent in this final federation of nations.

It is not Rome as it existed in John's day merely that is in view, but Rome as it will exist in the closing days of the dispensation, as is plain from the third verse, if it is rightly understood: "And I saw one of his heads as it were wounded to death; and his deadly wound was healed: and all the world wondered after the beast." We shall find help regarding the heads if we turn to 17:8–13, where we are told that the same beast is in view:

> The beast that thou sawest was, and is not; and shall ascend out of the bottomless pit, and go into perdition: and they that dwell on the earth shall wonder, whose names were not written in the book of life from the foundation of the world, when they behold the beast that was, and is not, and yet is [or, shall be]. And here is the mind which hath wisdom. The seven heads are seven mountains, on which the woman sitteth. And there [or, they] are seven kings: five are fallen, and one is, and the other is not yet come: and when he cometh, he must continue a short space. And the beast that was, and is not, even he is the eighth, and is of the seven, and goeth into perdition. And the ten horns which thou sawest are ten kings, which have received no kingdom as yet; but receive power as kings one hour with the beast. These have one mind, and shall give their power and strength unto the beast.

Now, in those brief words, you have a synopsis of the whole history of the

Roman Empire. For something like nine hundred years, it was the greatest earthly power with which men had to reckon. But a time came when it could be truly said that "the beast is not." It had been destroyed; its imperial head had been wounded to death. No man, for centuries, unenlightened by the Word of God, would have been bold enough to have predicted the return of imperial power to that fallen dominion. But Scripture had declared that it should come to pass, and although statesmen and carnal theorists have rejected what seemed to them a ridiculous assumption, students of prophecy, guided by the Spirit of God, have for nearly a century taught that the nations into which the Roman Empire had been divided should again come together under one head, and he would be a bold man today who would deny the likelihood of this very thing. But when statesmen talk of a coming world federation, how little they realize who it is who is going to bring it about. The Beast is to ascend out of the Abyss because it is satanic power that will bring into existence what is here pictured. It will be the Devil's last effort to make men believe that they do not need God's Christ, that they can have peace and security while they reject the Prince of Peace. But God will blow upon all of their plans because He has said, "I will overturn, overturn, overturn, . . . until he [shall] come whose right it is" (Ezek. 21:27).

But now notice two interpretations of the seven heads. We are told that they are seven *mountains* upon which the woman sits, and they "are seven *kings:* five are fallen, and one is, and the other is not yet come; and when he cometh he must continue a short space. And the beast that was, and is not, even he is the eighth, and is of the seven, and goeth into perdition."

The seven mountains have generally been taken as meaning the seven hills upon which the imperial city is built. I am inclined to think that this view is correct, even though some people would refuse the idea from the fact that the hills themselves are not in any sense mountainous in character, but the very fact that the Romans delighted to speak of their capital as the seven-hilled city would, naturally, bring this city to mind to anyone who read John's description.

As to the second interpretation, a king is the familiar symbol for a form of government. Livy, the Roman historian, shows us that Rome had passed through five very distinct forms of government before John's day. The sixth form, which was in existence in John's time, was the imperial. That was the form that was destroyed, and I am persuaded that this was the head wounded to death of our chapter. But that deadly wound is to be healed because the imperial form is to be restored, but under altogether different conditions, making it distinctly the seventh form. Ten nations, all banding themselves together, will elect one of their number as the head of the confederacy. This man is distinctly called "the Beast."

It reminds us of Louis XIV, who said, "I am the State." This Beast will continue to exercise authority, as the elected head, for but a short time, when he will throw off all restraint (as did Napoleon, who was first elected as consul and then later declared himself emperor), thus bringing about the eighth form, which is of the seventh.

So spectacular will be his *coup d'état* that men will be thrilled with admiration at his masterly genius. Accepting the principle that nothing but an imperial form of government can give them settled and continuous peace, they will readily acknowledge his pretensions, and in doing so will worship the dragon that gave power unto the Beast and do homage to the Beast himself, saying, "Who is like unto the Beast; who is able to make war with him?" I think that God has given us a wonderful illustration of this very thing in the history of Napoleon Bonaparte, as I mentioned earlier. Think of that Corsican—low born, utterly insignificant, and first coming into notice as a second lieutenant in the revolutionary army—suddenly, after the bloody reign of terror, emerging from his former obscure place and becoming the central figure of the world in that day. He was elected by an overwhelming majority as First Consul of France, proclaimed himself Imperator, and dazzled all of France and the world for a time, but ended his course on the isle of St. Helena.

A greater than Napoleon shall yet arise out of the chaotic conditions that will prevail in Europe after the church has been taken home. He will be a man of marvelous appearance and transcendent ability, wholly given up to Satan. He will be the great civil leader of the last days, the man who will have the final word in all matters, including religious issues. All of the civilized earth will wonder after him and do homage to him and his hidden master, the Devil. In his pride and folly, he will speak great and blasphemous things against God. He will doubtless consider himself the man of destiny whom no power, human or divine, can overthrow. But the God whom he denies has limited his sway because power will be given him only "to continue forty and two months." For three and a half years, the last half of Daniel's seventieth week, he will be in authority over the prophetic earth. During that time, he will open his mouth in blasphemy against God, and blaspheme His name and His tabernacle and all that dwell in heaven, namely, the saints who will have been caught up at the Rapture. With saints on earth, the faithful in God's restored Israel, he will make war and overcome them, power being given him over all countries, tongues, and nations.

This, then, is the manner in which the dragon will attempt the destruction of the remnant of the woman's seed. His effort will be completely to root out everything that is of God in the earth. To do this, he will have a trusty lieutenant dwelling in the land of Palestine itself, who will uphold him in all of his nefarious plans, but of this assistant I cannot speak tonight. We will be occupied with him in our next lecture.

There can be no question, I think, that the days of the Beast are the days to which our Lord Jesus Christ referred when He said that if it were possible the very elect would be deceived. But, thank God, He will preserve His own, even in that dreadful day, so we learn from verse 8 that none will be deceived by him, nor do homage to him, but those "whose names are not written in the book of life . . . from the foundation of the world." How solemn the challenge of 13:9–10: "If any man have an ear, let him hear. He that leadeth into captivity shall go into captivity: he that killeth with the sword must be killed with the sword. Here is the patience and the faith of the saints." These will be the days of the Great Tribulation, which, in all of its intensity, will be directed against Israel. But the Lord will be watching over His little flock, and, as scattered as they will be among the heathen, He will be to them a little sanctuary in every place that they may wander.

Only those who have exchanged the heavenly hope for an earthly hope will be deceived by this great leader. He is the coming man for whom the world is waiting. Mistaken and blinded statesmen will hail him as the head of the nations, the one who will solve the problems—social, political, and economic—that now disturb the world. How blessed to be warned by God Himself of all of these things beforehand, that we may walk apart from everything that savors of that day of reproach and blasphemy. And when it actually comes, who can question the value of this Scripture for the guidance and consolation of God's earthly people Israel, who otherwise might well be in despair at the apparent defeat of righteousness and the triumph of iniquity.

But "the triumphing of the wicked is short" (Job 20:5), and "the man of the earth" (Ps. 10:18) will be destroyed in due time, while faith will have its reward when the Lord appears from heaven to take vengeance on all who dare lift up their bloody hands against His afflicted people. "Here is the patience and faith of the saints."

THE PERSONAL ANTICHRIST

Revelation 13:11–18

The world is waiting for an authoritative religious leader. In an age of doubt and uncertainty, men are longing for one who can speak a final word on all of the ethical, religious, and political questions that today trouble so many people. Instructed Christians know that God has already spoken authoritatively in the person of His Son and revealed His mind in His holy Word. But they, too, are looking for a coming One, even the coming of the Lord Jesus Christ from glory to establish heaven's authority and power on the earth. He will descend from heaven and with all of His glorified saints will reign over the earth for a thousand years of peace and blessing. "The coming man" for whom unbelievers look is one whom they expect to be born on the earth—a man of the earth, earthy, and therefore not the Lord from heaven. This expectation is to have its fulfillment in "the man of sin," the personal Antichrist, the false Messiah, who will soon be manifested. In fact, it is a very solemn consideration that he may already be in this world—perhaps a babe in arms—possibly a precocious youth—not improbably a man of affairs! But he will not be made known until after the church of the firstborn has been raptured at the presence of the Lord.

The remarkable thing is that many people are waiting expectantly for the Antichrist who imagine that they are looking for a reincarnation of Christ Himself. They profess to wait for a savior and expect him to appear on earth, born after the course of nature. Theosophists and others are waiting expectantly for a great world teacher, despite the disappointment of Mrs. Besant's Order of the Star of the East, whose puppet Krishnamurti has fallen so far short of their hopes. They are really preparing the world for the advent of the Man of Sin, the son of perdition.

To be forewarned is to be forearmed: God's holy Word has predicted the coming of this false one and has clearly shown what will lead up to his manifestation. I desire to look into the Word with you on this subject tonight in connection with the passage we have read.

No Spirit-taught Bible student can fail to observe the shadow of the Antichrist falling athwart many pages of prophecy. "Ye have heard," writes the apostle of John, "that Antichrist shall come" (1 John 2:18). The only question that troubles many people has to do with the identification of the person or thing referred to. Is the Antichrist a person or a system? Many weighty names could be quoted in favor of either view, but, that our faith may not stand in the wisdom of men but in the power of God in this matter, as in all else, we desire to be guided by the written Word. But before turning to a number of definite Scriptures, let me remind you of this blessed fact: Christ is a person—a glorified, holy, all-powerful person—one member of the eternal Trinity, Who has taken humanity into union with Deity through being born on earth of a virgin, where He humbled Himself as man to the death of the Cross. Logically, one would expect that the Antichrist would also be a man, a definite personality, opposed to the Lord Jesus Christ, yet claiming to be all that He was—usurping the place of Christ.

But we would not forget that there is in the world a body united to Christ of which He is the glorified Head. There is also a great apostate system opposed to this divine body, falsely claiming to be the spouse of Christ and the only authorized custodian of the mysteries of God. Is this system the Antichrist, or is it rather Babylon the Great, the antichurch? I think we shall see as we go on that the latter view is the correct one.

The prophetic Scriptures outline two great religious deceptions, a false Christ, and a false church, but the one is not to be confused with the other. The Antichrist will be a *man,* as the Christ of God is a Man. Babylon is a vast organized *system,* even as the church of God is a divine organization. But the one is a satanic counterfeit of the other.

When the voice of prophecy speaks of the Antichrist, it uses the masculine pronoun *he.* When it speaks of the false church, it uses either the neuter or the feminine *it* or *she*, and for good reason. The Antichrist is the final head of the apostate system that bears the same relationship to him outwardly that the church does to Christ. Ever since the primeval promise of the Seed of the woman, who was to bruise the serpent's head, men have looked and longed for a deliverer to arise from among themselves. Such an expectation was grounded upon Scripture and was fulfilled in the birth of Christ. But since He has been rejected, this expectation has become a perversion of the truth because the God-sent deliverer, "the woman's Seed," has been caught up to God and to His throne. It is the *serpent's* seed who is coming (the *Anti*-Christ), and they who wait for him do not realize it! The serpent has for millennia been the symbol of esoteric religion, which stands for wisdom, and the coming one will claim to be the wisdom of God. Esoteric religion, I may say, is the religion *par excellence* of the Antichrist.

A man, then, is being awaited. His advent draws near. He will come when, at last, the restraining power, the Holy Spirit, has gone up to the heavens whence He came. This coming one is the Grand Monarch of the New Humanity cult. He is the coming Imaum, or Mahdi, of the Mussulmans, He is the long-expected last incarnation of Vishnu awaited by the Brahmins; the coming Montezuma of the Aztecs; the false Messiah of the apostate Jews; the great Master of all sects of yogis; the Ultimate Man of the evolutionists; and the *Übermensch* of Nietzsche, the Hun philosopher whose ravings prepared the way for the world war. He will be a Satan-controlled, God-defying, conscienceless, almost superhuman man—an individual whose manifestation will mean the consummation of the current apostasy and the full deification of humanity to his bewildered dupes.

Thus, the world will turn away from the Christ of God and stretch out eager hands to welcome the coming "Man of Sin." And, depend upon it, he will be on time! God's Word has declared his advent as surely as it predicts the second coming of the Lord Jesus Christ from glory.

Meanwhile, the great antichurch (the evil system that is but a counterfeit of the true church for which Christ died) is casting overboard every truth of Scripture and follows the lies that shall prepare them to receive *"the* liar" of whom 1 John 2:22 speaks—the Antichrist. The unalterable decree of the God of truth is that "whosoever loveth and maketh a lie" (Rev. 22:15) "shall have [his] part in the lake that burneth with fire and brimstone" (Rev. 21:8). That none here may be entangled in this awful iniquity is my sincere desire, and, to preserve from it, I earnestly ask your attention to a number of Scriptures.

The most complete description of Antichrist is found in Daniel 11:36–45.

And the king shall do according to his will; and he shall exalt himself, and magnify himself above every god, and shall speak marvellous things against the God of gods, and shall prosper till the indignation be accomplished: for that that is determined shall be done. Neither shall he regard the God of his fathers, nor the desire of women, nor regard any god: for he shall magnify himself above all. But in his estate shall he honour the God of forces: and a god whom his fathers knew not shall he honour with gold, and silver, and with precious stones, and pleasant things. Thus shall he do in the most strong holds with a strange god, whom he shall acknowledge and increase with glory: and he shall cause them to rule over many, and shall divide the land for gain. And at the time of the end shall the king of the south push at him: and the king of the north shall come against him like a whirlwind, with chariots, and with horsemen, and with many ships; and he shall enter into the countries, and shall overflow and pass over. He shall enter also into the glorious land, and many countries shall be overthrown: but these shall escape out of his hand, even Edom, and Moab, and the chief of the children of Ammon. He shall stretch forth his hand also upon the countries: and the land of Egypt shall not escape. But he shall have power over the treasures of gold and of silver, and over all the precious things of Egypt: and the Libyans and the Ethiopians shall be at his steps. But tidings out of the east and out of the north shall trouble him: therefore he shall go forth with great fury to destroy, and utterly to make away many. And he shall plant the tabernacles of his palace between the seas in the glorious holy mountain; yet he shall come to his end, and none shall help him.

Notice that here it is predicted that a king will arise in Jerusalem who will be an utter atheist, and yet, evidently, a Jew because it is distinctly predicted of him that "he shall not regard the God of his fathers, nor the desire of women." The expression "the God of his fathers" can mean nothing else than the God of Abraham, Isaac, and Jacob. It is frequently so used in Scripture whereas the expression "the desire of women" is recognized by both Jewish and Christian expositors as referring to the Messiah. This point is, I think, very important because the Antichrist could not be the false Messiah if he were not a Jew; otherwise, he would have no claim upon the allegiance of Israel. He will, I take it, be a great Jewish leader who will seem, at first, to be a wonderful lover of his people and who will establish them in their own land. But he will soon throw off all restraint and, exalting himself, will magnify himself against every god and speak marvelous things against the God of gods during the last three and a half years of Daniel's seventieth week, which we have had so constantly before us in our study of the book of Revelation.

This passage connects so intimately with the portion we have read tonight that I want you to notice the two passages in comparison. In Revelation 13:11 we read, "I beheld another beast coming up out of the earth, and he had two horns like a lamb, and he spake as a dragon." Observe that he does not arise from the Gentile nations as does the first Beast, but he comes up out of the earth, or land, that is, the land of Palestine, the very same land in which the king in Daniel 11 is to be manifested. He had "two horns like a lamb," for he seems, at first, to have both the meekness and the strength of the Lamb of God, but his dragonlike speech betrays him. It is the speech of self-exaltation, which indicates that his condemnation is the same as that of his master, the Devil, who fell through pride.

Now Daniel tells us that although the willful king will not regard any supernatural god, yet he will honor one who is called "the god of forces"—evidently a man, for he is one to whom he pays tribute: "a god whom his fathers knew not shall he honour with gold, and silver, and precious stones, and pleasant things." This mighty one will be the backer, if I may say so, of the Antichrist, and, in return for his protection, he will cause Palestine to submit to his authority and pay tribute to him. This "strange god shall he acknowledge and increase with glory, and shall cause him to rule over many, and divide the land for gain." Now this same thing is implied in verse 12 of our chapter: "And he exerciseth all the power of the first beast before him, and causeth the earth and them which dwell therein to worship the first beast, whose deadly wound was healed." He is, you see, the vicegerent of the first Beast; and this first Beast, whom the world recognizes as a god (in the sense, of course, in which it recognized the caesars of old as gods) is the master whom he enriches with Jewish wealth.

But he is not only an astute statesman and a crafty politician but also a wonder-worker, as verses 13–14 tell us:

> And he doeth great wonders, so that he maketh fire come down from heaven on the earth in the sight of men, and deceiveth them that dwell on the earth by the means of those miracles which he had power to do in the sight of the beast; saying to them that dwell on the earth, that they should make an image to the beast, which had the wound by a sword, and did live.

With this agrees the striking account of "the lawless one" in 2 Thessalonians 2:3–12:

> Let no man deceive you by any means: for that day shall not come, except there come a falling away first, and that man of sin be revealed, the son of perdition; who opposeth and exalteth himself above all that is called God, or that is worshipped; so that he as God sitteth in the temple of God, showing himself that he is God. . . . Even him, whose coming is after the working of Satan with all power and signs and lying wonders, and with all deceivableness of unrighteousness in them that perish; because they received not the love of the truth, that they might be saved. And for this cause God shall send them strong delusion, that they should believe a lie: that they all might be damned who believed not the truth, but had pleasure in unrighteousness.

Here is a prediction of the coming of the atheist king of Daniel 11 and the wonder-worker of Revelation 13.

One of the signs of the times in our own days is the unhealthful craving for marvels and wonders so prevalent in many quarters. It is a most dangerous condition of mind, and Christians might well beware of anything of the kind. We are too near the end of the dispensation to expect divine miracles in any number, but satanic signs and wonders will increase as we draw nearer the end, and when the Antichrist himself appears, he will give men all of the marvels for which they long—only to deceive them and to lead them to accept his ungodly pretensions.

Exactly what is meant by the "image" of the Beast I do not pretend to say. I have no doubt that it is linked with our Lord's warning about "the abomination of desolation" (Matt. 24:15; Mark 13:14) that is to be set up in the Holy Place. At any rate, it will be the culmination of the apostasy and the signal for all believing Jews, who in that day of great persecution cleave to the Lord, to flee from Jerusalem and hide themselves in distant parts among the nations until the appearing of the Messiah Himself. We are told that the lamb-like Beast will give life to the image, and it will speak and cause "that as many as would not worship the image of the Beast should be killed." A great society of apostate Jews and apostate Gentiles will be formed, patterned somewhat after our present-day labor unions and oath-bound organizations. This view is intimated in verses 16 and 17: "And he causeth all, both small and great, rich and poor, free and bond, to receive a mark in their right hand, or in their foreheads: and that no man might buy or sell, save he that had the mark, or the name of the beast, or the number of his name." It is well for Christians to keep themselves from all such worldly associations and unequal yokes.

Our Lord Jesus told the Jews of His day, "I am come in my Father's name, and ye receive me not; if another shall come in his own name, him ye will receive" (John 5:43). He was speaking of this awful person whom we have seen portrayed in these various Scriptures. With them we might also link Zechariah 11:16–17: "For, lo, I will raise up a shepherd *in the land* [note that he will arise in the land of Palestine], which shall not visit those that be cut off, neither shall seek the young one, nor heal that that is broken, nor feed that that standeth still: but he shall eat the flesh of the fat, and tear their claws in pieces. Woe to the idol shepherd that leaveth the flock! the sword shall be upon his arm, and upon his right eye: his arm shall be clean dried up, and his right eye shall be utterly darkened." This idol shepherd is put in contrast to the Good Shepherd, whom Zechariah was to impersonate or represent, as described in the first part of the same chapter and who was sold for thirty pieces of silver. This part of the prophecy has been fulfilled literally, and we may be certain that the rest will come to pass in due time.

The Jews are even now waiting for this idol shepherd, although they little realize it. At a Zionist Congress some years before the recent war, Max Nordau declared, according to the published reports, "We are ready to welcome any man as our Messiah who will lead us back to our own land and establish us there in prosperity." Max Nordau is a so-called reformed Jew, who has given up the Messianic hope as set forth in the Holy Scriptures. But only recently, when Dr. Mosinsohn, of the Hebrew College of Jaffa, was touring America in the interests of the same Zionist movement, I had the privilege of hearing him give an address at the University of California. In the course of his remarks, he said, "Think of all the great religious leaders who have come out of the East. Moses arose in the East, Buddha, Confucius, Jesus, and Mahomet all arose in the East. And we say to you people of the West, with confidence, that if you will restore the Jew to his ancestral home it will not be long until we will give you another great religious leader who will perhaps transcend all who have gone before." A Christian physician and I, who had gone there together, looked at one another in amazement. We felt that we were listening to a "John the Baptist" of the Antichrist, so startling was the announcement. And with the light that the prophetic word throws upon the now very near future, who can doubt that this Hebrew leader's declaration will indeed seem to an unbelieving world to be fulfilled in the willful one who is to be raised up in the land of Palestine and whom apostate Judaism and apostate Christendom alike will acknowledge as the Christ—the coming man. Toward this awful end all modern cults and -isms are tending, and when the personal presence of the Holy Spirit has been withdrawn from the earth, his manifestation will not long be withheld.

I know that the Reformers and many moderns have considered the papacy to be the fulfillment of the prophecies we have been considering. I do not wonder at that view because that unholy system is one of the most amazing counterfeits of what is of God that the world has ever seen. But it certainly does not meet all of the requirements of the case, although it is undoubtedly one of the "many antichrists" of which the apostle John writes when forewarning us of *"the* Antichrist" whose coming is still future.

I would direct your attention to six things predicted of this false one that have never been true of the papacy, and, it seems to me, are never likely to be.

1. The Antichrist must be a Jew; otherwise, he would not be acknowledged by Israel as their Messiah.
2. He is to rise up in the land of Palestine, not in Italy, and in Jerusalem, not in Rome.
3. He is to be subject to and in league with the civil power, not dominating it, as the papacy did for centuries.
4. He is to be acknowledged by the mass of the Jews as their king and religious leader, and it is well known that the Jews have never acknowledged the pretensions of the popes.
5. He is to be the patron of Israel, whereas the Romish church has ever been their persecutor.
6. He is not to be manifested until after the hindering Holy Spirit shall be removed, and that will be only when He goes up with the church at the return of the Lord Jesus Christ for His people, before the hour of judgment strikes for this godless world where the Word of God, the Christ of God, the Spirit of God, and the church of God have all been rejected.

Other systems are equally antichristian as the papacy, but none of them answer to the preceding requirements; therefore, none of them is to be confused with the personal Antichrist who is yet to arise and delude for a time those "[who refused] the love of the truth, that they might be saved" (2 Thess. 2:10). The many antichrists are but preparing the way for this incarnation of iniquity, and the avidity with which men and women drink in their evil teachings may give us some idea of how easy a thing it will be for the false Messiah to establish his claims.

Some people would ridicule the thought of vast numbers of people responding to such monstrous pretensions, but we must remember that God Himself is going "to give them up" (Deut. 31:5; Mic. 5:3), in retributive judgment, "to believe *the*[1] lie" because they would not have His truth. And, in our own day, how easily have deceivers such as Mrs. Mary Baker Glover Patterson Eddy, Mrs. Ellen G. White, Madame Blavatsky, Annie Besant, Katherine Tingley, John Alexander "Elijah" Dowie, and other charlatans, not to speak of Rome itself, been able to enslave the minds and consciences of vast multitudes of people who refuse the simple truth of the Word of God—and, mark you, all of this with the Holy Spirit still in the world, waiting to guide into all truth every honest soul who is willing to be led by Him and taught through the Word! How much easier it will be for error to assert itself when He is no longer here!

But time presses, and it is necessary that I touch briefly on the last verse of our chapter.

I know that many of you will be anxious to have me attempt to expound this verse and tell you plainly what is meant by its mystic number. "Here is wisdom. Let him that hath understanding count the number of the beast: for it is the number of a man; and his number is six hundred three score and six." All I can say is that *six* is the number of *man* and *three* of *manifestation.* In these three sixes I see the full manifestation of what is in the heart of man—man's last effort to attain to divinity and deity, to rob God of His glory, and to exalt himself. But, undoubtedly, when the Antichrist actually appears and the first Beast is manifested, the meaning will be so plain that everyone who turns to God in that day will be warned thereby to "have no fellowship with the unfruitful works of darkness," but will cleave to the Lord all the more earnestly because they know that the end has drawn so nigh. Guesses as to the meaning of 666 have been innumerable; I shall not add another.

In closing, I would again remind my hearers that time for us also is flying by quickly. If any of you is unsaved, it is well for you to remember that mercy's day is quickly gone. Gospel light already seems to be vanishing from the earth; the darkening apostasy is making rapid strides; a famine for hearing the Word of the Lord will soon be here. Oh, that now, in this day of grace, men would heed the testimony of the Scripture of truth, receive the virgin-born Son of God as Savior and Lord, and spurn the lies of every antichrist!

O earth, earth, earth, hear the word of the LORD. (Jeremiah 22:29)

Hear, and your soul shall live. (Isaiah 55:3)

He that heareth my word, and believeth on him that sent me, hath everlasting life, and [cometh not unto judgment]; but is passed from death unto life. (John 5:24)

THE HARVEST AND VINTAGE

Revelation 14

This fourteenth chapter forms a distinct section of the book. It consists of one vision divided into six parts and evidently has to do with the closing of the Great Tribulation and the introduction of the kingdom. It is as though God would give to John and us a heartening view of the consummation before depicting in detail the closing trials that will occupy the last half of the tribulation period.

The first part of the vision is that of the Lamb on Mount Zion. John tells us,

> And I looked, and, lo, a Lamb stood on the mount Zion, and with him an hundred and forty and four thousand, having his Father's name written in their foreheads. And I heard a voice from heaven, as the voice of many waters, and as the voice of a great thunder; and I heard the voice of harpers harping with their harps: and they sung as it were a new song before the throne, and before the four [living ones], and the elders: and no man could learn that song but the hundred and forty and four thousand, which were redeemed from the earth. These are they which were not defiled with women; for they are virgins. These are they which follow the Lamb whithersoever he goeth. These were redeemed from among

men, being the firstfruits unto God and to the Lamb. And in their mouth
was found no guile: for they are without fault before the throne of God.
(vv. 1–5)

This is a beautiful little prophetic picture, quite complete in itself. It sets
forth that which is to take place after the desolations of Israel are ended; the
glory is dawning in the land where Jesus lived and died and rose again and to
which He is coming back in person.

First, observe that Mount Zion is on the earth. The vision has to do with the
return of the Lamb to the city that once rejected Him. It is a very common thing
for Bible readers to spiritualize the various localities mentioned in the Bible.
Thus, Jerusalem, Mount Zion, and Israel are all made to mean the church, or
possibly even heaven itself, whereas they have no such application. When God
says Israel, He means Israel. When He speaks of Jerusalem, He does not intend
us to understand that either heaven or the church is in view. And Mount Zion is
that Mount Zion that David first set apart to God and is a distinct locality to
this day in the land of Palestine within the limits of the city of Jerusalem. It is a
place on earth, not in heaven, and there the Lord Jesus Christ is going to gather
the Israelitish remnant to Himself when He comes to set up His kingdom.

Although many people have taught the contrary, I have no question in my
own mind but that the 144,000 of this chapter are the very same as the sealed
144,000 of chapter 7. In the earlier chapter, John saw them sealed before the
Great Tribulation began; God had pledged Himself to protect them. No matter
how vindictively their enemies might assail them, He had set His own mark
upon them, and He had promised to bring them safely through those tempestu-
ous and difficult days. Now, in chapter 14, we see that same company gathered
about the Lamb on Mount Zion, the firstfruits of the kingdom age.

The Lord reveals His Father's Name to them; the seal of the living God upon
their foreheads is, in fact, this blessed revelation. They know God as Father and
rejoice in His protecting care and tender love. In heaven are those who rejoice
with them in a very special way, and these are distinguished from the elders, who
represent, as we have already seen, the entire priestly company caught up at the
Rapture. But, as the Great Tribulation continues, Jewish believers, who will be
martyred because of their faith, will also join that heavenly throng, and so we are
told that John heard "a voice from heaven, as the voice of many waters, and as
the voice of a great thunder: . . . the voice of harpers harping with their harps."
These "[sing] as it were, a new song before the throne, and before the [living
ones], and the elders: and no man could learn that song but the hundred and

forty and four thousand, which were redeemed from the earth." These in heaven and those on earth will have passed through the same experiences in measure. A sympathetic cord will be struck to which both respond. The new song is, of course, here, as elsewhere, the song of redemption.

The company on Mount Zion are next described as undefiled, a virgin band, who have kept themselves from the uncleanness everywhere prevailing in those fearful days. It is to be their hallowed privilege to follow the Lamb wherever He goes because they are described as being redeemed from among men, being the firstfruits unto God and to the Lamb. Thus, we have a firstfruits of the kingdom age, even as our Lord Himself is described as the firstfruits of the current dispensation, and His church, associated with Him, is "a kind of firstfruits of His creatures" (James 1:18).

The blessing of Psalm 32 pronounced upon the man in whom is no guile, the blessing that our Lord pronounced upon Nathanael, is the portion of this special company. A guileless man is not a sinless man; he is one who has nothing to hide. When sin is all confessed and judged in the presence of God, guile is absent. And so this guileless company are described as without fault before the throne of God; not, indeed, that they appear there in any righteousness of their own, but they are saved by the same precious blood that today makes faultless every believer in our Lord Jesus Christ.

The second section is that of the everlasting gospel, as recorded in verses 6–7.

> And I saw another angel fly in the midst of heaven, having the everlasting gospel to preach unto them that dwell on the earth, and to every nation, and kindred, and tongue, and people, saying with a loud voice, Fear God, and give glory to him; for the hour of his judgment is come: and worship him that made heaven, and earth, and the sea, and the fountains of waters.

This everlasting gospel is not to be distinguished from the gospel that has been proclaimed throughout the centuries. In truth, the very fact that it is called "everlasting" shows that it is identical with the gospel as proclaimed from the beginning. It is the good news of all the ages that God is sovereign, and man's happiness consists in recognizing His authority. To this blessed fact is added, in the current dispensation, the full truth of the gospel of the grace of God. The gospel of the kingdom is but another aspect of this same news from heaven, emphasizing particularly the lordship of Christ. There can be only one gospel because the apostle tells us, "Though we, or an angel from heaven, preach any other gospel unto you than that which we have preached unto you, let him be accursed" (Gal. 1:8). But that one gospel has different phases. In the epistle to the Galatians, Paul speaks of "the gospel of the circumcision" and the "gospel of the uncircumcision" (2:7)—the same gospel but presented in one way to the Jews and another to the Gentiles. When John the Baptist and the Lord were ministering here on earth, they preached the gospel of the kingdom, but men rejected the kingdom, so, for the time being, the kingdom is in abeyance. This is the day of the church.

The Son of Man is likened unto a man who has gone into a far country to receive for himself a kingdom and to return. When the word is given by the Father, He will descend to take the kingdom, to be proclaimed as King of kings, and Lord of lords. Throughout the current dispensation, He is taking out from among both Jews and Gentiles all who believe on His name, and He unites them in the one body, the church. After the church has gone, no Christian will be left on earth. Then it is that God is going to commence again to work among the Jews, and He will send them out to preach the gospel of the kingdom unto the ends of the earth. Finally, we have the very last phase of that gospel immediately preceding His coming. It is the final call for the guilty nations to prostrate themselves in the dust and pay homage to their Creator. It is mercy indeed to God's creatures everywhere that in that hour of judgment, before the last blow falls, the call will still go forth to men everywhere to acknowledge the claims of the Omnipotent One whose mercies they have rejected for so long. We do not hear, however, of any response, at least not in this chapter, but Scripture elsewhere warrants the thought that many who had never before heard and rejected the gospel will, in that day, open their hearts to the message and repent and thus be led to welcome the King.

The third section of the vision is that of verse 8:

And there followed another angel, saying, Babylon is fallen, is fallen, that great city, because she made all nations drink of the wine of the wrath of her fornication.

Babylon is more fully described for us in chapters 17 and 18, but we have to defer any detailed exposition of this subject until a later lecture, except to say that just as Babylon of old was the fountainhead of idolatry, so is mystic Babylon today the mother of all false religious teaching in Christianity. In the time of the end, it will be headed up in one great false church. That worldly church, which has proved so unworthy and false to her Lord, is to be broken absolutely to pieces, to be utterly destroyed. I have no doubt that all over the world will be such scenes as are now going on in Russia, with men crying, "No God; no church."

I know that many religious leaders are now very enthusiastic about what they call "the reunion of Christendom," but that reunion will simply be a great federation of Christless churches forming the most powerful religious association that has ever been known in this world—Catholic, Greek, Protestant, and all other systems united into one—after the true believers have gone. For a time, this great institution will dominate everything, until men will say at last, "What is the use of a church like this? Why not destroy the whole thing and be done with it once and for all?" And so they will destroy it throughout the world, as they once destroyed it in France, and as they are now destroying it in Russia.

Would that professed preachers of the gospel realized, before it is too late, that, when men take up religion in which there is no real conversion and which has no place for the work of the Holy Spirit, the whole thing will soon go on the rocks. In spite of the latitudinarianism of the times in which we live, it is still blessedly true that when faithful men preach the genuine old-time gospel of the grace of God in power, people are willing to go and hear. Speaking generally, even unsaved men and women have more respect for the old, old story of redeeming love than they have for these modern shams. When a man comes to the place where he no longer believes in the Bible, in the blood of Christ, in regeneration, he says to himself, "What a fool I am, paying money to keep up the church. I had better pay it to a lodge or a club. I can get more out of something like that than I can get out of the church."

Have you ever noticed that Unitarianism has never been a financial success? Therefore, when a preacher in one of our orthodox churches comes no longer to believe in orthodoxy, you will observe that generally he holds on to his position in the orthodox institution as long as he can. Loaves and fishes are commoner there, after all, than in the heretical systems that are languishing all about us. And so we can understand how it will be in the Great Tribulation. Babylon, for a while, will dominate everything. The head of the nations will be the head of the church. The Antichrist will be supreme in religious matters. But when Babylon falls, what a tremendous smashup there is going to be!

The next section gives us the third angel's message. We read in verses 9–13,

> And the third angel followed them, saying with a loud voice, If any man worship the beast and his image, and receive his mark in his forehead, or in his hand, the same shall drink of the wine of the wrath of God, which is poured out without mixture into the cup of his indignation;

and he shall be tormented with fire and brimstone in the presence of the holy angels, and in the presence of the Lamb: and the smoke of their torment ascendeth up for ever and ever: and they have no rest day nor night, who worship the beast and his image, and whosoever receiveth the mark of his name. Here is the patience of the saints: here are they that keep the commandments of God, and the faith of Jesus. And I heard a voice from heaven saying unto me, Write, Blessed are the dead which die in the Lord from henceforth: Yea, saith the Spirit, that they may rest from their labours; and their works do follow them.

What a solemn thing this is! A message from heaven declaring that those who turn away from the true God, who reject His Word, and who instead worship the Beast and his image will have to drink the very dregs of the cup of God's wrath.

I need not turn aside to animadvert upon the absurd interpretation given to this vision by the Seventh-Day Adventists. But they tell us that the third angel's message is the Sabbath message and that worshiping the Beast and receiving his mark consists in recognizing the holiness of the first day of the week. What can be the mental condition, not to speak of the moral state, of a man or woman who can conceive of a God of love and grace pouring out His wrath upon men because, with earnest desire to glorify Him, they keep the resurrection day, which from the earliest period of church history has been known as the Lord's Day? Surely, one must have lost all sense of moral values to advocate a theory so absurd, even though they were mistaken as to the proper day to hallow. But when one realizes that the judgment pronounced here is the doom of apostasy, for which, in retributive judgment, God will press the cup of His wrath to the lips of those who have refused the cup of salvation, all is perfectly clear. Nor is there any evidence that that judgment will come to an end, for verse 11 distinctly says, "The smoke of their torment ascendeth up for ever and ever: and they have no rest day nor night, who worship the beast and his image, and whosoever receiveth the mark of his name."

It will indeed require courage of a very high order to stand against all of that apostate condition and hold firmly to the truth of God as then revealed. And so we are told in verse 12, "Here is the patience of the saints: here are they that keep the commandments of God, and the faith of Jesus." This is strikingly in line with what we have been pointing out, that these converts will be Jewish believers. They keep the commandments of God, as made known in the Old Testament, and yet the faith of Jesus as declared in the New. Their part is not in the body of Christ; that glorious truth of the current dispensation is not for them, but they will have learned, at last, that Jesus is the promised Messiah, who was rejected by their nation when He came in grace, but He is coming again in mighty power. So they will bring forth fruits meet for repentance, manifested by their pious, godly lives and their desire to glorify the One whom their nation rejected.

And now we come to a very striking word in verse 13. Notice that little word *henceforth*. You have often heard this verse used in connection with funerals in the current dispensation, and I do not question that it may be so used, and very blessedly too; but its full application refers to a coming day. A voice from heaven says, "Blessed are the dead which die in the Lord from henceforth: Yea, saith the Spirit, that they may rest from their labours; and their works do follow them." The point, I take it, is this: the darkest part of the Great Tribulation is still before them. The storm clouds, heavy with judgment, may break at any moment, but immediately following, the kingdom is to be set up. Those who pass through the Tribulation will enter into the kingdom on earth. Those who die during its course will have their part in the heavenly kingdom, and so a special blessing will be theirs. In other words, from that point on it will really be better to die than to live. They will rest from their labors, be spared further tribulation on the earth, and have their place with their Lord in heaven, which will be far better than the highest place in the kingdom here on earth, as glorious as that will be.

And now let me press a question upon my hearers, whether saved or unsaved. You also must leave this scene shortly. What kind of works are going to follow you? If you are saved, what have you been doing for the Lord? If you are un-saved, oh then, I beg you to remember that your sins will follow after you—those sins you have been trying to forget; those sins from which you have fled; those sins for which, in your folly, you thought you could atone by your own effort. When you stand up, at last, poor and naked and miserable, before the Great White Throne, you will find all of your sins there, and they will fasten upon you like the hell-hounds that they really are and drag you down to the lake of fire. Do not, I beseech you, turn away from this solemn truth. The blood of Christ alone can wash you from all of those sins, and then, as a believer in the Lord Jesus, you can live for Him in this scene, and your works will follow you to heaven because all that is done for Christ will abide for eternity.

The fifth part of the vision is that of the harvest, and a most solemn one it is, as recorded in verses 14–16.

And I looked, and behold a white cloud, and upon the cloud one sat like unto the Son of man, having on his head a golden crown, and in his hand a sharp sickle. And another angel came out of the temple, crying with a loud voice to him that sat on the cloud, Thrust in thy sickle, and reap: for the time is come for thee to reap: for the harvest of the earth is ripe. And he that sat on the cloud thrust in his sickle on the earth; and the earth was reaped.

You will remember that our Lord Jesus spoke about the harvest, and He declared that it is the end of the age, the time when the wicked are going to be separated from the just, when He is going to gather the wheat into His garner but burn up the chaff with fire unquenchable. This is what you have here: discriminating judgment. The earth is reaped. Everything that is of God, the Son of Man will claim for Himself; all that is contrary will be given up to judgment. Observe that it is the Son of Man who sits upon the cloud and directs the reapers. All judgment is committed unto the Son; the One who once hung on Calvary's Cross is the same blessed person who is coming to execute judgment. This is, I take it, the same, in nature, as the judgment in Matthew 25. It is premillennial, and not, like the judgment of the Great White Throne, postmillennial. Jesus is coming back to the world that crucified Him, and He is going to gather for His kingdom, out of all nations, those who have heeded His message and cared for His messengers, but all who have heard His gospel, only to reject it, will be given up to judgment.

The last part of the vision is that of the vintage. It is very different from the harvest, in that the harvest is, as we have just seen, discriminatory whereas the vintage is unsparing judgment.

And another angel came out of the temple which is in heaven, he also having a sharp sickle. And another angel came out from the altar, which had power over fire; and cried with a loud cry to him that had the sharp sickle, saying, Thrust in thy sharp sickle, and gather the clusters of the vine of the earth; for her grapes are fully ripe. And the angel thrust in his sickle into the earth, and gathered the vine of the earth, and cast it into the great winepress of the wrath of God. And the winepress was trodden without the city, and blood came out of the winepress, even unto the horse bridles, by the space of a thousand and six hundred furlongs.

The vintage has to do with the vine—the vine of the earth—and this vine is apostate Israel. We are familiar with the figure, as used regarding Israel in the Old Testament. Isaiah uses it, and in Hosea we hear the Lord saying, "Israel is an empty vine, he bringeth forth fruit unto himself" (Hos. 10:1). The same figure is used in Psalms 80 and 81. When our Lord was here, He could say, "I am the true vine" (John 15:1). He was the only one in Israel bearing good fruit, and all who accept His message become branches in the living vine. By and by, the vine is going to be replanted in Palestine. In fact, we may go further and say that the vine is *being* replanted in Palestine. The Jews are going back to their own land. It stirs one's soul as Scripture is being fulfilled before our eyes. They are being replanted in their own vineyard, but replanted for what? For the vintage of the wrath of God. A remnant will be gathered out, separated to the Lord, but the rest will be given up to unsparing judgment in the Time of Jacob's Trouble. Fleshly Israel, the vine of the earth, can produce no fruit for God. But in that day of great distress, the clusters of the vine of the earth will be cast into the great winepress of the wrath of God. And we are told that the winepress was trodden without the city, and blood came out of the winepress, even unto the horse bridles, by the space of a thousand and six hundred furlongs. This is said to be the actual length of the land of Palestine. The picture is that of the entire land drenched in blood up to the horse bridles. What will the reality be? O Lord, how long?

Thank God, brighter things are ahead. In fact, the best days for Israel, and the whole earth, lie beyond that awful scene of wrath and carnage. But we need to remember that the people of the Jews brought their judgment upon their own heads by refusing the Prince of Peace when He came in grace to deliver them. In Pilate's judgment hall they cried, "His blood be on us and on our children." How dreadfully has this fearful imprecation been answered by a just God the centuries bear witness.

The scene depicted in these closing verses of the chapter shows that a more dreadful fulfillment is yet in the future. Immanuel's land, once stained with His own precious blood, will be red with the gore of those who reject Him and who, even in that day, when their own Scriptures will be so marvelously fulfilled before their very eyes, will still refuse Him and acknowledge instead the unholy claims of the Antichrist. Of old, they chose Barabbas in place of Jesus, which is called Christ. Unchanged in spirit to the very end, they will prefer the "son of perdition" (2 Thess. 2:3) to the Son of God and thus bring upon themselves swift destruction.

THE VIALS OF THE WRATH OF GOD

Revelation 15–16

My purpose this evening is to go over briefly chapters 15 and 16, which form one connected vision, depicting the final scenes of the dispensation of judgment that has been so largely occupying us in these addresses. We need to remember that the Revelation is primarily a book of judgment, and, although it might seem very pessimistic to be occupied with so many fearful scenes, all is bright at the end. The book does not close until the new heavens and the new earth, wherein righteousness shall dwell throughout a blissful eternity, are brought in. I need not apologize therefore for bringing so continually before you picture after picture of God's judicial dealings with the prophetic earth. He has given us these revelations out of kindness to us that we may be warned thereby to avoid what lies ahead of this guilty world, and to shun every form of the apostasy that He is so soon coming to judge.

The seven vials (more properly, *bowls*) of the wrath of God, with which chapter 16 deals, are all included in the judgments of the last half of the Great Tribulation. They show the intensive character that these judgments will take as the end draws near. I do not like to speak conclusively where I have no definite word of Scripture to guide me, but it seems to me that the series covers but a very brief period at the close of the last half of the week, thus setting forth the judgments that will fall upon the kingdom of the Beast and the sphere of the Antichrist's special sway at the very end of the Great Tribulation.

In our last address, we noticed that one particular company of saints in heaven responded very noticeably to the 144,000 Israelites standing on Mount Zion. In chapter 15, the scene is changed. The prophet sees what is going on in heaven, and this company at once comes before his vision. He says,

> And I saw another sign in heaven, great and marvellous, seven angels having the seven last plagues; for in them is filled up the wrath of God. And I saw as it were a sea of glass mingled with fire: and them that had gotten the victory over the beast, . . . and over the number of his name, stand on the sea of glass, having the harps of God. And they sing the song of Moses the servant of God, and the song of the Lamb, saying, Great and marvellous are thy works, Lord God Almighty; just and true are thy ways, thou King of saints. (15:1–3)

This redeemed company standing on the sea of glass and having the harps of God is not to be confused with the church of the current dispensation. We are told that they sing the song of Moses the servant of God and the song of the Lamb. Clearly, then, they are Israelites. They are singing the song of Moses, which is the celebration of Jehovah's victory over Israel's foes, and the song of the Lamb, which is the song of redemption. They are those who have been slain by the servants of the last great apostate power but who have been raised from the dead and raptured during the tribulation period. They are, perhaps, identical with the two witnesses of chapter 11, although I do not press this point. But they are at least like them in these particulars: they have been faithful witnesses on earth and, because of their witnessbearing, have been put to death. They are seen as raised from the dead and caught up to God and to His throne. Like the elders, they have in their hands the harps of God and are a worshiping company.

These are said to stand upon the sea of glass, which is here represented as mingled with fire. The sea of glass, as I pointed out in an earlier lecture, answers to the brazen sea in Solomon's temple and the brazen laver in the court of the tabernacle. It is the type of the Word of God, needed for cleansing here; in heaven, crystallized, a glassy sea upon which the glorified saints take their stand to praise Him who has redeemed them to Himself, and made them forever clean.

The glass is seen here as mingled with fire because of the fiery trial through which these martyrs have passed.

Observe that the rendering "King of saints," at the close of verse 3, is generally recognized as faulty. The better manuscripts read "nations," although some manuscripts have "ages" rather than "saints." Nowhere is the Lord spoken of as "King of saints." He is, however, "King of the nations" and the "Ruler of the ages." These glorified witnesses to His saving power praise and adore Him for His justice and truth, recognizing the righteousness of His ways and the holiness of His person. Consequently, all nations shall come and worship before Him in the day that His judgments are made manifest. Observe, it is not the grace of God that will thus bring the nations to acknowledge His authority and worship before Him; it is "when [his] judgments are in the earth [that] the inhabitants of the world will learn righteousness" (Isa. 26:9). Scripture nowhere teaches the conversion of the world through the preaching of the gospel in this dispensation. The world will, eventually, be converted, but it will be only after the unbelieving portion has been purged by judgment, and the remnant left for the kingdom will give glory to the God of heaven.

In the fifth verse, we have another of the "openings" of this marvelous book. We read, "And after that I looked, and, behold, the temple of the tabernacle of the testimony in heaven was opened." The mention of the tabernacle of the testimony brings Israel again before us and reminds us that these judgments are for the carrying out of God's covenant with His ancient people Israel, when the nations that have oppressed them must be punished.

"Jerusalem [is] a burdensome stone for all people: all that burden themselves with it shall be cut in pieces, though all the people of the earth be gathered together against it" (Zech. 12:3). Therefore, the nations who have vented their hatred upon Israel cannot escape the wrath of God.

The temple of the tabernacle of the testimony in heaven being opened, John tells us,

> The seven angels came out of the temple, having the seven plagues, clothed in pure and white linen, and having their breasts girded with golden girdles. And one of the four beasts [or, living ones] gave unto the seven angels seven golden vials [or, bowls] full of the wrath of God, who liveth for ever and ever. And the temple was filled with smoke from the glory of God, and from his power; and no man was able to enter into the temple, till the seven plagues of the seven angels were fulfilled. (15:6–8)

These seven angels are to complete the wrath of God. They introduce and close His final visitations in judgment upon the Gentiles. Then will be fulfilled the many prophecies of retribution with which Scripture abounds. "It is a righteous thing . . . ," says the apostle Paul, "to recompense tribulation to [those who] trouble you" (2 Thess. 1:6). If this could be said regarding saints of the church period, how much more regarding Israel. Many people have been troubled with what are called the imprecatory psalms. They cannot understand David's calling down the judgment of God upon His enemies, or what amounts to the same thing, Israel's prayer for the overthrow and destruction of all of their foes. But, in the righteous government of God, it must be that those nations that have oppressed and sought the destruction of His people shall themselves be visited with the fierceness of His wrath.

Joseph Cook tells how on one occasion a gentleman, in conversation with a minister of the gospel, was objecting to the imprecatory psalms because they did not seem to him to be in harmony with the spirit of Christianity. It was just at the beginning of the Civil War. As they talked together, a newspaper was brought in, and the minister read, "The Federal Army is marching upon Richmond."

"Good," exclaimed the other. "I hope they will destroy it."

"That," cried the preacher, "is an imprecatory psalm." The point is that it is thoroughly in keeping with God's mind to desire the triumph of righteousness and the overthrow of what is iniquitous.

God's glory is at stake; His righteousness demands the punishment of iniquity, both in this world and in that which is to come. He does not apologize for dealing thus with unrighteousness, nor do His servants need to apologize for Him.

Verse 8 indicates that when the seven angels are about to come forth to execute their awful mission, it will be one of intense concern in heaven. The temple is seen filled with smoke from the glory of God, and from His power, and man, though redeemed, is represented as standing without, in awe, awaiting developments. Then a great voice out of the temple is heard saying to the seven angels, "Go your ways, and pour out [or, empty] the [bowls] of the wrath of God upon the earth" (16:1). As in the case of the seven trumpets, and, in measure, of the seven seals, I do not profess to be able to tell you just how much we are to take as symbolic and how much as literal in this septenary series of judgments. We know that the book of Revelation is a book of symbols, and yet there may be a great deal more in it that is literal than many of us suppose. The literal judgments may be intimately linked with the symbolical. No one reading this chapter carefully can fail to observe how intimately the bowls of wrath are linked, in their results upon the earth, with the plagues that fell upon Egypt preparatory to Israel's deliverance. God is again about to deliver His people, and this for the last time. The outpouring of these bowls depict, in large measure, the woes that were visited upon the kingdom of Pharaoh. But, as I've already said, descriptions perhaps must be taken symbolically rather than literally, or perhaps both interpretations coalesce.

In verse 2 we read, "And the first went, and poured out his vial upon the earth; and there fell a noisome and grievous sore upon the men which had the mark of the beast, and upon them which worshiped his image." This answers to the plague in Egypt, where God smote man and beast with boils and blains. It perhaps symbolizes a spiritual plague, which will cause those who have received the mark of the Beast and worship his image, as great annoyance as the physical suffering that would follow such a noisome and grievous sore upon the bodies of men. Notice that the sphere of this plague is *the earth,* and it answers to the first trumpet of chapter 8. But it is very evident that, although the sphere is the same, the judgment is more intense.

In the same way, the second angel's bowl links with the second angel's trumpet, which affected *the sea.* But again we have greater intensity, for, in verse 3 we read, "And the second angel poured out his [bowl] upon the sea; and it became as the blood of a dead man: and every living soul died in the sea." What a scene of death and desolation, whether we think of it as physical or spiritual or both. "All they that hate me," says Wisdom in the book of Proverbs, "love death" (8:36). And so death is the portion for those who have refused the life that is in Christ Jesus.

The third angel's trumpet affected the rivers and fountains of waters, and in verse 4 we read, "The third angel poured out his [bowl] upon the *rivers and fountains* of waters; and they became blood." Thus, the very sources of life are destroyed, as in the plague that fell upon Egypt when the river itself became blood. In verses 5–7, God's righteousness in thus dealing with those who had slaughtered His servants is fully attested: "And I heard the angel of the waters say, Thou art righteous, O Lord, which art, and wast, and shalt be, because thou hast judged thus. For they have shed the blood of saints and prophets, and thou hast given them blood to drink; for they are worthy. And I heard another out of the altar say, Even so, Lord God Almighty, true and righteous are thy judgments." Every right-thinking person will add his "Amen" because God is righteous in all of His ways, whether in grace or in judgment.

The fourth angel's bowl is poured out upon *the sun,* even as at the sounding of the fourth trumpet the third part of the sun was smitten. But again we have greater intensity in the judgment than in the trumpet series because "Power was given unto him to scorch men with fire. And men were scorched with great heat, and blasphemed the name of God, which hath power over these plagues: and they repented not to give him glory." The sun is the supreme source of light, and this implies that that which should have been for man's comfort becomes a curse and the means of his bitter suffering instead. Although their anguish is so great, however, men are not brought to repentance by punishment. God's name is blasphemed, and His creatures refuse to give Him glory. This is a solemn consideration for those who teach that punishment is really only chastisement and is always corrective.

The next section intensifies this point remarkably. When the fifth angel empties his bowl upon the seat of the Beast, thus smiting the last great confederation at its center, filling his kingdom with darkness, we read that "they gnawed their tongues for pain, and blasphemed the God of heaven because of their pains and their sores, and repented not of their deeds." Darkness and anguish do not tend to soften men's hearts or to lead them to confess their sins. Their very suffering but stirs them up to blaspheme God the more. And so, in the outer darkness of a lost eternity, our Lord has told us that there shall be not only weeping and wailing because of suffering endured but also the gnashing of teeth, which implies rage and indignation against God. With permanency of character, he who rejects Christ is guilty of eternal sin, and eternal punishment necessarily follows.

At the sounding of the fifth angel's trumpet, we were told that the bottomless pit was opened, "and there arose a smoke out of the pit, as the smoke of a great furnace, and the sun and the air were darkened by reason of the smoke of the pit" (chap. 9:2). This, doubtless, explains the darkness that fills the kingdom of the Beast when the fifth angel's bowl of wrath is poured upon the seat of the Beast. It is judicial darkness brought about by demoniacal delusions.

We now come to a portion that has been very much before people in these past years of bloody warfare. Again and again the question has been raised whether this great world war is the Armageddon conflict predicted in the Bible. Teachers instructed by the Word have invariably assured anxious questioners that, although this war might be arranging the stage, if one may so speak, for Armageddon, it cannot be that great conflict itself. Armageddon is a definite locality in the land of Palestine. The word means "the mountain of Megiddo," and it refers to the mountain that overlooks the valley of Esdraelon—the great plain of Jezreel in the northern part of the land of Palestine, which Napoleon Bonaparte said would make an ideal battle ground for all of the armies of the world. There, the last great battle is to be fought, just before the appearing of the Lord in glory. And this the sixth angel's bowl introduces:

And the sixth angel poured out his vial upon the great river Euphrates; and the water thereof was dried up, that the way of the kings of the east might be prepared. And I saw three unclean spirits like frogs come out of the mouth of the dragon, and out of the mouth of the beast, and out of the mouth of the false prophet. For they are the spirits of devils [or, demons], working miracles, which go forth unto the kings of the earth and of the whole world, to gather them to the battle of that great day of God Almighty. Behold, I come as a thief. Blessed is he that watcheth, and keepeth his garments, lest he walk naked, and they see his shame. And he gathered them together into a place called in the Hebrew tongue Armageddon" (16:12–16).

The great river Euphrates was formerly the eastern boundary of the Roman Empire and later of the Turkish dominion, and it speaks, I believe, of the destruction of that power. Luther said, "When the Turk is driven out of Europe, then comes the day of judgment." And, in a certain sense, this will undoubtedly be true—not the day of judgment for the wicked dead, but the day of judgment for the living nations. The Turk is an intruder in Europe, the enemy of both God and man, but I am convinced that his hold upon Constantinople and surrounding country is very nearly ended. God will drive the Ottoman Empire from Europe[1] and punish that nation that has so well deserved the name of "The Unspeakable Turk." The cry of martyred Armenia and of other peoples who have suffered so fearfully from these Asiatic hordes will be answered by the destruction of the nation that wrought such havoc. It is very evident, I think, that God is already beginning to bring this to pass. If you have a map of Europe of one hundred years ago, notice the place that the Turkish Empire then had, and compare it with a map of the present day, and see how much of its territory has been wrested from it.

Turkey, long known as "the sick man of Europe," is sicker than ever now and is hanging on with the clutch of despair to one little corner of Europe. I am convinced that it will not be long before he is driven out altogether. Then, according to the book of Daniel, he will "[pitch his tent] between the seas in the glorious holy mountain; yet he shall come to his end, and none shall help him" (11:45). Driven into Asia Minor, he will finally, I take it, attempt to establish himself in the land of Palestine. And this will not only arouse the European powers in the league of the ten kingdoms but also stir up the eastern and northern nations besides. Turkey will, if I understand the prophetic scheme aright, be backed in the last days by Russia and possibly Germany, too, in opposition to the Western confederation. Both of these great powers will be anxious to hold the land of Palestine, which is admittedly the key to the so-called Eastern question. But the activity of these European nations will arouse the races of the Far East because, when the Euphrates is dried up, we are told it is "that the way of the kings of the East might be prepared." Who are the kings of the East? Various theories have been suggested. Some people consider they may be the so-called lost ten tribes of Israel returning to their land. Others, the dominions of Persia, Afghanistan, and so on. It is significant that the word rendered "the east" is really "the sun-rising." Is it only a coincidence that for a millennium at least Japan has been known as "the kingdom of the rising sun"? May not the Mongolian races, possibly allied with India, be the kings of the East here depicted as coming in conflict with the powers of the West? Thus, the whole world will be thrown into bloody warfare, and all nations will be gathered together against Jerusalem to battle. This great world conflict will be the direct result of the working of demons because we are told that three unclean frog-like spirits came out of the mouths of the dragon, the Beast, and the False Prophet—demons working miracles, visiting the kingdoms of the earth (that is, the prophetic earth), and of the whole world (that is, the nations outside the prophetic earth), to gather them to the battle of that great day of God Almighty. This will be the great and final Armageddon conflict—the place where they will meet one another in an attempt to settle the final issues.

Notice that there is a parenthesis, however, in verse 15, which comes in just before the close of this section, and thus preceding the seventh bowl. It is the voice of the Lord Himself, "Behold, I come as a thief. Blessed is he that watcheth, and keepeth his garments, lest he walk naked, and they see his shame." The time of His manifestation is very close. He would have those who look for His appearing watching, and keeping their garments undefiled, lest they be put to shame before the ungodly. The undefiled are those who keep themselves from all fellowship with the Satan-inspired movements of the last days, walking with God in holy separation from the abounding iniquity, as directed by His Word. The voice is for us as well as for the saints in a future day.

The seventh angel's bowl is poured out into the air, and, we are told,

> There came a great voice out of the temple of heaven, from the throne, saying, It is done. And there were voices, and thunders, and lightnings; and there was a great earthquake, such as was not since men were upon the earth, so mighty an earthquake, and so great. And the great city was divided into three parts, and the cities of the nations fell: and great

Babylon came in remembrance before God, to give unto her the cup of the wine of the fierceness of his wrath. And every island fled away, and the mountains were not found. And there fell upon men a great hail out of heaven, every stone about the weight of a talent: and men blasphemed God because of the plague of the hail; for the plague thereof was exceeding great. (vv. 17–21)

This indicates the utter destruction of every spiritual and religious institution that man has built up apart from God. It is the absolute overthrow of civilization, and the complete wreck of all man's hopes to bring in even livable conditions in this world while rejecting the Lord Jesus Christ. The scene is one of anarchy and confusion, but, despite the signs of divine wrath resting on the souls of men, they still blaspheme God and give no sign of repentance.

Time forbids our taking up great Babylon's judgment tonight. It will, however, come before us in our next address.

In closing, let me remind you that the church of God is to be caught up before these scenes take place upon the earth. We are looking for the Lord Jesus Christ, who is our Savior from the coming wrath. Do you know Him? If not, I plead with you in the light of all that we have had before us, "Flee from the wrath to come" (Matt. 3:7; Luke 3:7).

LECTURE 18

BABYLON: ITS CHARACTER AND DOOM

Revelation 17

I am to address you tonight on a theme the wonder of which grows upon me every time I speak of it, namely, the Mystery of Iniquity in its final form: Babylon the Great. It is that vast system of error that is so like Christianity in some respects that thousands of apparently spiritually minded people such as Fénelon, Pascal, Faber, and others have not been able to distinguish it from Christianity; yet, when tested by the Word of God, it is seen to be but a *counterfeit* of the church that God has purchased with the blood of His own Son.

Twice already in the course of this book we have heard of Babylon's fall, but as yet we have not learned to what city or system it referred. But the chapter now before us is entirely devoted to that interesting and solemn subject, and a careful study of what is here revealed ought to leave us free from all doubt or perplexity as to the identity of Babylon.

This chapter and the one that follows make up another of the great parentheses of this book. Chronologically, chapter 19 immediately follows chapter 16. But before he continues with the direct order of events, John is taken aside, as it

164

were, to see this remarkable vision of the false church before he beholds the union of the true church with the Lamb in the glory.

I ask your careful attention to the apostle's own words as recorded in verses 1–6:

> And there came one of the seven angels which had the seven vials [or, bowls], and talked with me, saying unto me, Come hither; I will show unto thee the judgment of the great [harlot] that sitteth upon many waters: with whom the kings of the earth have committed fornication, and the inhabitants of the earth have been made drunk with the wine of her fornication. So he carried me away in the spirit into the wilderness: and I saw a woman [sitting] upon a scarlet coloured beast, full of names of blasphemy, having seven heads and ten horns. And the woman was arrayed in purple and scarlet colour, and decked with gold and precious stones and pearls, having a golden cup in her hand full of abominations and filthiness of her fornication: and upon her forehead was a name written, MYSTERY, BABYLON THE GREAT, THE MOTHER OF HARLOTS AND ABOMINATIONS OF THE EARTH. And I saw the woman drunken with the blood of the saints, and with the blood of the martyrs of Jesus: and when I saw her, I wondered with great admiration [or, amazement].

I have quoted this somewhat lengthy portion in full that we may have the complete description before us. The beast is beyond question the same as that of chapter 13 and is therefore indubitably the Roman Empire. It is the empire as a whole but with the last phase especially emphasized. The woman is a religious system who dominates the civil power, at least for a time. The name upon her forehead should easily enable us to identify her. But to do that we will do well to go back to our Old Testament and see what is there revealed concerning literal Babylon, for the one will surely throw light upon the other. We have also the added instruction of secular history, which supplies us with some very important facts in this connection, and throws a flood of light upon the succession of spiritual Babylon of the Apocalypse to literal Babylon of the Old Testament.

As we go back into the dim twilight of history with Scripture, we learn that the founder of Bab-el, or Babylon, was Nimrod, of whose unholy achievements we read in Genesis 10. He was the archapostate of the patriarchal age. He is described as "a mighty hunter before the LORD" (Gen. 10:9)—"a hunter of the souls of men," the rabbis said. Going out from the presence of the Lord, he impiously sought to gather a multitude about himself, and, in defiance of the express command of God to spread abroad upon the face of the earth, he persuaded his associates and followers to join him in "building a city and a tower which should reach unto heaven" (Gen. 11:4). Not surely, as some of us were taught in our childhood, a tower by which they might climb up into the skies to escape another possible flood, but a tower of renown, rising to a great height, to be recognized as a temple or rallying center for those who did not walk in obedience to the word of the Lord. With all of the effrontery of our modern apostates, they called their city and tower Bab-El, "the gate of God"; but it was soon changed by divine judgment into Babel, "confusion." It bore the stamp of unreality from the first, for we are told "they had brick for stone, and slime had they for mortar" (Gen. 11:3). An imitation of that which is real and true has ever since characterized Babylon in all ages.

Nimrod, or Nimroud-bar-Cush, as he is called on the monuments, was a grandson of Ham, the unworthy son of Noah, whose character is revealed in his exposure of his father's shame. We know that Noah had brought through the flood the revelation of the true God because he was a preacher of righteousness, and his utterances on more than one occasion show that he had the prophetic gift. Ham, on the other hand, seems to have been all too readily affected by the apostasy that brought the Flood because he shows no evidence of self-judgment but the very opposite. His name, as spelled out upon Egyptian monuments, is Khem, and this agrees with the literal sound of the Hebrew word rendered Ham in our Bibles. It means "swarthy," "darkened," or, more literally, "the sun-burnt." And the name indicates the state of the man's soul. For what is a sun-burned person? One who is darkened by light from heaven. Ham had been granted wonderful mercies; he was saved from the Flood because of his father's faith, but he abused his privileges and "[turned] the grace of God into lasciviousness." He was actually darkened by the burning rays of the light that God caused to shine upon his soul. Thus, his conscience became seared as with a hot iron, and he became the founder of a race that departed from the living God and led the way into idolatry, worshiping and serving the creature more than the Creator.

We know something of what this means. We speak of people today who have become, as we say, gospel-hardened. They, too, have been darkened by the light, and they are often the ringleaders in apostasy: "If . . . the light that is in thee [become darkened], how great is that darkness!" (Matt. 6:23). Many people in the world tonight used to listen with tears in their eyes to the story of the matchless grace of God as revealed in the Cross of Christ, but they are unmoved now though that story be told never so tenderly; they have become hardened in their sins, and their seared consciences no longer feel the Spirit's breath. It is a most dangerous thing to trifle with light from heaven.

But to proceed with our theme. Ham became darkened by the light. We know his failure and sin. But when Noah had recovered himself and knew what his son had done unto him, he pronounced, by the spirit of prophecy, a curse upon Canaan, not on Ham. Do you wonder at that? I did, until I saw that God had already pronounced a blessing upon all three of the sons of Noah—Shem, Ham, and Japheth. So Noah passes over his unworthy son and utters a curse upon Canaan, who we can well believe was, as we say, "a chip off the old block." Ham begat a son named Cush, "the black one," and he became the father of Nimrod, the apostate leader of his generation.

Ancient lore now comes to our assistance and tells us that the wife of Nimroud-bar-Cush was the infamous Semiramis the First. She is reputed to have been the foundress of the Babylonian mysteries and the first high priestess of idolatry. Thus, Babylon became the fountainhead of idolatry and the mother of every heathen and pagan system in the world. The mystery religion that originated there spread in various forms throughout the whole earth, and, as we shall see in a few minutes, it is with us today. It is identical to the mystery of iniquity that wrought so energetically in Paul's day and shall have its fullest development when the Holy Spirit has departed and the Babylon of the Apocalypse holds sway.

Building on the primeval promise of the woman's Seed who was to come, Semiramis bore a son, whom she declared was miraculously conceived! When she presented him to the people, they hailed him as the promised deliverer. This was Tammuz, against whose worship Ezekiel protested in the days of the Captivity. Thus was introduced the mystery of the mother and the child, a form of idolatry that is older than any other known to man. The rites of this worship were secret; only the initiated were permitted to know its mysteries. It was Satan's effort to delude mankind with an imitation so like the truth of God that they would not know the true Seed of the woman when He came in the fullness of time. To this fact Justin Martyr bears definite witness.

From Babylon, this mystery religion spread to all of the surrounding nations as the years went on and the world was populated by the descendants of Noah. Everywhere the symbols were the same, and everywhere the cult of the mother and the child became the popular system, and their worship was celebrated with the most disgusting and immoral practices. The image of the queen of heaven with the babe in her arms was seen everywhere, although the names might differ as languages differed. It became the mystery religion of Phoenicia, and the

Phoenicians carried it to the ends of the earth. Ashtoreth and Tammuz, the mother and child of these hardy adventurers, became Isis and Horus in Egypt, Aphrodite and Eros in Greece, Venus and Cupid in Italy, and many other names in more distant places. Within one thousand years, Babylonianism had become the religion of the world, which had rejected the divine revelation.

Linked with this central mystery were countless lesser mysteries, the hidden meanings of which were known to only the initiates, but the outward forms were practiced by all of the people. Among these mysteries were the doctrines of purgatorial purification after death; salvation by countless sacraments such as priestly absolution; sprinkling with holy water; the offering of round cakes to the queen of heaven, as mentioned in the book of Jeremiah; dedication of virgins to the gods, which was literally sanctified prostitution; and weeping for Tammuz for a period of forty days before the great festival of Istar, who was said to have received her son back from the dead, for it was taught that Tammuz was slain by a wild boar and afterward brought back to life. To him, the egg was sacred, depicting the mystery of his resurrection, even as the evergreen was his chosen symbol and was set up in honor of his birth at the winter solstice, when a boar's head was eaten in memory of his conflict and a yule-log burned with many mysterious observances. The sign of the cross was sacred to Tammuz, symbolizing the life-giving principle and the first letter of his name. It is represented upon vast numbers of the most ancient altars, and temples, and did not, as many have supposed, originate with Christianity.

The patriarch Abraham was separated from this mystery religion by the divine call. With this same evil cult the nation that sprang from Abrahem had constant conflict, until under Jezebel, a Phoenician princess, it was grafted onto what was left of the religion of Israel in the northern kingdom in the day of Ahab and was the cause of their captivity at the last. Judah was polluted by it because Baal worship was but the Canaanitish form of the Babylonian mysteries; only by being sent into captivity to Babylon itself was Judah cured of her fondness for idolatry. Baal was the sun god, the life-giving one, identical with Tammuz.

When Christ came into this world, the mystery of iniquity was everywhere holding sway, except where the truth of God as revealed in the Old Testament was known. Thus, when the early Christians set out upon the great task of carrying the gospel to the ends of the earth, they found themselves everywhere confronted by this system in one form or another; although Babylon as a city had long been but a memory, her mysteries had not died with her. When the city and the temples were destroyed, the high priest fled with a company of initiates and their sacred vessels and images to Pergamos, where the symbol of the serpent was set up as the emblem of the hidden wisdom. From there, they afterward crossed the sea and emigrated to Italy, where they settled in the Etruscan plain. There, the ancient cult was propagated under the name of the Etruscan Mysteries, and eventually Rome became the headquarters of Babylonianism. The chief priests wore miters shaped like the head of a fish, in honor of Dagon, the fish-god, the lord of life—another form of the Tammuz mystery, as developed among Israel's old enemies, the Philistines. When the chief priest was established in Rome, he took the title Pontifex Maximus, which was imprinted on his miter. When Julius Caesar (who, like all young Romans of good family, was an initiate) had become the head of the State, he was elected Pontifex Maximus, and this title was held henceforth by all of the Roman emperors down to Constantine the Great, who was, at one and the same time, head of the church and high priest of the heathen! The title was afterward conferred upon the bishops of Rome and is today borne by the pope, who is thus declared to be, not the successor of the fisherman-apostle Peter, but the direct successor of the high priest of the Babylonian mysteries, and the servant of the fish-god Dagon, for whom he wears, like his idolatrous predecessors, the fisherman's ring.

During the early centuries of the church's history, the mystery of iniquity had wrought with such astounding effect, and Babylonian practices and teachings had been so largely absorbed by that which bore the name of the church of Christ, that the truth of the Holy Scriptures on many points had been wholly obscured whereas idolatrous practices had been foisted upon the people as Christian sacraments and heathen philosophies took the place of gospel instruction. Thus was developed the amazing system that for a thousand years dominated Europe and trafficked in the bodies and souls of men, until the great Reformation of the sixteenth century brought in a measure of deliverance.

It was this that filled the apostle with such amazement. It seemed incredible that the glorious movement with which he had been identified for a generation should ever become so perverted as to become the mother of harlots and of every abomination and should even become the slaughterer of the saints of God and the martyrs of Jesus. But her bloody history during the dark days of persecution bears awful witness to the truth of the vision. The angel, however, goes on to show that the future has more marvelous things in store than we should otherwise have dared to imagine; no other period of Rome's history fully answers to what is brought before us in the rest of the chapter.

We hear a great deal about the desirability of church federation now, but men seem to forget—or never to have known—that it is God Himself who has rent

Christendom asunder because of her unfaithfulness and apostasy. We are told that it would be a most excellent thing if the different denominations of Protestants could be united in one great body, and then join hands with the three so-called Catholic churches—Anglican, Greek, and Roman. It is pointed out that such a vast united church could dominate the world. Besides, it would make for such increased efficiency and would simplify the financial problems that have so troubled and perplexed our boards and officials for so long. But we must remember that such a union would not be the body of Christ at all. It would simply be a worldly confederacy of saved and unsaved—just great Babylon over again. The body of Christ remains undivided in spite of Christendom's unhappy schisms because it is composed of all truly saved people who have by the Spirit's baptism been made one in Christ. Although outward unity is desirable, it would not be a blessing if it occurred at the expense of the truth.

But we must now consider the angel's interpretation of the vision. He said to John,

> Wherefore didst thou marvel? I will tell thee the mystery of the woman, and the beast that carrieth her, which hath the seven heads and ten horns. The beast that thou sawest was, and is not; and shall ascend out of the bottomless pit, and go into perdition: and they that dwell upon the earth shall wonder, whose names were not written in the book of life from the foundation of the world, when they behold the beast that was, and is not, and yet is. (vv. 7–8)

We have already seen in our study of chapter 13 that this Beast sets forth the Roman Empire as revived in a Satan-inspired league of nations after the church dispensation is over. This will be a very different thing to any league that might be formed in our times and that might result from the recent war while the church is still here. The federation of the future will be utterly godless and God defiant. When that league is formed, it will be but natural that a confederacy of all religious systems be wrought out, and this, too, will be satanic in character. It will be a union of Christless professors, inheriting all of the human and demoniacal mysteries of Babylon. In other words, all sects will be swallowed up in the one distinctively Babylonish system that has ever maintained the cult of the mother and the child. This system will for the first part of the tribulation period dominate the civil power. Thus, the woman will be in the saddle again and ride the Beast! He who has eyes to see and a heart to understand can readily discern the preparations now in progress, with this very end in view.

From verses 9–11, we learn the identity of the city where Babylon has her seat and also that it is when the final form of the empire appears that she will attain the position of preeminence that she has sought so long. Rome alone answers to the description given. On a previous occasion, we saw that the eighth head, who is of the seven, is the last great world ruler who will dominate the League of Nations in the time of the end and whose capital will be the so-called eternal city.

It would seem, however, from verses 12–14 that the other ten kings act in fullest harmony with the Beast, and this point completely nullifies the theory that the vision refers to any past history of the nations into which the Roman Empire was divided. Never have they thus acted in unison, but Europe has ever been a scene of conflicting nations and warring powers since the breakup of the Empire itself. We must look to the future for a time when the ten kings shall receive power for one hour with the Beast. Then they will impiously make war with the Lamb only to be overcome by Him who is King of Kings and Lord of Lords.

The similitude of the waters is explained for us in verse 15: "The waters which thou sawest, where the harlot sitteth, are peoples and multitudes, and nations and tongues." Over all nations has Babylon borne sway in the past, deceiving them with the wine of her fornication. Over all nations will she again bear rule, until, wearied with her blandishments, the world, whose favor she courted, will spurn her at last. The angel continues his explanation of the mystery by saying,

> And the ten horns which thou sawest *and* the beast [not, *upon* the beast, as in the AV], these shall hate the [harlot], and shall make her desolate and naked, and shall eat her flesh, and burn her with fire. For God hath put in their hearts to fulfill his will, and to agree, and give their kingdom unto the beast, until the words of God shall be fulfilled. And the woman which thou sawest is that great city, which reigneth over the kings of the earth. (vv. 16–18)

There is no mistaking her identity. Pagan Rome was the lineal successor of Babylon. Papal Rome absorbed the Babylonian mysteries; and the Rome of the Beast in the last days will be the seat of the revived satanic system that began with Nimrod and his infamous consort Semiramis, which has from that day to this been opposed to everything that is of God and which changed the truth of God into a lie, worshiping and serving the creature more than the Creator.

Babylon of old, as we have seen, was the mother of idolatry. In Jeremiah 50:38, we read, "It is the land of graven images; they are mad upon their idols." It was she who taught the nations to substitute idolatry for spiritual worship, and to-day one-third of Christendom has followed her in the adoration of images, and another third worships icons, or pictures. There can be no question as to the Babylonish origin of these abominations. Nothing of the kind was known in the churches of God until the heathen mysteries were grafted unto Christianity. The images of the mother and child that are enshrined in Rome's temples are only different in name from the images worhsiped in the groves and temples of Semiramis, Ashtoreth, Isis, and other so-called "queens of heaven." In many instances, the old idols were simply renamed and adored as before. There is in one place in southern Europe a statue of Apollo, the sun god, that is identical to Tammuz and Baal, which is worshiped by deluded Romanists as St. Apollos; and the *S* is carved upon the pedestal by a later hand than carved the original name.

The mother of the Lord Jesus Christ assumed no such place among the early Christians as she has now been given in Rome's mysteries. She is seen as a lowly worshiper and as joining with others in prayer in Acts 2, which is the last mention of her in Scripture. Of the fable of her assumption and crowning as Queen of Heaven the Bible gives no hint. It is Babylonianism pure and simple.

The Word of the Lord to His people of old is most instructive for us now in the light of all that we have been studying:

> *Flee out of the midst of Babylon,* and deliver every man his soul: be not cut off in her iniquity; for this is the time of the LORD's vengeance; he will render unto her a recompense. Babylon hath been a golden cup in the LORD's hand, that made all the earth drunken: the nations have drunken of her wine; therefore the nations are mad. Babylon is suddenly fallen and destroyed: howl for her; take balm for her pain, if so be she may be healed. *We would have healed Babylon, but she is not healed: forsake her,* and let us go every one to his own country: for her judgment reacheth unto heaven, and is lifted up even to the skies. (Jeremiah 51:6–9)

It is a lamentable fact that Babylon's principles and practices are rapidly but surely pervading the churches that escaped from Rome at the time of the Reformation. We may see evidences of it in the wide use of high-sounding ecclesiastical titles, once unknown in the reformed churches, in the revival of holy days and church feasts such as Lent, Good Friday, Easter, and Christ's Mass, or, as it is generally written, Christmas. I quite admit that some of these festivals, if divested of any ecclesiastical character, may be observed in innocence in the home, but when they are turned into church festivals, they certainly come under the condemnation of Galatians 4:9–11, where the Holy Spirit warns against the observance of days and months and times and seasons. All of them, and many more that might be added, are Babylonish in their origin and were at one time linked with the Ashtoreth and Tammuz mystery worship. It is through Rome that they have come down to us, and we do well to remember that Babylon is a mother with daughters who are likely to partake of their mother's characteristics because it is written, "As is the mother, so is the daughter" (Ezek. 16:44). Therefore, it behooves all who love the Lord and desire His approbation to "depart from iniquity" (2 Tim. 2:19) and seek to "follow righteousness, faith, [love], and peace, with them that call [upon him] out of a pure heart" (v. 22).

We shall have a fuller account of Babylon's doom in our next study and shall perhaps see some things more clearly the details into which we could not well go tonight.[1]

BABYLON: ITS CHARACTER AND DOOM (CONT.)

Revelation 18:1–19:5

In my last address, I sought to identify the Babylon of the Apocalypse and to show just how it was linked with Babylon of old, the literal city in the land of the Chaldeans on the plain of Shinar. Tonight we have more details as to its unholy character and its awful doom. We also get a better idea of the marvelous way in which its principles have permeated the very warp and woof of civilization, affecting the entire civil and commercial fabric of the age in which we live, all of which must be destroyed to prepare the way for a higher and happier condition of society to be ushered in at the Lord's return. We read,

> And after these things I saw another angel come down from heaven, having great power; and the earth was lightened with his glory. And he cried mightily with a strong voice, saying, Babylon the great is fallen, is fallen, and is become the habitation of devils [or more properly, demons, as there is but one devil, but many demons], and the hold of every foul spirit, and a cage of every unclean and hateful bird. For all nations have drunk of the wine of the wrath of her fornication, and the

kings of the earth have committed fornication with her, and the merchants of the earth are waxed rich through the abundance of her delicacies. (vv. 1–3)

This, I take it, synchronizes with the second angel's message of chapter 14:8 and introduces the judgment of the seventh vial as foretold in 16:19. Babylon will therefore continue to the very end of the tribulation period, its destruction by the Beast and his ten kings being a last frantic effort to rid themselves of this dreadful incubus just before *they* are destroyed by the appearing of the Lord in glory. The Antichrist will be the pretended incarnation of the woman's Seed and will be accepted as such by apostate Christendom and apostate Judaism. Thus, Satan's masterpiece will seem to carry all before it—but only until the true Seed of the woman appears from heaven, descending with all of His holy ones to the consternation of His enemies and the joy of His suffering saints, the persecuted remnant of Israel and those from among the nations who will receive their testimony in that day. Note again that these are not people who in this current dispensation of grace have refused the message of the gospel, but those to whom that message will not have gone until after the rapture of the church. To this, 2 Thessalonians 2 bears a clear and convincing testimony.

The description of fallen Babylon as the habitation of demons and the hold of evil spirits and a cage of unclean birds is most graphic, and it strikingly depicts the horrible end of the apostasy. That which professes to be the spouse of Christ, and which issues its oftentimes blasphemous decrees as under the direction of the Spirit of God, is seen to be but a Satan-inspired and demon-directed system in which every unholy thing flourishes and evil men can find shelter and are protected in the promulgation of their evil doctrines and practices. To this, the papacy has fully answered in the past, and its character remains unchanged to this present hour. It would be practically impossible to find a viler history than that of the medieval popes and their emissaries. It was a Roman Catholic writer who said of this period, "The annals of the church are the annals of hell."

The proverb "The corruption of the best thing is the worst of corruptions" is strikingly illustrated in the history of the church. It seems almost impossible to believe that the church to which the apostle Paul addressed his epistle could, in a few centuries, degenerate into the Roman church as it is now known. But this is the mystery of Babylon, as we have already seen. And a more amazing thing, if that were possible, is the solemn fact that the Reformation churches, once delivered from this vile system, should now look hopefully for reconciliation with it, so readily be able to forget its dreadful past and overlook its current wicked pretensions! We in America, and our brethren in Britain, see Rome at its best because men do not readily do in the light what they will do in the dark. But, as it has been said, "Character is what a man is in the dark," and we may test this system by the same principle. If, then, you want to know the true character of Romanism, go to the lands where the light of the Reformation has barely penetrated; look at the countries south of us, to the great Latin American republics, where the papacy has borne sway and poisoned the morals of the people for centuries. There you will see the results of Babylonianism unchecked by enlightened Christianity. What a horrible cesspool of iniquity it is. Let those tell who have seen it for themselves. There idolatry reigns in most abhorrent form, and the gospel is a proscribed teaching, which would be absolutely prohibited had the church full power as it did in the days of old.

In the Old Testament, idolatry is branded as spiritual fornication. In the New Testament, it is the unhallowed union of the church and the world. We see *both* in this evil system. Who is so unblushingly idolatrous as Rome? And who has so persistently courted the world's favor as she? And even now we may see how brazenly she is coquetting with the kings of the earth, and by her blandishments she is endeavoring once more to win their admiration and attentions. Nor will she stop until the scarlet woman again rides the Beast—until the church dominates the State. Subtly, she is enlarging her sphere of influence. By devious ways, she seeks to "make America catholic" and to undo the work of the Reformation in England. She largely controls a venal press; even the theater, which, alas, is all the church that some people attend, is being pressed into her service. I am told on good authority that it is becoming more and more common, both on the regular stage and in the picture palaces, to caricature Protestant ministers and to introduce on suitable occasions representations of Romish priests and nuns in a most attractive and solemn way. All this is part of a studied and far-reaching propaganda that is insidiously working in our midst to turn this nation toward Rome.

Commercialism has always flourished under the patronage of the popes, and this is another powerful weapon that Rome knows well how to use. Commerce is the goddess of the current feverish age, and to her everything must be sacrificed. And the Babylon of the future is not only a great church but also a great commercial system; to her men will finally turn for the solution of the problems that now perplex them. How largely is union labor today under the power of Rome! And while she is the professed enemy of socialism, she delights to be regarded as the patron of the working classes on the one hand and as the protector of capital on the other. She has a veritable genius for the commercial. "In

Rome," cried Luther, "they sell everything. They would sell the Father, and sell the Son, and sell the Holy Ghost." The stamp of simony is on her brow, and it behooves all who would glorify God to avoid her principles and flee from "the error of Balaam" (Jude 11).

The call of verse 4 is, if I understand it aright, not merely a warning to saints in a coming day who may be in danger of being deceived by her, but it is a message for all who even now discern her true character: "I heard another voice from heaven, saying, Come out of her, my people, that ye be not partakers of her sins, and that ye receive not of her plagues." Separation from evil is imperative for all who would have the Lord's approval. This was the call that the Reformers of the sixteenth century heard. But, alas, alas, many who are supposed to be their successors have returned in spirit to that which their fathers left behind, and many a Babylonish garment today is hidden in Protestant tents or even displayed upon Protestant shoulders. How else can we account for the widespread return to principles and practices once abhorrent to those who boasted, "The Bible and the Bible alone is the religion of Protestants"? Where that Bible is losing its hold upon the consciences of the people (because its inspiration and authority is being so widely denied by those who have solemnly sworn to teach it and defend it) we need not wonder that Babylonish ways and teachings are coming into vogue again. Men want something stable, something infallible; if they cannot have the infallible Word of the living God, they will turn to a professedly infallible church.

But the hour of God's judgment draws on apace. He will not forever be a silent spectator of all of these abominations. Soon, He will pour out the bowls of His wrath upon spiritual Babylon as He did of old upon the city of idolatry on the Euphrates, "For her sins have reached unto heaven, and God hath remembered her iniquities." Then will go forth the sentence,

> Reward her even as she rewarded you, and double unto her double according to her works: in the cup which she hath filled fill to her double. How much she hath glorified herself, and lived deliciously, so much torment and sorrow give her: for she saith in her heart, I sit a queen, and am no widow, and shall see no sorrow. (vv. 6–7)

A comparison of the prophecies of Isaiah and Jeremiah regarding the fall of ancient Babylon will show how plainly the doom of the spiritual counterpart is there prefigured. In several instances, the same identical figures are used, and this has led some commentators to suppose that the doom of the literal city was not final. So some people taught that Babylon is to be rebuilt on her ancient site, to flourish for a few years as the religious and commercial metropolis of the world, only to be again destroyed, and that finally, at or immediately preceding the Lord's second coming. These teachers generally agree in making this restored Babylon the seat of the Antichrist, whom they, as a rule, identify with the future world emperor. But I think we have already shown that a careful comparison of the Old and New Testament Scriptures on these subjects make this view untenable. The city of old has fallen to rise no more. The system that succeeded it is to be judged by God and destroyed as literally as her predecessor, according to the word now before us: "Therefore shall her plagues come in one day, death, and mourning, and famine; and she shall be utterly burned with fire: for strong is the Lord God who judgeth her" (v. 8).

And we learn that although God will use the ten kings and the Beast to bring this about, yet they will themselves bewail her fall when they find to their horror that the whole fabric of civilization is falling with her. Something like this was seen in the days of the French Revolution and has been seen in measure in other lands of late. With the destruction of the church, no matter how corrupt, came the breakup of all social barriers, and a flood of anarchy and violence seemed likely to involve the entire nation in ruin, so that even Napoleon the First saw the necessity of reestablishing the church—though largely shorn of its power—on the ground that a poor religion is better than none at all in holding the masses in restraint.

We can readily understand, therefore, how Babylon's fall will send a thrill of horror through all who have been in any way linked with her, causing the kings of the earth who have enjoyed her favor to bewail her and lament for her when they see the smoke of her burning. Standing afar off, they cry, "Alas, alas, that great city Babylon, that mighty city! for in one hour is thy judgment come." It would seem that coincident with the fall of the system comes the fall of the city where she has had her seat, and that, by some act of God, perhaps such as a great earthquake, will be forever destroyed that proud and haughty capital that has borne the title of "The Eternal City" for two millennia but whose doom is sure because of her impiety and hateful pride. It is a well-known fact that all southern Italy is of a peculiarly volcanic character. The very soil seems to be "stored with fire," to use a scriptural phrase that is applied in 2 Peter 3:7 (literal rendering) to the heavens and earth as a whole. In a very remarkable manner is this true of the vicinity of Rome, and it may yet prove to be the means of its complete destruction. In such a case, the words "the smoke of her burning" may be far more literal than some people have supposed.

This seems to be intensified in the lament of the merchants of the earth in verses 11–19. It is a magnificent elegy and deserves more careful consideration than our limited time will permit. It pictures the destruction of the great commercial system that men are building up with such painstaking care and that some people look upon fondly as the panacea for all of the disturbances that have wrought such distress among the nations. How often was it said before the outbreak of the great world war that labor would not fight and that capital dare not. It was claimed that there was too much at stake. But how false have all such predictions proved. We may, however, be assured that when it is over, for a time, a tremendous effort will be put forth to build up a financial system that will be world embracive and that will unite the nations in the bonds of commercial self-interest so securely that the danger of such another world conflict will be at an end. We know that all such schemes are doomed to disappointment because the prophetic word has clearly foretold their failure. There can be no lasting peace until the Prince of Peace becomes the Governor among the nations.

And so we are permitted in this portion of our book to stand by as it were and look on as Bablyon falls and to hear her merchants bewailing her doom and their own tremendous losses. As her merchandise is tabulated, now with none to buy, we notice among the precious things mentioned are the bodies and souls of men—not merely "slaves," as in the Authorized Version. And this is the awful thing about Babylon. She has made merchandise of the bodies and souls of her dupes, who, turning away from the rich grace revealed in the gospel, have sought to purchase what God was freely offering, only to find at last that they have sold their souls to a cruel and avaricious system that is conscienceless and as remorseless as the grave. How fearful must be the accounting at the judgment bar of God of those responsible for such terrible deceptions!

No wonder Babylon's fall brings joy in heaven, although it involves the earthdwellers in selfish sorrow. "Rejoice over her, thou heaven, and ye holy apostles and prophets; for God hath avenged you on her" (v. 20). She had shed their blood like water, but the vengeance of God, though it seems to slumber long, shall awaken at last, and every upright soul will justify God when He visits her in His wrath and indignation with the judgments here symbolized.

The figure used in Jeremiah 51:63 is repeated in depicting this end. A mighty angel is seen casting into the sea a great stone, like a tremendous millstone (fit symbol indeed of that mysterious power that had crushed the nations and ground the saints of God beneath it for so long). He cast it into the sea, crying,

Thus with violence shall that great city Babylon be thrown down, and shall be found no more at all. And the voice of harpers, and musicians, and of pipers, and trumpeters, shall be heard no more at all in thee; and no craftsman, of whatsoever craft he be, shall be found any more in thee; and the sound of a millstone shall be heard no more at all in thee; and the light of a candle shall shine no more at all in thee; and the voice of the bridegroom and of the bride shall be heard no more at all in thee: for thy merchants were the great men of the earth; for by thy sorceries were all nations deceived. (vv. 21–23)

How solemnly do the angel's words fall on the ear, and how solemnly do they contrast with the lamentations of the merchants of the earth, whose only grief is that no man buys their merchandise any more.

It is the destruction of the greatest schemes and works of man to make way for that which has been in the mind of God and promised through His prophets from the beginning of the world. Cain went out from the presence of the Lord and built a city after the murder of his brother Abel. This was the beginning of man's boasted civilization. All of the arts and sciences had their origin there. There were artificers in brass and iron; trade and barter, the pursuit of the unrighteous mammon began there; and there, too, dwelt those who handled the harp and the organ. Music charmed the weary sons of Cain as they sought to make themselves happy and this world attractive apart from God. The Lord blotted out all of this in the Deluge, but it is evident that Ham, Noah's son, had learned the same ways. In his family, the world as an ordered system of things, apart from God, had a new beginning. Nimrod built a city and a tower, as we have seen, and it became the mother city from whence others went out and built a godless and selfish civilization. That system eventually crucified the Lord of Glory, and His accusation was written above Him in Hebrew, the language of religion; Greek, the language of culture; and Latin, the language of world politics—the world, as such, arrayed against God and His Christ. And this is the world that is to reach its culmination in Babylon the Great, presided over by the greatest geniuses that earth has ever produced but only to be judged by God because of its inveterate enmity to everything holy and its constant rejection of His Son. Its downfall will prepare the way for the establishment of the kingdom of God and the reign of righteousness and peace for which humanity has sighed so long. Man's city must fall to give place to the city of God, which shall stand forever; hence, the joy in heaven at Babylon's destruction.

"And in her," that is, in Babylon, "was found the blood of prophets, and of saints, and of all that were slain upon the earth." This closing verse of chapter 18, I think, should make manifest that although, as I have been trying to show, Rome is the inheritor of the mysteries of ancient Babylon, it also is a world-inclusive system of apostasy. This, and this alone, fully meets the requirements of this last verse. When God makes inquisition for blood, He finds it all shed by this guilty thing, Babylon the Great. Had man not gone out from the presence of the Lord, this earth would never have been stained with human blood; brotherhood and righteousness would everywhere have prevailed. "Babylon," therefore, is guilty of all of the corruption and violence that have darkened the history of the human race; it caused the death of the Christ of God Himself. May grace be given to all to whom this message comes to "flee [from] the midst of Babylon, and deliver every man his soul" (Jer. 51:6).

In the opening verses of chapter 19, we get another look into heaven and can note the exultation that the judgment of the great harlot causes up there:

> And after these things I heard a great voice of much people in heaven, saying, Alleluia; Salvation, and glory, and honour, and power, unto the Lord our God: for true and righteous are his judgments: for he hath judged the great [harlot], which did corrupt the earth with her fornication, and hath avenged the blood of his servants at her hand. And again they said, Alleluia. And her smoke rose up for ever and ever. And the four and twenty elders and the four [living ones] fell down and worshipped God that sat [upon] the throne, saying, Amen; Alleluia. (vv. 1–4)

All of the redeemed of every age, who when on earth knew something of this awful power of iniquity, will then rejoice that it is forever overthrown. This is the last time the twenty-four elders are seen in the book. The symbol changes in the next section, and the bride, the Lamb's wife, takes its place. The elders represent the heavenly saints as a worshiping company of holy and royal priests. But when the harlot-church is off the scene, the true bride appears and the elders are never again mentioned. It is noteworthy that on this their last appearance, as upon their first appearance in chapter 4, they are seen in the attitude of worship. They adore the Lamb as Creator and as Redeemer in chapter 4, and here they adore God as moral Governor of the universe for the display of His righteous judgment.

In response to their note of praise comes a voice from the throne itself, saying, "Praise our God, all ye his servants, and ye that fear him, both small and great."

This concludes the solemn and soul-stirring portion under consideration in which the character and doom of the great mystery of Babylon have been so vividly portrayed. Happier scenes lie before us, scenes, however, that could be introduced only by the judgment of that which had so grievously departed from the living God. Happy will it be for us if we learn to judge not only the unclean system upon which we have been dwelling but also every tendency in ourselves to partake of its spirit.

LECTURE 20

THE TWO SUPPERS

Revelation 19:6–21

We are to be occupied with two opposite scenes on this occasion, one of which is to take place very shortly in heaven and the other on earth. Both events are called *suppers*. The one is the Marriage Supper of the Lamb; the other is the Great Supper of God. The first is all joy and gladness; the second is a scene of deepest gloom and anguish. The Marriage Supper of the Lamb ushers in the fullness of glory for the heavenly saints; the Great Supper of God concludes the series of judgments that are to fall upon the prophetic earth and opens the way for the establishment of the long-awaited kingdom of God.

When I use the term *the prophetic earth*, I refer to the Roman earth; that is, to that portion of the world that lies within what were once the confines of the Roman Empire, and in addition to this, that part of the world where Babylon will hold sway at the time of the end. As I understand it, the heathen nations that have not yet taken professedly Christian ground will not be included in the scene upon which God's heaviest judgments will fall, though necessarily all of the world will suffer in measure when Christendom and Judaism are visited by the fires of His wrath. "The day of God's red heavens" will be worldwide, but its intensity will be upon the prophetic earth.

After the harlot Babylon has passed out of the vision of the apostle, his attention is transferred to heaven, and he tells us,

> I heard as it were the voice of a great multitude, and as the voice of many waters, and as the voice of mighty thunderings, saying, Alleluia: for the Lord God omnipotent reigneth. Let us be glad and rejoice, and give honour to him: for the marriage of the Lamb is come, and his wife hath made herself ready. (vv. 6–7)

The hour for the heavenly nuptials will then have struck. But who is the bride, or the wife of the Lamb, thus mentioned for the first time? Is this special dignity the portion of Israel, or is it that of the church of the current dispensation? Both views have been advocated by godly and able teachers, and one should perhaps speak with diffidence when dwelling on a theme concerning which there has been so much controversy.

In the Old Testament, Israel certainly is the wife of Jehovah, but is that the same thing as "the bride, the Lamb's wife"? Are not two different glories revealed in these two expressions—the one to be manifested on earth and the other in heaven? It seems very plain to me that the Marriage Supper of the Lamb takes place in heaven just before the Lamb descends with all of His saints to take His great power and reign. When He reigns, His bride will reign with Him. And this is certainly the church, which He has called out of the world for that very purpose. There will be other heavenly saints, as we know, but these are distinguished for us from the bride.

It also seems clear that a very real difference exists between the wife of Jehovah (now put away for her sins but to be owned by God as His own in the day of her repentance) and the heavenly bride of the Lamb, the incarnate Son, now espoused as a chaste virgin unto her absent Lord and waiting for her marriage nuptials until He calls her home. But some people have objected to this view as, to use their own words, a kind of spiritual polygamy. My answer would be that where we are speaking only in figures the objection does not apply, and the church, which is His body, is distinctly identified with His wife in Ephesians 5:30–32; otherwise, the figures used there become meaningless. So it seems plain that we are warranted in viewing Israel as the earthly bride and the church as the heavenly bride, both alike dear to His heart who purchased them with His precious blood but each having a special character of her own.

The Marriage Supper of the Lamb is the time of displayed glory, when the results of the judgment seat of Christ will be fully manifested in the saints. That event itself, as we have seen, takes place immediately after the rapture of the church, for the Lord's Word is clear: "Behold, I come quickly; and my reward is with me, to give every man according as his work shall be" (Rev. 22:12). But the full manifestation of the saints in the same glory with their Head and Lord, their heavenly Bridegroom, can only be after the false church has been exposed and judged; then the Lamb's marriage day shall come. And so we are told concerning the bride that "to her was granted that she should be arrayed in fine linen, clean and white: for the fine linen is the righteousness of saints" (v. 8). Students of the original text well know that the word rendered "righteousness" in this verse is in the plural and therefore should be translated "righteousnesses," or "righteous acts." It is not imputed righteousness that is here in view, nor is it the believer being made the righteousness of God in Christ. It is that which we have already seen in connection with the elders; the fine linen sets forth the righteous acts of the saints themselves, right-doing while here on earth that the judgment seat of Christ will make manifest and that will form the wedding garment of the bride on her nuptial day.

In light of this Scripture, we may well be exercised as to our own ways. Are you, dear fellow believer, preparing any fine linen for that coming day? You are no doubt familiar with the thought of the prospective bride's hope chest. How interested the engaged damsel is in preparing beautiful and spotless articles of apparel in view of her wedding day. May I say that we, too, have a spiritual hope chest to fill? Everything that is really done for Christ is something added to that bridal chest. Some of us, I am afraid, will have rather a poor supply. The wedding garments are to be prepared here on earth, as the Spirit of God Himself works in us to will and to do of His good pleasure. Let us not be neglectful of this task because the time is short, and the night cometh when no man can work. It is true that even our very best deeds, our most devoted service, need to be washed and made white in the blood of the Lamb, but He will not fail to value aright and to reward richly everything that was for His own glory in our poor straitened lives. But all that is done for self, all that springs from unholy motives, will disappear in that day whereas that which was the result of His Spirit's working within us will abide forever to His praise and glory and for our own eternal joy as we see what pleasure we have given Him.

But we must now move to verse 9. "And he saith unto me, Write, Blessed are they that are called unto the marriage supper of the Lamb. And he saith unto me, These are the true sayings of God." Here we have a class of people who are certainly to be distinguished from the bride. These are all friends of the Bridegroom, who rejoice in His joy and share in His gladness. I understand them to be the Old Testament saints and the Tribulation saints, who, though they form no part of the church, are sharers in the heavenly glory. They are pictured as wedding guests who participate in the general gladness of the occasion and whose presence, too, adds to the happiness of the bride and Groom. Thus, we have a scene of unalloyed delight and holy mirth, a mirth that shall never have an end because sin shall never enter there to destroy that hallowed joy.

So ravished and enraptured was John's heart as this vision passed before him that he tells us that he fell down to worship at the feet of the angel who showed him these things, only to have the glorious messenger rebuke him for his grave mistake by crying, "See thou do it not; I am a fellow servant with thyself and thy brethren that have the testimony of Jesus: worship God: for the testimony of Jesus is the spirit of prophecy." Our Lord Himself, because He was God, received worship and blessed the worshiper in the case of Thomas when he was convinced of Christ's resurrection, but the angel here scrupulously refuses what belongs to Deity alone.

But the rapidly changing prophetic pictures hurry us on, and neither does time stay. So we ask, What will follow the Marriage Supper of the Lamb? What will be the next great event? Verses 11–16, which I must quote in full, will give the answer.

> And I saw heaven opened [and this is the last of those wondrous "openings" to which I drew attention in an earlier lecture], and behold a white horse; and he that sat upon him was called Faithful and True, and in righteousness he doth judge and make war. His eyes were as a flame of fire, and on his head were many crowns [or, diadems]; and he had a name written, that no man knew, but he himself. And he was clothed with a vesture dipped in blood: and his name is called The Word of God. And the armies which were in heaven followed him upon white horses, clothed in fine linen, white and clean. And out of his mouth goeth a sharp sword, that with it he should smite the nations: and he shall rule them with a rod of iron: and he treadeth the winepress of the fierceness and wrath of Almighty God. And he hath on his vesture and on his thigh a name written, KING OF KINGS, AND LORD OF LORDS.

How the heart thrills and the pulses bound as we read this description of the descending Christ of God and His saints! It is the coming of the Lord to the earth with His redeemed, as before we have been occupied with His coming in the air to rapture them to Himself.

You will remember that we read of a rider on a white horse when the first seal was broken: but that one did not come from heaven. He went forth on the earth and was of the earth, and his plans were doomed to disappointment. This rider, however, comes from heaven, and His plans shall never miscarry. And right here is the safety of the Christian: he knows that no future earth-born man can ever be the Christ for whom the Word has taught him to wait. Jesus came once in lowly guise, born of a woman, albeit a virgin; He comes again, descending from heaven, and all who come in any other way saying, "I am Christ" are but deceivers and antichrists. "As it is appointed unto men once to die [and] after this the judgment: so Christ was once offered to bear the sins of many; and unto them that look for him shall he appear the second time without sin [or, apart from sin, having nothing to do with the sin question], unto salvation" (Heb. 9:28).

This is the appearing that is depicted here. It is the manifestation of the Son of God to take vengeance on His enemies and to deliver His earthly people, who will be looking for Him with longing hearts and eager, anxious eyes. The description of the descending Lord is most striking. He rides a white horse as the Prince of Peace. He is called Faithful and True, as in the message to the church in Laodicea. He comes to execute righteous judgment and thus to establish the divine authority over all the earth. His eyes, as a flame of fire, tell, as in the vision of the Son of Man in the midst of the lampstands, of His readiness to detect and deal with all iniquity. The many diadems upon His head proclaim His authority over all of the kingdoms of the earth. The reign of misrule is to end when He takes the scepter, and all of the crowns are given to Him. "A name written, that no man knew, but he himself" speaks of His essential glory as the Eternal Son, concerning which He declared that "no man knoweth the Son, but the Father" (Matt. 11:27). The mystery of His glorious person is beyond all human ken. We rightly sing,

> The Father only Thy blest name
> Of Son can comprehend.

His garments are to be reddened with the blood of His enemies, as we are told by the prophet Isaiah, but the vesture dipped in blood with which He is here seen clothed, is, I take it, like the rams' skins, dyed red in the tabernacle, the sign of His consecration unto death. It is His own blood that is here in view, the price of our redemption.

It is noteworthy that He is said to have three names. One, we have already seen, is beyond man's comprehension. The second name is "The Word of God." And we know what is involved in that because it is as "the Word made" or, more literally, "become flesh" that He has revealed God to us. That Word was spoken in time, of which we read, "In the beginning was the Word, and the Word was with God, and the Word was God. The same was in the beginning with God" (John 1:1–2). Here we have eternity of Being, one Substance with the Father, but distinct Personality— true Deity and eternal Sonship. This was the Word unspoken; but when the Son became incarnate, God spoke in Him, according to the first chapter of Hebrews, and so we read, "No man hath seen God at any time, the only begotten Son, which is in the bosom of the Father, he hath [revealed] him," or "told him out" (John 1:18). This is just a little of what is involved in this second glorious name.

So as not to break the connection, we might look now at the third name or title that He bears. Verse 16 tells us that "He hath on his vesture and on his thigh a name written, KING OF KINGS, AND LORD OF LORDS." This is His official title, and it belongs to Him as Son of Man, the rightful Heir of all things. Earth would not recognize His claims when He was here the first time, and in derision they crowned Him with thorns and gave Him a cross instead of a throne; but soon God is going to reverse all of that. He is to "be exalted and extolled, and be very high" (Isa. 52:13). All of the kingdoms of earth are to be His, and He will rule the nations with the iron rod of unswerving justice.

Notice, then, that in these three names we have set forth, first, our Lord's dignity as the Eternal Son; second, His incarnation—the Word become flesh; and last, His second advent to reign as King of Kings and Lord of Lords.

The armies in heaven who follow Him comprise (1) the church, which we have just seen as the bride; (2) the saints of former dispensations; and (3) the Tribulation saints who had been slain under the Beast and the Antichrist. All of them ride forth with Him, their now triumphant Lord, when He comes to take His great power and reign.

The sharp sword that proceeds from His mouth is His word. This we have already seen in the first chapter, and we remember His warning to the church in Thyatira, that if they did not repent He would fight against them with the sword of His mouth.

We are told that He treads the winepress of the wrath of God. The winepress is the figure of unsparing judgment. This we have also become familiar with in chapter 14. In Isaiah 63:1–6, we have a remarkable passage that bears on what we have here:

> Who is this that cometh from Edom, with dyed garments from Bozrah?
> this that is glorious in his apparel, traveling in the greatness of his

strength? I that speak in righteousness, mighty to save. Wherefore art thou red in thine apparel, and thy garments like him that treadeth in the [winefat]? I have trodden the winepress alone; and of the people there was none with me: for I will tread them in mine anger, and trample them in my fury; and their blood shall be sprinkled upon my garments, and I will stain all my raiment. For the day of vengeance is in [my] heart, and the year of my redeemed is come. And I looked, and there was none to help; and I wondered that there was none to uphold: therefore mine own arm brought salvation unto me; and my fury, it upheld me. And I will tread down the people in mine anger, and make them drunk in my fury, and I will bring down their strength to the earth.

This marvelous prophecy, which had a partial fulfillment in judgments meted out to Israel's foes in the past, will have its complete fulfillment when the Lord comes the second time to tread the winepress of wrath and to destroy all who are His own and His people's foes, as depicted in the last part of our chapter.

From verse 17 to the end, we have a graphic portrayal by the Master-Artist of the closing scene of judgment—the Great Supper of God—because it is not exactly "the supper of the great God." The adjective has become transposed in our English version and is there made to qualify God Himself whereas, as any critical version will show, it should rather qualify the supper. An angel standing in the sun (the source of light that seemed to be blotted out under the bowls of wrath is now seen resplendent in glory) summons the fowls of the air that fly in the midst of heaven to feast upon the flesh of the great ones of earth and their vast armies who are seen gathering together for the Armageddon conflict, the location of which we previously noticed.

The Beast is seen marshalling his hosts, and with him his blasphemous ally and satellite, the False Prophet—that is, the Antichrist. The kings of the earth, with all of their hordes, are hurrying to the fray, all combining in one last desperate effort to make successful war against the Lord Jesus Christ and everything that is of God. But, like the hosts of Sennacherib of old, they are palsied and stricken by the blast of His mouth, and their armies become food for the birds of prey. It is an awful picture—the climax of man's audacious resistance to God—a picture, too, that may fill the heart with gladness as it tells of the end of unrighteous rule on this planet and the ushering in of the Golden Age for which all nations have sighed.

Note that two men are taken alive. They are the two arch-conspirators who have been so prominent in this book—the Beast and the False Prophet, the civil and religious leaders of the last league of nations, which will be Satan inspired in its origin and Satan directed until its doom. These two men are "cast alive into [the lake burning with fire and brimstone]," where a thousand years later they are still said to be "suffering the vengeance of eternal fire" (Jude 7), thus incidentally proving that the lake of fire is neither annihilation nor purgatorial because it neither annihilates nor purifies these two fallen foes of God and man even after a thousand years under judgment.

In the Old Testament, we read of two men who went to heaven without passing through death; Enoch and Elijah were translated that they should not see death. And here, before we come to the close of the New Testament, we have two men brought before us who are cast into hell fire without undergoing physical death. Their awful doom is for the warning of all who turn away from Him who speaks from heaven, whose indignation is soon to fall upon all who refuse the message of His grace.

> Lamb of God, when Thou in glory
> Shalt to this sad earth return,
> All Thy foes shall quake before Thee,
> All that now despise Thee, mourn;
> Then shall we, at Thine appearing,
> With Thee in Thy kingdom reign:
> Thine the praise and Thine the glory,
> Lamb of God, for sinners slain.

And now as I close, I would seek solemnly to impress upon each of my hearers that *you* may have a part in one or the other of these two Suppers that we have been considering. If you are saved, I know that you will have a place at the Marriage Supper of the Lamb because every blood-redeemed one of this dispensation will be there. Not one will be missing because our blessed Lord, in grace, became the Lamb of God to die for your sins upon the Cross, and you will share in that scene of bliss with Him. But you who refuse His grace, what will you do when the things of which we have been speaking take place? You might be among those deceived by Satan, accepting the leadership of the Beast and the claims of the Antichrist. In that case, you would have part in "the great Supper of God!" May God draw you to Himself now. Resist not the pleadings of the Holy Spirit, but flee at once for refuge to Him who said, "Him that cometh to me I will in no wise cast out" (John 6:37).

THE MILLENNIUM AND THE GREAT WHITE THRONE JUDGMENT

Revelation 20

Those who object to the doctrine of an earthly Millennium often say that the term itself is not found in the Bible. They insist that in neither the Old nor the New Testament do we ever read of a millennium, and they argue from this fact that the teaching is manmade, not derived from the Word of God. We might reply that the mere fact that a certain *term* is not used in Scripture does not necessarily prove that the *doctrine* for which the term stands is not taught there. The word *trinity* is not found in the Bible, but all sound Christians admit the doctrine of one God in three persons. The word *substitution* is not there either, but it is written, "He was wounded for our transgressions," and that is substitution. Where will you find the terms *eternal sonship, deity, fall of man, depravity, incarnation, impeccability* (as applied to Christ), and many more terms of similar character? Certainly not on the pages of the Authorized Version of our English Bibles. But all of these terms stand for great truths that are unmistakably taught in the Book and are a vital part of the teaching of Christianity. So the mere omission of a title or name of a doctrine does not prove the absence of the doctrine itself, nor does it prove that it is but manmade.

However, we are not shut up to reasoning of this kind regarding the Millennium because the word in question is but the Latin equivalent of an expression that is found *six times* in the chapter that now demands our attention. It simply means "a thousand years," just as *century* means "one hundred years," or *jubilee* indicates the expiration of fifty years.

A millennium, then, is a time period. It does not necessarily carry with it any thought of perfection or happiness nor of an era of manifested divine government. Six millennia have almost elapsed since God put man upon this globe, and another millennium and a fraction is yet to run before the course of time is finished. That last thousand years is the period with which we are now to be occupied, and I trust to show that it is the predicted kingdom age of the prophets and the "dispensation of the fulness of times" (Eph. 1:10) of the New Testament. It is not in only what some people have called an obscure passage in the Revelation that we read of this "good time coming"; it is taught everywhere in Scripture.

The binding of Satan, the arch foe of God and man, is the first notable event of this reign of righteousness. The seer says,

> And I saw an angel come down from heaven, having the key of the bottomless pit [or, the Abyss] and a great chain in his hand. And he laid hold of the dragon, that old serpent, which is the Devil, and Satan, and bound him a *thousand years,* and cast him into the bottomless pit, and shut him up, and set a seal upon him, that he should deceive the nations no more, till the *thousand years* should be fulfilled, and after that he must be loosed a little season. (vv. 1–3 emphasis added)

Without attempting to explain all of the symbols here used, it is enough to say that the passage very definitely indicates that there is a coming time when men will no longer be deceived and led astray by the great tempter who, ever since his victory over our first parents in Eden, has been the persistent and malignant foe of mankind and by whose wiles untold millions have been defrauded of their birthright privileges. If men sin during the Millennium, it will not be on account of having been deceived; it will be simply because of self-will and their yielding to the lusts of their own hearts. We must remember that the kingdom age is not to be a dispensation of sinlessness. There will be some people, even in that blessed time, who will dare to act in defiance of the will of God, but such will soon be dealt with in condign judgment. Such cases will, I take it, be very exceptional, but Scripture makes plain that there will be offences even when God's King reigns over the earth.

In the current dispensation of grace, those who will live godly in Christ Jesus suffer persecution; righteousness *suffers*. But in the Millennium, righteousness will *reign:* "A King shall reign in righteousness." In the eternal state, which follows the Millennium, righteousness will *dwell.* It will be at home, and every adverse thing will be forever banished from the new heavens and the new earth.

Daniel prophesied of the time coming when "the saints . . . [will] possess the kingdom" (7:18). To this agree the words of verse 4: "And I saw thrones, and they sat upon them, and judgment was given unto them: and I saw the souls of them that were beheaded for the witness of Jesus, and for the word of God, and which had not worshiped the beast, . . . and they lived and reigned with Christ a *thousand years.*"

We have here, if I understand the passage aright, the last cohort of the first resurrection. With our Lord Himself, the saints raised at the rapture of the church, and the witnessing remnant that were slain and raised up in the last, the seventieth, week of Daniel, they all share in the "administration of the fulness of the seasons," as the late William Kelly translated the expression rendered in our Bibles "the dispensation of the fulness of times." These saints appear in glory with the Lord, but we are not to understand by that fact that either He or they are to return to earth to live. Their relationship to the earth will be, I presume, very much like that of the angels in the patriarchal dispensation—able to appear and disappear at will and exercising a benevolent oversight on behalf of those who live in this scene. "Unto the angels hath he not put [into] subjection the world to come, whereof we speak" (Heb. 2:5). That world will be subjected to the Son of Man, and associated with Him will be all who have shared with Him in His rejection. These are the thronesitters first mentioned. With them will be the rest of the Tribulation saints, who will suffer death rather than deny their God in the awful days of Antichrist's ascendancy. Their rapture will be when the Lord appears for the establishment of the kingdom.

"But the rest of the dead," we are told in the verse that follows, "lived not again until the *thousand years* were finished. This is the first resurrection." This does not militate against the teaching already advanced that the first cohort of the first resurrection will be summoned from their graves before the Tribulation and the second in the midst of that time of trouble; rather, we have here a summary. All of these classes together make up the first resurrection—the resurrection of life—which is thus distinguished from the resurrection of judgment. Between these two will elapse the entire millennial age. The unsaved will remain in their graves until the heavens and the earth pass away. Their souls in hades (erroneously rendered "hell" in our version but really the state between death and resurrection) and their bodies in the grave, they await the day of judgment at the end of time.

"Blessed and holy is he that hath part in the first resurrection: on such the second death hath no power, but they shall be priests of God and of Christ, and shall reign with him a *thousand years*" (v. 6). This is the kingdom described in such glowing terms by Isaiah, who throughout his entire prophecy sees, through faith's telescope, the glorious time when Israel and Judah shall be one people in their own land, restored in soul to God, every man dwelling in peace under his own vine and fig tree, and the glory of the Lord covering the earth as the waters cover the sea. He tells how even nature itself shall respond to Messiah's rule, and the wilderness and the solitary place shall be glad for them, and the desert shall rejoice and blossom as the rose. The brute creation, too, shall be delivered from the Curse. They shall not hurt nor destroy in all God's holy mountain. The lion shall eat straw like the ox. The lamb shall lie down with the lion, and "a little child shall lead them" (Isa. 11:6). All nations will then ask the way to Zion, and Jerusalem shall become the metropolis of not only a rejuvenated Palestine but also the whole earth.

Jeremiah takes up the same happy strain and foresees the God of Israel sending "fishers" out into the sea of the nations, fishing out His people no matter where they may be hidden and bringing them back to the land of their fathers. He sees the city built again and inhabited by a peaceful, happy nation under the reign of the righteous *Branch* whom God has promised to raise up unto David, and "in his days Judah shall be saved, and Israel shall dwell safely: and this is his name whereby he shall be called, THE LORD OUR RIGHTEOUSNESS" (Jer. 23:6). Then they shall no longer need to "teach every man his neighbor, and every man his brother, saying, Know the Lord: for [they shall all] know [him], from the least to the greatest [of them]" (Heb. 8:11).

Ezekiel adds to the wondrous story, tells of the Spirit's being poured out from on high, and *describes* the service of the regenerated Israel, a priestly nation, through whom the Law of God goes forth to all of the lands of the nations. He depicts the millennial temple, even tells us how the land is to be divided among the tribes, and does not close his remarkable book until he can say, "The name of the city from that day shall be, [*Jehovah-Shammah*] The LORD is there" (Ezek. 48:35).

All of the visions of Daniel's companion apocalypse conclude with the bringing in of the fifth universal kingdom, and this, he tells us, is the kingdom of the Son of Man, which is to displace every other and is to stand forever. This is the Stone cut out without hands that falls upon the feet of the Gentile image and grinds it to powder, and then it becomes a great mountain and fills the *whole earth*. This is the kingdom conferred upon the Son of Man by the Ancient of Days when the bodies of the beasts (symbolizing the four great empires that have borne rule over all of the civilized earth) shall be cast into the burning flame.

Hosea shows how Messiah would come in lowly grace, but, rejected by Israel, He would go and return to His place until they acknowledged their sin and sought His face, when He will return to restore their souls and to ransom them from the power of the grave, bringing in everlasting righteousness and making them a blessing to all nations.

Joel sees the Great Tribulation in all of its intensity but beholds the glory that shall follow and predicts the outpouring of the Spirit on not only Israel but also all flesh.

Amos bears witness to the gathering again of the outcasts of Israel and their resettlement in their land under Jehovah's perfect rule.

Obadiah, who wrote the shortest of all of the prophecies, although he speaks chiefly of judgment upon Edom, declares triumphantly, "The kingdom shall be the Lord's" (v. 21).

Of all of the prophetic brotherhood, only Jonah seems to include no reference to that day of Jehovah's power; yet, we may learn through him how wonderfully God will own the testimony of Hebrew missionaries in the beginning of the kingdom age, as they go forth to spread the gospel among those who have neither heard His fame nor seen His glory.

But Micah joins with Isaiah in describing the time when "the mountain of the LORD's house shall be established in the top of the mountains, . . . and all nations shall flow unto it" (Isa. 2:2) when "the law shall go forth [from] Zion, and the word of the LORD from Jerusalem" (Mic. 4:2). Then "the nations . . . shall beat their swords into plowshares, and their spears into pruninghooks . . . and shall learn war [no] more" (Isa. 2:4).

Nahum predicts the judgments that shall befall the enemies of Jehovah in the day of His preparation while Habakkuk, standing on his watchtower, sees the coming King bringing in the glory.

Zephaniah and Haggai point onward to the restoration of Israel and, through them, the blessing of the whole world when the Lord their God is enthroned in the midst of them and they serve Him with one consent.

Zechariah, the prophet of glory, gives minute details that no others have touched upon and even tells of the provision to be made for children's playgrounds in the restored capital of Palestine because he says, "The broad places of the city shall be full of boys and girls, playing in the broad places thereof" (Zech. 8:5, literal rendering). He sees every spot in Jerusalem as holy to the Lord and all nations wending their way thitherward from year to year to keep the feast of the tabernacles. And Malachi completes the series and announces the soon-coming of the King, heralded by the prophet Elijah, to tread down the wicked and sit as a refiner of silver to purify the sons of Levi and to make His name great from the rising of the sun to the going down of the same.

Thus, "to him give all the prophets witness" (Acts 10:43), not only that through His name remission of sins is now to be proclaimed among all nations but also that He is to reign in righteousness over all the world when He comes the second time to claim the inheritance that is His by divine fiat, as Son and Heir of all things. Then will all the earth rejoice. The eyes of the blind shall be opened, the tongue of the dumb shall sing, the lame man shall leap as the hart, sorrow and sighing shall flee away, and the Lord alone shall be exalted for a thousand glorious years!

> And when the *thousand years* are expired, Satan shall be loosed out of his prison, and shall go out to deceive the nations which are in the four quarters of the earth, Gog and Magog, to gather them together to battle: the number of whom is as the sand of the sea. And they went up on the breadth of the earth, and compassed the camp of the saints about, and the beloved city: and fire came down from God out of heaven, and devoured them. And the devil that deceived them was cast into the lake of fire and brimstone, where the beast and the false prophet are, and shall be tormented day and night for ever and ever. (vv. 7–10)

This is indeed an amazing anticlimax to the story of human life on this earth. Who but God could have foreseen such an ending? But it shows us the incorrigible evil of the heart of man if he is left to himself. While Satan is shut up in the Abyss, many people will be born into the world whose obedience to the King will be only feigned; their hearts will not be in it. When the Devil is loosed for a little season at the end of the Millennium, he finds a host of these people ready to do his bidding and to join him in the last great rebellion against Omnipotence.

It is the old story of satanic hatred to God, and man's frailty told out again, but this time under the most favorable circumstances as far as man is concerned. Therefore, his sin is absolutely inexcusable. Tested *in the garden of delight* man broke through the only prohibition laid upon him. Tested under *conscience*, corruption and violence filled the earth, and the scene had to be cleared by the deluge. Tested under the restraining influence of divinely appointed *government,* man went into idolatry, thus turning his back upon his Creator. Tested under *law,* he cast off all restraint and crucified the Lord of Glory. Tested under *grace* in this current dispensation of the Holy Spirit, he has shown himself utterly unable to appreciate such mercy and has rejected the gospel and gone ever deeper into sin. Tested under the *personal reign* of the Lord Jesus Christ for a thousand years, some people will be ready to listen to the voice of the tempter when, at the close, he ascends from the pit of the Abyss bent upon one last defiant effort to thwart the purpose of God. It is a melancholy history indeed and emphasizes the truth that the heart of man is incurably evil. "The carnal mind . . . is not subject to the law of God, neither indeed can be" (Rom. 8:7); therefore, the need, in all ages, of a second birth through the Word and the Spirit of God.

"The heavens and the earth [that] are now, . . ." we are told by the apostle Peter, "[are] reserved unto fire against the [judgment of the great day]" (2 Peter 3:7). This pent-up fire that breaks forth from the heavens will destroy the hosts of Satan's dupes and purify the very globe itself, as once before it was cleansed by water. This event closes the course of time and introduces the unending ages of eternity, during which the Devil will be confined in the great prisonhouse of the lost, who have resisted God's mercy and spurned His grace. What an end for him who was once "the anointed cherub" (Ezek. 28:14) that covered the throne of God but whose heart was lifted up because of his beauty and who, thus falling through pride, became the most accursed creature in all of the universe of God! Our Lord tells us that the Devil "abode not in the truth" (John 8:44). He is the prince of all apostates, and apostasy has ever been the great sin into which he has malignantly sought to lead the human race.

The Great White Throne Judgment is the final scene before the new heavens and the new earth are introduced. It is, as a careful study makes exceedingly clear, not "the general judgment" at the end of the world, as many people have supposed, but the judgment of the wicked who, during Christ's reign of a thousand years, have been left in the realms of the dead. The righteous who share in heavenly glory are to be manifested, as we have seen, at the judgment seat of Christ, there to be rewarded according to their service while in this world; the living nations will be summoned to appear before the Son of Man when He comes in His glory at the beginning of the Millennium, as Matthew 25 makes clear. The wicked dead are to be raised at the end of that reign of righteousness and dealt with according to their works. The condemnation now is that men reject the Lord Jesus Christ, who has made full atonement for sin that all may be freed from wrath through Him. But if He is rejected finally, of very necessity men must face the penalty of sin themselves.

Solemn indeed is the description of that last great assize.

> And I saw a great white throne, and him that sat on it, from whose face the earth and the heaven fled away; and there was found no place for them. And I saw the dead, small and great, stand before God; and the books were opened: and another book was opened, which is the book of life: and the dead were judged out of those things which were written in the books, according to their works. And the sea gave up the dead which were in it; and death and hell [or, correctly, *hades*—the unseen world, the abode of departed spirits] delivered up the dead which were in them: and they were judged [everyone] according to their works. And death and hell [*hades*] were cast [literally, emptied] into the lake of fire. This is the second death. And whosoever was not found written in the book of life was cast into the lake of fire. (vv. 11–15)

We know from other Scriptures that the august occupant of the throne will be none other than our Lord Jesus Christ because "the Father judgeth no man, but hath committed all judgment unto the Son: that all men should honour the Son, even as they honour the Father" (John 5:22–23). He who once hung on Calvary's Cross is to be the judge of both the living and the dead. We have already been largely occupied with the first aspect of the judgment. It is, as we have already mentioned, the doom of the wicked dead that now engages our attention.

When the throne is set, the heavens and the earth as we now know them shrink away, as though the material universe were awed by the face of Him who summons the dead to their accounting. What a sea of faces will appear before Him in that solemn hour of tremendous import! All of the lost of all of the ages, all who preferred their sins to His salvation, all who procrastinated until for them the door of mercy was closed, all who spurned His grace and in self-will chose the way "[that] seemeth right unto a man" but that was in truth "the way of death" (Prov. 14:12; 16:25)—all such people are to be summoned to stand before that inexorably righteous throne. No condoning of sin then and no palliating or excusing in that day because the judgment of God will be according to truth, and every circumstance shall be taken into account. Nothing shall be overlooked. Therefore, some people will be beaten with many stripes and others with few stripes, according to the measure of light given and rejected. "The

Judge of all the earth shall do right" (see Gen. 18:25). And there shall be no appeal from His decisions because His court is the Supreme Court of the Universe. "What a magnificent conception," exclaims Thomas Carlyle, "is that of a last judgment! A righting of all the wrongs of the ages." And, I may add, the tracing back of every evil act to its source, and the placing of responsibility for every offence against the moral law, where it belongs.

No one will be great enough to escape that assize; no one will be too insignificant as to be overlooked. The dead, both "small and great," will be there. Although their bodies have been buried for centuries—yea, for millennia—in the depths of the sea, they shall come forth at His bidding, who when He speaks will not be denied. Death, the grave that has claimed what was mortal of man, his body, will give up its prey. Hades, the world unseen, will surrender the undying spirits and souls of the lost. With his body, soul, and spirit reunited, the man will stand trembling before the judgment bar. The books of record will be opened. Memory will respond to every charge. The Word of God, too, will be opened there because Jesus declared that both Moses' words and His words will judge men in the last day. And the Book of Life will be unfolded there, too, because many people in that vast throng have taken for granted that their names are there because, perchance, they have been listed on the roll of some church or religious society. Let them search and look; it will bear witness against them. The Lamb has not inscribed their name in that book. "And whosoever was not found written" in that book will be "cast into the lake of fire."

Will any people be saved who stand before the Great White Throne? Not one, if we read the account aright because death and hades are to be "[emptied] into the lake of fire." All of the lost, whose spirits and bodies they have held in durance so long, will be emptied out into the pit of woe. And God's Word says, "This is the second death." Death is the separation of body and spirit, we are told in James 2:26. The second death is the final separation of the lost from God, who created man. Like living planets, which, possessed of will, have swung out of their orbits, they dash off into the outer darkness, never to find their way back to that great central Sun.

The lake of fire is the symbol of sorrow immeasurable and of torment eternal. It is a divine picture intended to make the soul of the sinner shrink with dread as he contemplates the end of those who obey not the gospel. It is human character made permanent, abiding in eternal sin, and therefore under the wrath of God forever. Not until Judas Iscariot and John the Beloved, who wrote this book, clasp hands in heavenly glory, will the woes of the wicked come to an end. As to Judas, the Master he betrayed has declared, "[It were good] for that man if he had never been born" (Mark 14:21). Were there salvation ahead at last, even after ages of suffering, as another commentator has strikingly pointed out, even Judas might well thank God that he had ever been permitted to live. But over the portals of the lost they inscribed of old, "Abandon hope, ye who enter here."

Now is the time acceptable. Now a gracious Savior waits to catch the first breath of repentance, and He answers the feeblest cry of faith. Trifle not with His mercy and hope not for some vague second chance, but close with Christ now, and know for a certainty that you will have no part in the doom pronounced at the Great White Throne. The Lord Himself has said, "Verily, verily, I say unto you, he that heareth my word, and believeth him that sent me, hath eternal life, and cometh not into judgement, but hath passed out of death into life" (John 5–24 RV).

CLOSING SCENES

Revelation 21–22

My desire in this final address of the current series is to outline briefly the truth presented so vividly in these last two chapters, which include three distinct divisions. In chapter 21:1–8, we have the eternal issues. In verses 9–27 and the first five verses of chapter 22, we have a supplementary portion giving us a detailed symbolic description of the Holy Jerusalem, the city of God, holding sway over the earth during the Millennium. Then, from 22:6 to the end of the book, we have the divine epilogue, consisting mainly of practical messages from the glorified Lord to all of those to whom this book may come in the course of time.

Regarding the first division, it is important to note that prophecy does not properly relate to the eternal state. It is particularly occupied with this earth up to and including the Millennium. Only occasionally do we find in the prophetic Scriptures any reference to the unending ages that are to follow. Here we are told, "And I saw a new heaven and a new earth: for the first heaven and the first earth were passed away; and there was no more sea" (v. 1). This reminds us of Isaiah's prophecy, "For, behold, I create new heavens and a new earth: and the former shall not be remembered, nor come into mind" (Isa. 65:17), and in 66:22, Isaiah says, "For as the new heavens and the new earth, which I will make, shall remain before me, saith the LORD, so shall your seed and your name remain." Now the two chapters from which these verses are quoted have to do with the Millennium, but I take it that we have here faith's telescope looking out, even in that past dispensation, to the unchanging and unchangeable condition that shall abide forever. I have no doubt that it is to these promises that the apostle Peter refers in his second epistle. After describing the destruction by fire of the heavens and the earth that now are, he says, "Nevertheless we, according to his promise, look for new heavens and a new earth, wherein dwelleth righteousness" (3:13).

This, then, is the glorious consummation to which the opening verses of our current chapter introduce us. And the most marvelous object of that unending condition, next to the blessed Lord Himself, will be the church that has been redeemed to God by the precious blood of His Son. Observe that the bridal condition does not cease at the close of the Millennium. Verse 2 says, "And I John saw the Holy City, new Jerusalem, coming down from God out of heaven, prepared as a bride adorned for her husband." A thousand years of the reign of righteousness will have rolled by before the fulfillment of this verse, and yet the Holy City is seen in all of the freshness and loveliness of an adorned bride. And this happy state will abide forever because the next two verses describe a scene of blissful communion that is never to be terminated.

> And I heard a great voice out of heaven saying, Behold, the tabernacle of God is with men, and he will dwell with them, and they shall be his people, and God himself shall be with them, and be their God. And God shall wipe away all tears from their eyes; and there shall be no more death, neither sorrow, nor crying, neither shall there be any more pain: for the former things are passed away. (vv. 3–4)

The passage is beautiful in its simplicity, and comment would only seem to be like an attempt to paint the rose. How longingly must every believing heart look forward to that glorious day!

A voice from the throne cries, "Behold, I make all things new." And John is again commanded to write, and assured that "these words are true and faithful." The voice then exclaims solemnly, "It is done. I am Alpha and Omega, the beginning and the end." It is the proclamation that all of the ways of God have found their final issue in the full glory of His blessed Son, who is the first and the last.

In verse 8, we are told of those who shall never enter the Holy City and who will have no part in the bright glories depicted earlier. But, before giving the awful list, the Lord graciously extends another gospel invitation, that all to whom these words shall come may know that there is mercy still if they will but avail themselves of it. "I will give unto him that is athirst," He says, "of the fountain of the water of life freely." And He follows this with a word of encouragement to the overcomer, "He that overcometh shall inherit all things; and I will be his God, and he shall be my son." The world might bid for us now, and the treacherous flesh within might seek to act in concert with that world and its god, and thus woo our souls from Christ, but who with the glorious promises of this book before him, but must long to rise above the power of current things, and, in the energy of the Holy Spirit overcome the world by faith, in view of what He is preparing for those who love Him!

How gladly would we believe that not one soul of man will fail of the joy that is kept in store for those who know Christ; but, alas, alas, sin has made this impossible of realization; so this part of our chapter closes with the tremendously solemn announcement that "the fearful, and unbelieving, and the abominable, and murderers, and whoremongers, and sorcerers, and idolaters, and all liars, shall have their part in the lake which burneth with fire and brimstone: which is the second death" (v. 8). The list includes not only those who are generally looked upon as discreditable sinners but also the cowardly—those who were fearful of confessing Christ because, perhaps, of the sneers of professed friends or the consequences of turning from the world—together with the unbelieving, who refused to credit the testimony that God had given and to rest their souls upon the work of Christ—these both are linked with the unclean and unholy of all classes. Inasmuch as "all have sinned, and come short of the glory of God" (Rom. 3:23), there can be no difference in their final doom if Christ is rejected, although, as we have already noted in our last lecture, every transgression and disobedience will receive its just recompense of reward.

Beginning with the ninth verse, we have a marvelous description of the New Jerusalem. Note that this comes upon the conclusion of the prophetic outline. It is a kind of appendix or supplementary description. Just as one of the seven angels that had the seven bowls full of the seven last plagues gave to John a vision of Babylon the Great in chapters 17–18, so here one of the same angels now bids him come and view the bride, the Lamb's wife. Carrying him away in the Spirit to a great and high mountain, he shows him that great city, the holy Jerusalem, descending out of heaven from God. Babylon was both a city and a woman—both a great system and a company of people professing to be in bridal relation with the Lamb, so here the holy Jerusalem is both a city and a woman. The city is the bride as well as the home of the saints, just as we speak of Rome both when we mean the church that has her seat there and when we mean the city where she sits.

By this great city *descending* out of heaven from God, I understand then the diffusion of heavenly principles by the heavenly saints because through His saints over all of this earth during the Millennium the Lord is going to claim His inheritance. We may learn in this symbolic description of the city the great guiding principles that are to hold full sway in that coming age and that are full of instruction for us now. The city has the glory of God, and her light is described as "like unto a stone most precious, even like a jasper stone, clear as crystal" (v. 11). The church is to be the vessel for the display of the glory of God throughout that age of righteousness, and, indeed, as verse 2 has already informed us, throughout all of the ages to come. The "wall great and high" speaks of separation, a divine principle that runs throughout the Word of God, from the time that sin entered to the close. A wall is for protection, too, and the separation of God's people is not an arbitrary principle, to their discomfort, as some people seem to think, but it is manifestly for their blessing and protecting them from the evil without. Although the wall is great and high, it has twelve gates, the number of administrative completeness, and the gate itself, you will remember, is in Scripture the place of judgment. So the thought would seem to be that we have here righteousness reigning and provision made for entrance and egress, holy and happy liberty in accord with the holiness of God's nature. At the gates are twelve angels, divine messengers, and on the gates are written the names of the twelve tribes of the children of Israel. In the Millennium, government is to be maintained, as we have already seen, through God's earthly people being restored to their own land and to unbroken fellowship with the Lord. Thus, the heavens will respond to God's earthly people, Jezreel (the seed of God), in a way that means blessing for all of the world. Three gates on each of the four sides of the city speak of the universality of the divine government thus fully manifested.

The wall, we are told, had twelve foundations, and in them the names of the twelve apostles of the Lamb. This fact accords strikingly with our Lord's promise to the Twelve that, inasmuch as they had followed Him in His rejection, when the day of the earth's regeneration comes they will sit upon twelve thrones, judging the twelve tribes of Israel. Just as in Ephesians 2 the church is pictured as a holy temple, built upon the foundation of the apostles and prophets, so here the Holy City rests upon the chosen messengers, who are to be the representatives of that authority in the age to come.

The angel who talked with John measured the city with a golden reed, and the dimensions are given in verses 16–17: "And the city lieth foursquare," the length being equal to the breadth, and this, in each instance, is twelve thousand furlongs, while the wall itself is 144 cubits high. We are told that the length, the breadth, and the height of the city are equal. It has been suggested from this that the city is a cube, which may indeed be, but I frankly confess that I find the symbolism in that case exceedingly difficult to visualize before the mind's eye. I rather think of that Holy City as the mountain of God, a vast pyramid resting on a foursquare base, twelve thousand furlongs each way, and rising to a height as great as its length and breadth, the throne of God and of the Lamb being the very apex of it, from which flows the river of the Water of Life, winding about the mountain in the midst of the one street of gold on either side of that river. In either case, whether we think of a cube or a pyramid, the thought is the same: it is a city of absolute perfection. Twelve, the number, as previously mentioned, of governmental completeness, is seen everywhere. Who can attempt to depict any more clearly than the verses themselves describe it a city whose wall is of jasper—the glory of God built of pure gold, like unto clear glass—the divine glory maintained by righteousness.

The foundations of the wall are garnished with all manner of precious stones, answering to the stones seen in the breastplate of the high priest. These tell of the particular and peculiar preciousness that each believer has in the eyes of the Lord.

The twelve gates are twelve pearls, every several gate of one pearl, thus reminding us at every entranceway of that one pearl of great price for which our Lord, the heavenly merchantman, sold all that He had with which to buy the church because, although He was rich, yet He became poor that He might make it His own forever.

The street of pure gold reminds us that our feet shall stand on the righteousness of God forever; in His justice, we shall stand and walk forever. It is not mere mercy that is the ground of our salvation, but God's glory has been fully and righteously maintained in the work of Calvary's Cross, and thus He is faithful and just in receiving all who trust His Son.

Whereas on earth the church is pictured as a holy temple unto the Lord, in that day there will be no temple seen because the Lord God Almighty and the Lamb are the temple of it. Nearness to God will characterize every saint; none will be shut out. Our Lord said, "Thou . . . hast loved them, as thou hast loved me" (John 17:23), so that we can sing even now,

> So near, so very near to God,
> I could not nearer be;

> For in the person of His Son,
> I am as near as He.

And when we get home there will be no separating veil, no outer court, beyond which we dare not come, but we shall all be at home with God and the Lamb forevermore. That city will have no need of created lightbearers such as the sun and the moon to shine in it. Those bodies are for this world, not for that which is to come. The glory of God will be the light, everywhere displayed, and the Lamb Himself is the lamp thereof. The rendering "the Lamb is the *light*" hardly conveys the full thought. The glory of God is the light, and the Lamb is the One on whom that glory is centralized; He is the *lamp* from which it all shines. The glory of God in the face of Christ Jesus is our light even now, a light that has shone into our darkened hearts, and that light we will enjoy eternally in the home of the saints above. The nations that are spared to enter the millennial kingdom shall walk in its light, and all of earth's rulers will bring their glory and honor unto that throne city and light their tapers at that celestial fire.

The gates, we are told, shall not be shut at all by day, and night will be unknown there. I do not dwell on this fact now because we have the same expression repeated in the next chapter. In that city of holiness and blessing, no unclean thing shall ever enter to defile. No deceiving serpent shall enter that paradise of God, nor will any who manifest kinship with Satan, the father of lies. Only those who are written in the Lamb's Book of Life and all who have judged themselves in the presence of God and put their trust in Him who shed His precious blood for our sins on that Cross of shame may rest assured that in His book their names are written even now, and shall be there displayed, in the Holy City.

Moving to chapter 22 we read,

> And he showed me a pure river of water of life, clear as crystal, proceeding out of the throne of God and of the Lamb. In the midst of the street of it, and on either side of the river, was there the tree of life, which bare twelve manner of fruits, and yielded her fruit every month: and the leaves of the tree were for the healing of the nations.

David sang of a river, the streams of which shall make glad the city of God. This river is the Holy Spirit's testimony to the glory of Christ. It proceeds from the throne of God and of the Lamb because the Holy Spirit proceeds from the Father and the Son. Whoever has tasted on earth of that refreshing stream longs to drink to the full of its living stream throughout the unending day!

When man sinned in the garden on earth, God drove him forth and set the cherubim with a flaming sword to guard the way to the Tree of Life, lest man should eat and live forever. But that sword of flame has been sheathed in the heart of the Lord Jesus Christ Himself. And now the blessed truth is made known that He who died and rose again is that Tree of Life, the leaves of which shall be for the healing of the nations during Messiah's glorious reign and the fruit of which shall be for the refreshment and gladness of His redeemed saints as they gather by that river of joy. The Curse shall be unknown there because the throne of God and of the Lamb shall be established in unquestioned authority, and His servants will find delight in ever serving Him who, in the hour of their deepest need, served them so faithfully. They shall serve not as hirelings, seeing not the Master's face, but with holy gladness in His presence, beholding the light of His countenance and having His name stamped upon their foreheads.

The wonderful description closes with verse 5: "There shall be no night there; and they need no candle, neither light of the sun; for the Lord God giveth them light: and they shall reign for ever and ever." Oh, the nights of darkness and of anguish that many of God's beloved people have known in this poor world! The night is the time of mystery, suffering, and unfulfilled desire. The day will bring the glad fruition of all of our hopes, and, in the full blessing of that uncreated light, we shall reign in light through the ages of ages—at home in the city of God!

The closing verses need not detain us long. They are so plain and so simple that they require but little, if any, comment. And yet, they are so intensely solemn that we must not pass by them lightly but would desire that each added message might sink in deeper into our hearts.

Verse 6 links us again with the opening of the book: "He said unto me, These sayings are faithful and true: and the Lord God of the holy prophets sent his angel to show unto his servants the things which must shortly be done." How soon may all be fulfilled that we have been studying of late! Three times the Lord speaks announcing His near return. In verse 7, He says, "Behold, I come quickly: blessed is he that keepeth the sayings of the prophecy of this book." In verse 12, "And, behold, I come quickly; and my reward is with me, to give every man according as his work shall be." And again, in verse 20, the last word sent down to us by our Lord from heaven, before the canon of Scripture was closed, was this: "He which testifieth these things saith, Surely I come quickly," to which John, as representing all the saints, replies, "*Amen. Even so, come, Lord Jesus.*"

We can scarcely wonder that a second time the beloved apostle, overwhelmed by the abundance of the revelation given to him, fell down to worship before the feet of the angel who showed him these things, but again, as on the previous occasion, he is forbidden to do so, and the angel declares that he is a fellow servant of both John and his brethren the prophets—and of us, in like manner, if we are among those who keep the sayings of this book. "Worship God," he commands, and in worshiping our Lord Jesus Christ we worship God, "For in him dwelleth all the fulness of the Godhead bodily" (Col. 2:9).

Daniel's prophecy closes with the admonition, "Go thy way, Daniel: for the words are closed up and sealed till the time of the end" (Dan. 12:9). In a former verse, the word to him was, "But thou, O Daniel, shut up the words, and seal the book, even [until] the time of the end" (12:4). But to John the angel says, "Seal *not* the sayings of the prophecy of this book: *for the time is at hand.*"

In verse 11, we have set before us the great truth that science itself demonstrates, equally with the Word of God, namely, that character tends to permanence. "He that is unjust, let him be unjust still: and he [that] is filthy, let him be filthy still: and he that is righteous, let him be righteous still: and he that is holy, let him be holy still." It is a divine emphasis upon the solemn truth that as a man is found in that coming day, so shall he remain for all eternity. In this world, God is calling men to repent. Here and now, He waits to renew, by divine grace, those who commit themselves to Him. But in the eternal world, there will be no power that has not been in exercise here, to make the unjust righteous or the filthy clean.

Notice that verse 14 is rendered differently in the Revised Version, and that in accordance with the best manuscripts: "Blessed are they that [wash their robes], that they may have right to the tree of life, and may enter in through the gates into the city." The promise rests on no legal grounds. It is not *doing* that gives one title to that home of the saints. It is only the precious blood of Christ, by which the acts of the saints (however well intentioned) must be washed, that fits anyone for entrance there. Outside forevermore will be the false, apostate teachers, designated as dogs, with those trafficking with evil spirits, the unclean, all murderers and idolaters, and "whosoever loveth and maketh a lie." They will be outside because they would not prepare to enter inside while God was offering mercy through His Son's atoning work.

Noteworthy is the fact that, when the blessed Lord introduces Himself by His personal name and declares His official title in connection with Israel and His special title in connection with the church, the Spirit and the bride alike are aroused to send up the invitation shout, "Come." We read, "I Jesus have sent mine angel to testify unto you these things in the churches. I am the root and the offspring of David." He is the *root* of David because David sprang from Him—

David's Creator and Lord, who called him to guide His people Israel. And He is the *offspring* of David because He was born as man from a daughter of David. And He is "the bright and morning star."

Immediately, the Spirit and the bride respond, saying, "Come." It is an invitation to Him to return to shine forth and gather His own to Himself. And all who hear are urged to join in this cry, "Come." To all of those who do not yet know Him, the gospel invitation goes forth for the last time in view of His near return: "Let him that is athirst come. And whosoever will, let him take the water of life freely."

In verses 18–19, in unmistakable solemnity, the glorified Lord Himself testifies unto every man who hears the words of the prophecy of this book,

> If any man shall add unto these things, God shall add unto him the plagues that are written in this book: and if any man shall take away from the words of the book of this prophecy, God shall take away his part out of the book of life, and out of the holy city, and from the things which are written in this book.

Oh, how unspeakably awful must be the fate of those who reject this testimony and its message! Better far never to have been born than thus to refuse the Word of the living God.

Surely every believing heart can join with the apostle in the prayer, "Even so, come, Lord Jesus." But while we wait for His return, we would still seek to make known the message of His grace to a guilty world.

And so, with the apostolic benediction, this book, and with this book the entire canon of Scripture, comes to a close: "The grace of our Lord Jesus Christ be with you all. Amen."

ENDNOTES

Lecture 2

1. The peculiar metal referred to was really a very hard copper alloy, but I use the word *brass* because that is the word used in our English Bible.

Lecture 4

1. It is always a pleasure for me to commend the writing of trustworthy servants of Christ who are true to the Book. There are a number of excellent expositions of Revelation, each of which would, I am sure, be a help in the further study of the subject: Walter Scott, *Exposition of the Revelation* (London: Pickering and Inglis, n.d.); William Kelly, *Lectures on Revelation* (n.p., n.d.); and A. C. Gaebelein, *The Revelation: An Analysis and Exposition of the Last Book of the Bible* (New York: Our Hope, 1915). On the seven churches, I especially commend F. W. Grant, *The Prophetic History of the Church* (New York: Loizeaux Brothers, 1945).

Lecture 6

1. I thought at first of recasting this lecture because it seemed somewhat too colloquial and localized. But I decided to let it remain largely as given. The reader will understand that it was delivered during the armistice year and while the influenza plague was still in progress.

Lecture 13

1. Walter Scott.

Lecture 15

1. In the original, it is the definite article, *"the* lie," that is, the lie of the Antichrist.

Lecture 17

1. Since this was written, the Ottoman Empire has fallen, and the Angora Republic has taken its place.

Lecture 18

1. For those who desire to make a fuller investigation of Babylonianism, I commend Alexander Hyslop's monumental work, *The Two Babylons* (New York: Loizeaux Brothers, 1959), to which I am indebted for many of the preceding facts.